Building trust in government

Trends and Innovations in Governance Series

This book forms part of a series on trends and innovations in governance in Asia; the 2010 launch of which coincides with the fiftieth anniversary of the East-West Center.

The Trends and Innovations in Governance series is the result of collaboration between the East-West Center's Asia-Pacific Governance and Democracy Initiative (AGDI) and the United Nations University Institute for Sustainability and Peace. Contributors to the books include leading scholars from around the world specializing in governance, political science and the Asia-Pacific region.

Other titles in this series are:

Engaging Civil Society: Emerging Trends in Democratic Governance, edited by G. Shabbir Cheema and Vesselin Popovski

Cross-Border Governance in Asia: Regional Issues and Mechanisms, edited by G. Shabbir Cheema, Christopher A. McNally and Vesselin Popovski

Building trust in government: Innovations in governance reform in Asia

Edited by G. Shabbir Cheema and Vesselin Popovski

United Nations University Press

TOKYO · NEW YORK · PARIS

United Nations University Press
United Nations University, 53–70, Jingumae 5-chome,
Shibuya-ku, Tokyo 150-8925, Japan
Tel: +81-03-5467-1212   Fax: +81-3-3406-7345
E-mail: sales@unu.edu   general enquiries: press@unu.edu
http://www.unu.edu

United Nations University Office at the United Nations, New York
2 United Nations Plaza, Room DC2-2062, New York, NY 10017, USA
Tel: +1-212-963-6387   Fax: +1-212-371-9454
E-mail: unuony@unu.edu

United Nations University Press is the publishing division of the United Nations University.

Cover design by Andrew Corbett

Printed in the United States of America

ISBN 978-92-808-1189-6

Library of Congress Cataloging-in-Publication Data

Building trust in government : innovations in governance reform in Asia / edited by G. Shabbir Cheema and Vesselin Popovski.
    p.   cm.
Includes bibliographical references and index.
ISBN 978-9280811896 (pbk.)
1. Trust—Political aspects—Asia. 2. Political alienation—Asia—Prevention. 3. Organizational change—Asia. 4. Asia—Politics and government—21st century. I. Cheema, G. Shabbir. II. Popovski, Vesselin.
JQ36.B85 2010
320.9501'9—dc22   2010015352

In memory of

Ledivina V. Cariño
for her enduring contribution to the study of
democratic governance reform,
trust and accountability, and participatory governance.

Contents

Figures

Tables

Preface

Over the past few decades, four transformations – globalization, democratization, information and communication technologies, and the end of Soviet-style centralized planning – have had major impacts on the expectations of citizens and the roles of the state. Democratization and increased access to information led to greater demands on the state to deliver services. Many states around the world have been under tremendous stress to meet the rising expectations of citizens. One consequence of the shortfall in the capacity of governments to provide adequate economic opportunities, skills, and access to services has been declining citizen trust in government institutions dealing with representation, law and order, and economic management.

Recognizing the significance of declining trust in government, the United Nations organized the 7th Global Forum on Reinventing Government in 2007 to identify constraints on building trust in government, good practices and innovations around the world, and the role of effective and democratic governance – including the government, civil society, and the private sector – in rebuilding trust in government. Although there is a wide body of literature on the concept of trust based largely on the experiences of the developed world, relationships between democratic governance and trust in the developing countries have not been adequately examined, especially in view of ongoing innovations and reforms introduced by many governments in the developing world.

This book argues that various dimensions of effective and democratic governance and the promotion of trust in government are interdependdent. It examines the reforms undertaken by governments in Asia and the Pacific region to improve electoral and parliamentary processes, to decentralize governance, and to develop service delivery and access. It also reviews civil society engagement, the accountability and transparency of governance, and public sector capacity. It reviews the literature related to relationships between governance and trust, and presents sub-regional reviews of trust and governance in Northeast Asia, Southeast Asia, South Asia, and the Pacific Islands. It also presents some country studies.

We hope the book will enhance our understanding of the practice of trust in government and of the effectiveness of governance reforms and innovation, while at the same time contributing to ongoing discussion and dialogue on the need to strengthen citizen trust in government.

We are profoundly grateful to several individuals who supported the compilation of the volume: Ho Young Kim, former Director of the UN Project Office on Governance in Seoul and Secretary General of the 6th Global Forum; Guido Bertucci, former Director of the Division for Public Administration and Development Management of the United Nations; Meredith Rowen, UN Programme Officer; Gerard Finin, East-West Center Senior Fellow; and Cameron Lowry, East-West Center Project Assistant. We are particularly thankful to the contributors to the book for making major revisions to the papers they presented to the Asia-Pacific Workshop on Building Trust in Government, which was held in Honolulu in January 2008.

The views expressed in the book are those of the authors and do not necessarily reflect the views of the United Nations University or the East-West Center.

G. Shabbir Cheema
East-West Center
Honolulu, Hawaii

Vesselin Popovski
United Nations University
Tokyo, Japan

Contributors

Peride K. Blind is currently an Associate Expert in Governance and Public Administration in the United Nations Department of Economic and Social Affairs. She obtained her PhD in Comparative Government and has published on the questions of governance, democratization, and economic reform.

Ledivina V. Cariño held the rank of university professor at the University of the Philippines (UP). She had served as dean of the UP National College of Public Administration and Governance and was the director of what is now the Center for Local and Regional Governance. She was a member of the International Advisory Committee of the Ash Institute for Democratic Governance and Innovation, JFK School of Government, Harvard University, USA.

G. Shabbir Cheema is director of the Asia-Pacific Governance and Democracy Initiative and a senior fellow at the East-West Center, Honolulu, Hawaii. He has been a visiting fellow at Harvard University's Ash Institute for Democratic Governance and Innovation and was previously programme director in the United Nations Department of Economic and Social Affairs (2001–2007).

Gerard A. Finin is a senior fellow and since 2004 has served as deputy director of the East-West Center's Pacific Islands Development Program. He conducts research on contemporary social and economic issues in the Pacific Islands region, with ongoing projects focusing on governance and globalization. Finin received his PhD from Cornell University, USA.

Sukehiro Hasegawa is currently Professor, Hosei University, Tokyo, and Visiting Fellow at the United Nations University, Tokyo. Previously, he was Special Representative of the Secretary-General of the United Nations for Timor-Leste and Resident Co-ordinator of the United Nations' operational activities for development. During his United Nations career, which extended over 30 years, he served in senior positions at the United Nations Development Programme, the United Nations Volunteers, and UN peacekeeping organizations.

Byong Seob Kim is Chairman of the Presidential Committee on Government Innovation and Decentralization, Republic of Korea, and is also currently Professor of Public Administration at Seoul National University. He received his PhD from the University of Georgia, USA, in 1990. He previously served as program manager of the Korean Association for Public Administration.

Pan Suk Kim is Director of the Institute for Poverty Alleviation and International Development and Professor of Public Administration in the College of Government and Business at Yonsei University in South Korea. He is currently a member of the UN Committee of Experts on Public Administration. In 2009, he received the International Public Administration Award from the American Society for Public Administration.

Sajjad Naseer, currently serving as Senior Fellow and Professor of Political Science at the Lahore School of Economics, Pakistan, served twice as Chairperson of the Political Science Department, Punjab University. As a Consultant for the United Nations Development Programme and the International Fund for Agricultural Development, he handled various governance-related assignments. He is a regular at prestigious national institutions and is a political analyst in both print and electronic media in Pakistan and abroad.

Vesselin Popovski is senior academic programme officer and head of section for Peace and Security in the Institute for Sustainability and Peace at the United Nations University, Tokyo. He has published on intervention, human rights, the International Criminal Court and UN reforms. His most recent book is *Human Rights Regimes in the Americas* (UNU Press, 2010).

Meredith Rowen is a visiting fellow at the East-West Center, Honolulu. She served previously as the governance and public administration officer at the Division for Public Administration and Development Management, United Nations Department of Economic and Social Affairs. She is the co-author of *Towards Participatory and Transparent Governance: Reinventing Government* (United Nations, 2007).

Prijono Tjiptoherijanto is a professor of economics at the University of Indonesia. He holds a PhD degree in Human Resources Economics from the University of Hawaii. He has held several governmental positions, such as deputy minister of the State Secretariat, deputy minister at the State Ministry for Population, and Head of the National Civil Service Agency (BKN).

Teresa Wright is a professor of Political Science and Graduate Coordinator at California State University, Long Beach, USA, and a Visiting Scholar at the East-West Center, Honolulu. She is the author of *The Perils of Protest: State Repression and Student Activism in China and Taiwan* (University of Hawai'i Press, 2001).

1

Building trust in government: An introduction

G. Shabbir Cheema

"Building trust in government is at the core of the world's quest for peace and well-being. The ability of the global community to achieve the Millennium Development Goals, ensure security, and promote adherence to basic standards of human rights depends on whether or not people have confidence in their governments."

Ban Ki-moon, United Nations Secretary-General, at the 7th Global Forum on Reinventing Government, 2007

Despite its importance, public trust in government and political institutions has been declining in both developing and developed countries in the new millennium. According to the BBC/Gallup International in 2005, global dissatisfaction with government had reached 65 percent in Western Europe, 73 percent in Eastern and Central Europe, 60 percent in North America, 61 percent in Africa, 65 percent in Asia and the Pacific, and 69 percent in Latin America (see Reynolds 2005). In particular, global citizenry has insufficient confidence in political parties, parliaments, and judicial systems, while more trusted institutions are churches, universities, and order institutions, such as the armed forces. Lower levels of trust in government raise the question of why they have fallen and how they can be strengthened. This situation has prompted a new look at the role of trust, as well as its relationship with governance and ways of restoring and rebuilding trust in different contexts.

This publication seeks to answer many of the questions raised in reference to means of strengthening trust in government within the Asia-Pacific region; trust deficits can depend upon country- and region-specific

Building trust in government: Innovations in governance reform in Asia, Cheema and Popovski (eds), United Nations University Press, 2010, ISBN 978-92-808-1189-6

variables. In developing countries, weak systems and processes of democratic governance, as well as inadequate access to services and economic opportunities, tend to erode trust in government. In the developed countries, however, citizens have greater access to information and higher levels of education and thus demand more transparency, accountability, and participation. In most of the developed countries, trust in government is associated with citizen disagreement with government policy (United Nations 2007a).

To explore these considerations, the contributors to this book provide various perspectives on the causes of declines in trust, on countries and institutions that have managed to maintain higher degrees of confidence, and on measures that have played an important role in strengthening trust once it has faltered. Following an introduction to trust at the theoretical level (Chapters 1 and 2), more in-depth analyses of trends within the four sub-regions of Northeast Asia, Southeast Asia, South Asia, and the Pacific Islands are undertaken (Chapters 3–6). These reviews are then complemented by country studies of specific innovations and reform measures that have influenced the process of building trust in government (Chapters 7–10). The final chapter presents conclusions.

Global and regional context

The search to strengthen trust in government takes place within a global context of the United Nations conferences and summits that were held in the 1990s, as well as the historic UN Millennium Summit Declaration. These events have led to a vision of shared development priorities, a normative framework, and time-bound targets encapsulated in the Millennium Development Goals; i.e. the eradication of extreme poverty and hunger, the achievement of universal primary education, the promotion of gender equality, the reduction of child mortality, the improvement of maternal health, the fight against HIV/AIDS and other diseases, environmental sustainability, and the promotion of a global partnership for development.

As the world population increases and becomes more interconnected, the need to strengthen understanding, ensure mutually beneficial interdependence, and promote cooperation has become the principal challenge of the twenty-first century. At the same time, a related challenge has arisen as to how to incorporate marginalized groups, including the poor, into the policy process to ensure that governance is truly representative and participatory and benefits all members of society. Where governance processes are exclusionary, intrastate conflicts and violence within the country can negatively impact regional security and peace. Within this context, the issue of how to build trust in government and trust between socioeconomic actors has emerged as an increasingly relevant issue in both developed and developing economies. In particular, there is an essential need for strategies that help develop and strengthen trust as the basis for social cooperation and joint advantage.

Following the publication of Fukuyama's *Trust: The Social Virtues and the Creation of Prosperity* in 1995, levels of trust in government in Asia, and particularly in East Asia, were generally considered to be higher than in many other regions of the world and therefore not requiring additional attention. However, several new issues emerged over the course of the 1990s that illustrated new challenges within the region that had indirectly and directly decreased the confidence of citizens in their governments.

In particular, many countries within Asia had begun to experience a divergence between citizens' increased expectations for the role of the state and the functional capacities of governments. This divergence was deemed to be directly responsible for the growing trust gap. The increased expectations of citizens were a product of globalization, liberalization processes, and the information and communication revolution, which had led to greater demands from citizens in terms of the way governments should perform and what they should accomplish.

Coupled with this phenomenon, many countries within the region had experienced a process known as the "hollowing out of the state." Although many countries had begun to implement widespread reform measures, such as decentralization and privatization, these reforms were not accompanied by a sufficient strengthening of capacities. Hence, even though the degree of reform is very high within the region, the capacity to carry out these reforms is low in many cases. This situation has led to greater fragmentation, complexity, and interdependence while weakening the power of the executive branch.

One of the central conclusions emerging from recent regional conferences organized by the United Nations on reinventing government has been that most countries within Asia and the Pacific, as elsewhere, are not fully capable of responding to citizen demands. Significant governance capacity development is needed alongside reform processes in order to improve transparency and accountability and ensure that the public sector is both ready and able to embark upon a more collaborative approach, based on the contributions of all governance partners.

Many current human development challenges within the Asian region are closely linked to the need for improvements in governance. For example, in cases where populations have insufficient access to basic services, this disconnect has been attributed to: a failure of accountability at different points in the service delivery chain; the bulk of public spending in healthcare and education often going to the non-poor; considerable "leakage" tending to occur before subsidies reach their intended targets; and often high absentee rates for service providers (Chaudhury and Devarajan 2006). In coming years, such factors as population growth and climate change will provide additional obstacles to the maintenance and reconstruction of trust in government within the region, taxing both infrastructure and governance systems. Over the next few decades, hyperurbanization is expected to continue and the region may account for some 60 percent of the world's population by 2050 (UN-HABITAT 2009).

Within this general context, it will be essential to start prioritizing both governance and trust as better means to confront existing and emerging challenges – including the need to develop and evolve joint understandings on the role of the state, civic responsibilities, the importance of transformative and collaborative leadership, and human resource development.

Defining trust

Trust as a multifaceted concept refers to a basic consensus among members of a society on collective values, priorities, and differences and on the implicit acceptance of the society in which they live. It also refers to citizens' expectations of the type of government that they should have, how government should operate and interact with other social and economic institutions and citizenry, and the behavior of political leaders, civil servants, and citizens. When citizens have higher expectations, as is often the case in relation to parliaments and elected representatives, these expectations are less easily met and often result in a decline in confidence. In contrast, lower expectations for a specific institution can mean that it is relatively easier to maintain trust.

When trust has been damaged, the restoration process can be slow and difficult. Institutions and policymakers then face the challenging task of setting achievable goals, using sustainable processes, ensuring the legitimacy of policy objectives through participation in policy formation, transparently communicating these objectives and implementation measures to the populace, demonstrating accountability for measures taken, and maintaining their commitment to the process as a whole, when new circumstances and contingencies arise that make continued implementation difficult. As such, trust is closely linked to the credibility of public policy and institutions.

To embark upon a discussion of trust in government, the definition of trust must first be qualified. Contributors to this publication have offered five alternative trust dimensions as an entry point for discussions on trust: moral trust, with a focus on ethics and morality; economic trust, with an emphasis on economic efficiency and non-partisanship; political trust, with the stress on political legitimacy; social trust, focusing on the catalyzing effects of social capital; and technological trust, concentrating on how technology can bring about more democratization.[1] Governance strategies that address these five dimensions are expected to strengthen citizen trust in government.

Trust in government can be further evaluated via four additional subdimensions: goodwill trust, competency trust, procedural trust, and performance trust. First, citizens have goodwill trust when leaders and organizations have made an effort to be participatory, inclusive, and reliable in their responsiveness to citizens. As a result, citizens believe that the leader or institution is looking out for their best interests. Second, citizens have competency trust when leaders and institutions appear capable of fulfilling their mandates and carrying out their responsibilities, irrespective of whether or not the citizens believe that the leaders and institutions are governing in their own best interests. Hence, competency trust relates to the perceived expertise of the leader or institution, as well as to speed or accuracy in fulfilling duties and mandates. Third, procedural trust refers to the regularity and consistency with which leaders and institutions follow established rules, laws, regulations, guidelines, and stated procedures. Finally, performance trust implies confidence in the overall productivity, output, and outcomes of the leader or institution. Different types of innovations can be selected to address specific trust deficits in each of the four areas.

A further distinction exists between types of trust in different government institutions. Citizens commonly have markedly different expectations of representational institutions, such as the parliament, and order institutions, for example the military, the police, and the judicial system (Rothstein and Stolle 2003). Although order institutions may tend to receive greater trust, according to results from the sub-regional reviews, this is not because their governance practices are necessarily better. Good governance, including good public sector management, helps to reduce uncertainty, because citizens understand public policy and have faith that their basic environment will remain stable or even improve. Order institutions, such as the military and the police, often rank highly in trust surveys because their main concern is increasing order, reducing uncertainty, and handling risk management. In contrast, representational institutions, such as parliaments, often face higher and more varied expectations from their constituencies.

Demographics can also provide a partial explanation for changes in levels of trust. On the one hand, studies of advanced industrialized countries have indicated that skepticism toward government tends to increase with age and income level. This phenomenon may help to provide part of the explanation for the recent declines in trust in Japan and the Republic of Korea mentioned in the sub-regional review for Northeast Asia. On the other hand, the sub-regional review for the Pacific Islands indicates that generational issues might be having a different impact in this area, because the "younger generation" is thought to have less trust in traditional leaders than their forefathers.

Determinants of trust

There are many determinants of trust in government. Their relative effect on promoting or inhibiting trust depends upon global, regional, and country contexts. Factors that determine an increase or a decline in trust in government can be divided into five categories.

First, effective policies and implementation mechanisms yield positive results for society and create an environment of trust in government. The credibility of and support for public policies inspire public trust and create a level playing field for businesses, thus contributing to efficient markets and economic growth. In the advanced democracies of the West, for example, a significant part of trust in government can be explained by the extent of public support for a set of policies. With high levels of access to information, citizens are well positioned to hold the government accountable to the results of its policies. Where policies are ineffective, public cynicism and distrust increase, even when the government in power has political legitimacy and there are structures and processes for citizen participation. Government waste and negative perceptions of governmental performance also contribute to the decline in trust in government.

Second, committed and inspiring political leaders can promote trust in government (Rondinelli and Heffron 2009). Trust in government is enhanced where leaders have a vision of the future and the ability to take actions to bring about change through decisiveness, persuasion, and coalition-building. Though leadership attributes are culturally conditioned and depend upon country-specific circumstances, many leadership attributes contribute to trust in government. For example, in the context of globalization, political leaders at the national level and government officials at the organizational level have to reconcile short-term political necessities with long-term development goals in complex political environments and institutional arrangements. This requires leaders with attributes such as technical ability, cultural sensitivity, and an ability to forge partnerships. Because of the conflicting interests and priorities of different groups in a society, there is the tendency towards a lack of trust if the priorities of one group are not included in government policies. In such situations, leaders can play a vital role in promoting the trust of all citizens by forging partnerships among diverse groups, mediating differences, and consulting with different interest groups.

Third, economic growth and economic opportunities available to citizens are conducive to greater trust in government (Wright 2007). Where the economy is growing, greater employment opportunities are available, and the resource base in relation to population size is favorable, citizens are more likely to accept public policy and program weaknesses. This explains why trust in government is higher in some non-democratic states with booming economies than in democratic states with poor economic performance. In stagnant economies with limited economic opportunities for citizens, a culture of cynicism and a lack of trust in government are more likely to emerge.

Fourth, the provision and delivery of services such as water, sanitation, healthcare, and education are essential to inspire confidence and trust in government because these services affect citizens directly and in most cases immediately (Clark 2008). In many cities in developing countries, between 10 and 30 percent of urban residents live in slums and squatter settlements, with inadequate access to shelter and basic urban services. In rural areas, especially in remote regions, the poor lack basic services. To gain the support of citizens, governments need to explain how policy choices are debated, adopted, institutionalized, and finally implemented. Management innovations in public sector organizations, the elimination of "rent-seeking" practices, and the development of core public service values are critical in facilitating the access of citizens, the poor in particular, to basic public services.

Finally, good governance and effective public administration are increasingly receiving recognition from the international community as the foundation for the successful achievement of a wide range of international and domestic policy objectives, including items on the United Nations development agenda, and thereby enhancing trust in government. As the basis for effective policy selection and implementation, governance – including public administration and civil service, rule of law, human rights, macroeconomic policies and regulatory frameworks, and transparent and participatory decision-making processes – is a necessary condition to achieve the Millennium Development Goals (Cheema 2005). In view of this, the Millennium Project's Report to the Secretary-General, *Investing in Development: A Practical Plan to Achieve the Millennium Development Goals*, made a strong case for investing in governance, including public administration (UN Millennium Project 2005).

Good governance and trust

Governance is the process of interaction between three sets of actors – the state, civil society, and the private sector – in making political, administrative, economic, and social decisions that affect citizens. It is how a society organizes itself to make and implement decisions, mediate differences, and exercise legal rights and obligations. It comprises the rules, institutions, and practices that set limits and provide incentives. It operates at every level of human enterprise. The state creates an enabling political and legal environment. Civil society facilitates political and social interaction. The private sector generates jobs, income, goods, and services. The essence of effective governance is fostering and strengthening the interactions, relationships, roles, and capacities of the three sets of actors to achieve the universally accepted principles of good governance – participation, accountability, access, subsidiarity, justice, equity, effectiveness, efficiency, and sustainability. Experience suggests, however, that institutional designs and structures of governance are necessary but not sufficient to improve the quality of governance as a process. Because of differences in the internal and external contexts of each country, similar institutional designs and structures sometimes produce different results in terms of the quality of the process.

Building trust is both the result and the determinant of inclusive governance. Where governance is both effective and democratic, citizens are more likely to trust public officials, politicians, and political institutions. The ineffectiveness of governance institutions and processes – such as parliamentary and electoral processes, the accountability and transparency of the public sector, decentralization and local governance, the roles and capacity of civil society, and people's access to justice – gradually erodes citizen trust. Enhanced trust facilitates effective functioning of governance institutions, and hence improves the quality of governance.

Citizens expect public servants to serve the public interest with fairness and to manage public resources properly on a daily basis. Fair and reliable public services, as well as credible policies and institutions, inspire public trust. In this context, corruption in matters such as procurement should be viewed not only as an individual act but also as the result of systemic failure and an indication of "weak governance." Publicized corruption cases have had a major negative impact on trust in public decision-making.

Key components of good governance that affect trust in government are: public sector capacity; decentralization and local governance; electoral and parliamentary processes; civil society engagement and partnerships with the government and the private sector; accountability and transparency of governance; and conflict management and recovery. Together, these components allow governments to promote legitimacy, enable citizen empowerment, strengthen the credibility of policies and institutions, provide opportunities for participation in government processes and decision-making, and ensure efficient and accessible service delivery (see Figure 1.1).

Public sector capacity

In order to enhance trust in government, the public sector must have the capacity to design and implement programs to protect the rights of citizens, mobilize resources through taxes and other sources, and ensure the delivery of and access to basic social services (Rondinelli and Cheema

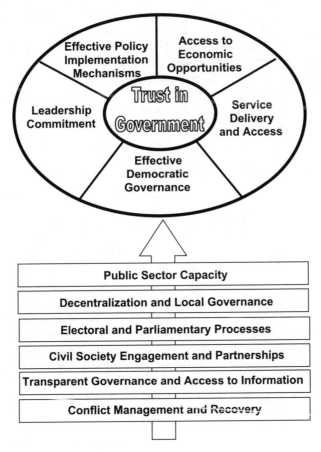

Figure 1.1 Understanding trust: A conceptual framework.

2003). Furthermore, the public sector must have the capacity to maintain law and order, promote and protect public goods such as the environment, and establish well-coordinated and complementary mechanisms to ensure that government agencies and departments work together effectively. Equally important is the "capacity to govern" – to make important policy choices, to design and implement programs and actions to achieve policy objectives, and to anticipate emerging trends and challenges. Qualified and motivated staff, recruited on the basis of merit, are central to enhancing public sector capacity.

Over the past few decades, improving public sector management capacity has been one of the most critical issues facing the developing economies of Asia. With the rapid pace of globalization, the public sector is under even greater pressure to increase its capacity to deal with new challenges and opportunities presented by globalization – new information and communication technologies, the expansion of trade and investment, an increased focus on such public goods as the environment and human rights, and the proactive role of global institutions such as the World Trade Organization, which affect development processes at the country level. Not only must the public sector have the capacity to provide an enabling environment for enterprises to take advantage of the opportunities provided by globalization; it must also provide safety-nets for those segments of society who are negatively affected by changes emanating from globalization.

Decentralization and local governance to bring government closer to people

Within the framework of democratic governance, decentralization and local autonomy are crucial in fostering more participatory governance and enhancing trust in government. They allow citizens to "voice" their demands in a more effective way and to become active partners in all stages of policy decision-making, implementation, and evaluation – thereby bringing government closer to the people and enhancing trust between the government, civil society, and the private sector. Decentralization provides an institutional framework for the engagement of individuals and groups in local decisions affecting their lives. It also creates a system of checks and balances at the local and sub-national levels and devolves resources to local areas. Decentralization thus contributes to the empowerment of local communities and trust in government at all levels (Cheema and Rondinelli 2007).

Over the past few decades, many countries have adopted decentralization policies and programs. Many driving forces at the global, national, and local levels have influenced recent trends toward greater political devolution and the transfer of financial authority from the center to regions and local areas: the demise of the former Soviet Union and the end of the Cold War, an increase in ethnic conflicts and demands for greater recognition of cultural, religious, and regional traditions, and the focus of bilateral donors, multilateral agencies, and non-governmental organizations (NGOs). Other factors have included the demand by groups and individuals within countries for greater control over local political processes, greater transparency, better access to services, and more openness in political decision-making processes.

However, the results of decentralization policies and programs have been mixed. Successful experiments in decentralization have yielded many benefits, such as improved access to services, citizen participation, and the mobilization of local resources, and the institutionalization of democratic political processes at the local level. Decentralization's limitations have also been highlighted by the skeptics, including "elite capture" of local governments, the weak financial and administrative capacity of local governments, widening economic and social disparities between regions, and increased levels of local corruption and nepotism (United Cities and Local Governments 2007).

Trust in government can be enhanced or impeded by the way decentralization programs are designed and implemented. Of particular importance are legal frameworks for decentralized governance, the redistribution of functions and resources between central and local governments, and relationships between local governments and NGOs. Trust in government is also affected by the extent to which central government provides technical and financial support for strengthening local capacity; the ways in which the system of checks and balances between central and local governments works in practice; and the role of community-based organizations in local decision-making and service delivery and access. Where there are effective mechanisms for local participation, citizens are more likely to trust government actions than they are in highly centralized systems of governance. Local government accountability mechanisms – including procurement procedures, social audits, and codes of conduct for public officials – are also conducive to creating a culture of trust in government.

Electoral and parliamentary processes for legitimacy and participation

Effective electoral and parliamentary processes ensure that elected representatives are responsive to the needs and priorities of their constituencies, including marginalized communities and the poor. Free and fair elections, parliamentary oversight of the executive, and freedom of the press create the necessary conditions for enhanced trust between citizens and government and facilitate partnerships between governance actors.

One of the primary reasons for the breakdown of trust among groups and regions in a country is the perceived lack of effective representation in electoral and parliamentary processes. Adequate representation of minorities and economically backward regions in political institutions at the national and local levels, perceived fairness of electoral processes, and proactive parliamentarian–constituent exchanges and dialogue are essential to promote political legitimacy and, thus, trust in government institutions. Trust in government is also enhanced by the capacity and impartiality of electoral management bodies, bipartisanship among the competing political parties in the legislature, and smooth working relationships between the executive and legislative branches of government.

There are many constraints on the effectiveness of electoral and parliamentary processes in the developing countries of Asia and the Pacific. There are a few good examples of mature and established democracies such as Japan, South Korea, and India. In many other countries of the region, however, the effectiveness of parliaments is constrained by low levels of interface between parliamentarians and their constituents, weak internal capacity and resource base, a historical legacy of executive control of the legislative branch, and weak oversight institutions. In some countries, military dominance in the political process and the lack of parliamentary control over the budgetary process limit the effectiveness of parliaments as institutions of democratic governance. In new and restored democracies, a culture of political tolerance is usually lacking, which creates cynicism among citizens.

Electoral processes in many countries in the region have in the past been marred by allegations of fraud, vote-buying, violence, and the unwillingness of defeated political parties to accept the results of elections. Trust in the electoral process, especially in new democracies in Asia, is negatively affected by a lack of agreement among political parties on the legislative framework within which elections are held. It is also diminished by the low level of capacity and lack of independence of electoral management bodies and the dominance of elites with the resources to fund election campaigns. As in the case of the parliamentary process, however, there have been recent examples of elections perceived to be free and fair by internal and international monitors.

Civil society engagement and partnerships

Civil society has been widely recognized to be an essential "third" sector. Along with the state and the private sector, civil society is instrumental in promoting good governance and trust in government. As an agent of change, civil society can actively engage in policy analysis and advocacy, monitor the state's performance, including the actions and behavior of public officials, build social capital and enable citizens to identify and articulate their values and civic norms. Civil society can also mobilize particular constituencies, such as vulnerable and marginalized groups and minorities, to participate more fully in politics and public policy. Another important role of civil society is to undertake local developmental activities, including the provision of shelter and basic social services to the poor in urban and rural areas.

Participation in various groups and local-level political and developmental activities improves not only mutual trust between members but also trust in government, because citizens in increasingly tight-knit communities tend to cooperate for their public interests (Putnam 2000). The longer constituents belong to a voluntary organization, the higher the level of trust becomes (Stolle 2001). Also, there are many research results showing that participation in various civic groups has a close relationship with trust in government, administrative responsiveness, and political efficiency (Rosenstone and Hansen 1993; Axelrod 1984). The type of organization also matters.

Studies also show that those who actively participate in politics, by, for example, enrolling in labor unions and political parties, demonstrate higher levels of confidence in other constituents and government than those who do not (Rothstein 2001). Researchers who emphasize the value of Western civil society (Almond and Verba 1963; de Tocqueville 1984; Putnam 1993, 1995) claim that the culture and values of civic groups and political participation will increase social capital-like trust, cooperation, and interaction, which leads to the development of democracy and economic prosperity. Where there is low trust in the political system, illegitimate political participation could occur; where there is low trust in government, people do not feel it necessary to participate in politics themselves.

Over the past few decades, the number of civil society organizations in Asia has rapidly increased. They are engaged in political, social, developmental, and cultural activities at local, sub-national, national and regional levels. Non-governmental organizations in Asia have become important in securing a democratic political system through their roles as watch groups as well as voluntary organizations pursuing further participative democracy. They have promoted political participation, voluntary social service participation, and policy participation.

Civil society organizations play a pivotal role in promoting democracy and good governance, which in turn can contribute to trust in government. Major democratic transitions in Asia (in South Korea, the Philippines, and Pakistan) have emanated from pressures from civil society.

Once democratic governance institutions are introduced, civil society organizations continue to play an important role in ensuring the accountability of political leaders and public officials and in promoting the interests of the poor and marginalized groups. They monitor elections, undertake public interest litigation, and provide paralegal services to the poor. They check the abuse of government power by public officials at national and local level through their access to the media, monitoring the government mechanisms for service delivery and access. They also protect the human rights of minorities, women, and marginalized groups. Where the government responds positively to pressure from civil society organizations, citizen trust in government is likely to be enhanced.

Accountability and transparency to promote confidence in government

Accountable and transparent governance allows the public to remain informed about policy, enables greater opportunities for participation, increases the efficient allocation of resources in both the public and private sectors, and minimizes corruption and unethical practices. It increases stability and consensus. These aspects are conducive to building trust between the government and citizens.

Corruption and a lack of accountability affect political processes and outcomes. Corruption bypasses due process, constrains the capacity to design and implement appropriate policies and programs, and weakens political institutions such as the judiciary, parliaments, and electoral management bodies. All of this can lead to the loss of people's trust in government. Where corruption is prevalent and mechanisms for government accountability and transparency are ineffective, citizens' trust in government is negatively affected in many ways. If civil servants are corrupt and are not responsive to citizens, public distrust and cynicism can emerge. If the electoral and parliamentary processes are not transparent and accountable, people lose faith in them. Corruption in the judiciary can lead to a lack of faith in the rule of law and access to justice.

In a society where corruption is rampant and the rule of law is ignored, people rarely trust each other and this in turn increases the cost of social transactions. In such situations, citizens are likely to develop distrust of the entire society (Rothstein and Stolle 2003). Social trust can be built only when the general public consider their government trustworthy (Levi 1998). Therefore, it is important for public officials to conduct their duties in a fair and just manner. In particular, the integrity of law enforcement authorities such as police and the prosecution have strong effects on social trust. When the law enforcement authorities fail to abide by the rule of law, people will have distrust not only in the authorities but also in society as a whole (Rothstein and Stolle 2003)

Conflict management and recovery through inclusion and dialogue

The emergence of conflict situations can be viewed as evidence that a significant erosion of trust has occurred over a period of time. A lack of social trust inhibits the development of effective partnerships for the achievement of mutually beneficial objectives and can have serious implications for the well-being of the population as a whole.

Experience suggests that the restoration of governance and the rebuilding of trust in government in crisis and post-conflict countries can be attributed to several factors (United Nations 2007b). First, each crisis-hit country has a unique history, culture, political tradition, and level of capacity to recover from hostilities. The solutions for restoring governance and build trust should depend on each country's specific situation. What is needed is to tailor, adjust and implement programs according to the conditions in the conflict and post-conflict countries.

Second, initial efforts to restore governance and trust should focus on strengthening the capacities needed for carrying out the most urgent reconstruction programs – establishing safety and security, strengthening constitutional government, reconstructing infrastructure and restoring services, stabilizing and developing the economy, and strengthening justice and reconciliation organizations.

Third, public–private partnerships can mobilize private financial, managerial, technical, and knowledge resources for providing public services more effectively. The use of NGOs and civil society organizations can extend the reach of weak governments in providing services to the poor, to remote rural areas, and to regions subject to continued tensions. NGO partnerships can help build the capability of the public administration to take over functions carried out by parallel structures and to manage public–private partnerships and strengthen administrative capacity in the private sector or civil society organizations to deliver services that supplement those of the public sector.

Fourth, rebuilding trust among fractured communities in conflict and post-conflict countries is essential through such mechanisms as supporting community-based groups, promoting dialogue and discussion among community members, making civil society more actively engaged, and providing basic social services.

About this book

The central argument of this book is that various dimensions of effective and democratic governance and the promotion of trust in government are interdependent. This volume examines the reforms undertaken by governments in the Asia-Pacific region to improve electoral and parliamentary processes, decentralize governance, and service delivery and access. It also reviews civil society engagement, the accountability and transparency of governance, and public sector capacity. After a review of the literature on the concept of trust and the decline in trust in government (Chapter 2), four sub-regional reviews analyze government reinvention and reforms in Northeast Asia, South Asia, Southeast Asia, and the Pacific Islands (Chapters 3–6). This is followed by country experiences with innovation and government reinvention in the People's Republic of China, the Republic of Korea, Indonesia, and Timor-Leste (Chapters 7–10). The main conclusions are presented in the final chapter.

In Chapter 2, Peride K. Blind presents a literature review on the concept of trust. She suggests that trust is a complex construct that can be categorized in many ways – including political trust and social trust – and at many levels – individual, group, institutional, sub-national, and systemic. She examines the relationship between trust and the new social, political, and economic requirements of globalization by drawing on survey results and examples. Many mechanisms to promote and strengthen trust receive particular attention. These include the rule of law; an independent judiciary; free, fair, and regular elections; legitimate parliamentary processes; a healthy civil society; fighting corruption; local governance and decentralization; and e-governance. Other mechanisms are performance management, e-government, and participatory mechanisms. When these mechanisms are used effectively, political legitimacy and trust are strengthened. Democratic governance is more likely to be enduring and stable where the trust of citizens becomes the norm. The author further explores innovation and good practices in governance reform that selected developed and developing countries have designed and implemented to promote trust in government. These innovations were presented to the United Nations 7th Global Forum on Reinventing Government, held in June 2007.

In Chapter 3, Pan Suk Kim examines the status of trust in government in Northeast Asia within the context of globalization, as well as the ways through which different dimensions of governance are affecting citizens' trust in government. In a discussion on recent findings from trust surveys, he notes that, even though Japan and the Republic of Korea have made significant progress in democratic governance and economic performance, trust in political parties and parliaments remains low. This is partly attributed to the higher expectations of well-informed citizens as well as the perceived ineffectiveness of some of the political leaders. Despite the remarkable economic performance of China and Vietnam, politics and administration are monopolized by the Communist Party in both countries. Kim points out that, to varying degrees, each country has shown a commitment to public sector reform, civil society engagement, decentralization and local governance, and transparent legal and judicial reform. Together with the notable economic performance, these will continue to positively affect citizen trust in government.

In Chapter 4, Ledivina V. Cariño provides an analysis of the status of trust and governance within the countries of Southeast Asia. She suggests that there is greater trust in government and order institutions than in representative institutions. In her opinion, trust in government does not seem to be merited when viewed in the context of ineffective service delivery, the quality of citizens' access, the performance of the police, and the provision of justice in most of the countries in the region. She describes the many challenges governments in the region face to strengthen trust, especially in the representative institutions, including the need to improve service delivery and access through innovations, to promote better-performing human resources, and to emphasize customer satisfaction and transparency. Other important dimensions of governance for strengthening trust are better civic education, civilian pre-eminence and respect for human rights, the integrity of electoral processes, and improved performance by legislatures and local governments. She makes a strong plea for the governments in the region to place more trust in citizens through greater transparency and accountability, the elimination of favoritism in the public decision-making process, and incorporating citizen evaluations of policy where possible.

In Chapter 5, Sajjad Naseer offers a review of governance reform and trust in South Asia with a focus on three variables: participation, development, and security. He argues that many factors have negatively influenced the decline in trust in government. With the exception of India, governance practice does not reflect effective use of governance instruments such as the rule of law, decentralization, representative institutions, and anti-corruption strategies. Moreover, participatory mechanisms at the local level have not been effective. Development performance in the sub-region has been poor, leading to an inequitable distribution of economic benefits and cynicism in government programs. Security issues, including intra-state conflicts and tensions between India and Pakistan, have complicated the situation. Major issues raised include the relationship between trust, legitimacy, and national identity.

In Chapter 6, Meredith Rowen and Gerard A. Finin examine the traditional institutions of governance in the Pacific Island region and the links between globalization and government reinvention. They emphasize that government reinvention processes should incorporate indigenous forms of governance, customs, and leadership. Traditional and modern institutions should be viewed as a continuum, where both types complement and support one another. The assessment of governance practice in the region shows that not all of the indigenous institutions are democratic; in some cases, the indigenous institutions serve as a source of stability and continuity by filling the gaps created by the modern institutions; sometimes tensions exist between elected non-traditional leaders and traditional leaders. The authors further discuss recent innovations that have been successfully implemented within small island developing states within the Pacific. They conclude that further strengthening trust in government in the region would require working with the existing institutions over a longer period of time and an approach that places the people at the center of developmental efforts.

In Chapter 7, Teresa Wright comments on the important distinction between trust in central government, in local government, and in the Communist Party in the People's Republic of China. She argues that there is popular trust in national leaders and political institutions, even amongst citizens who have previously demonstrated against the government. Often citizens show anger against local officials but express support for the central authority and party. Furthermore, citizens who have greatly benefited from recent economic development have shown increasing interest in joining the party. Wright then looks into the impact of recent reform measures on different socioeconomic groups, emphasizing the evidence of a strong preference for socialist economic benefits. Based on the most recent surveys, the author notes that, although the younger generation of citizens is less likely to support the Communist Party, they appear to be very nationalistic. Therefore, she concludes that high trust in government is likely to continue.

In Chapter 8, Byong Seob Kim presents a case study of the National Tax Service in the Republic of Korea. Under the Roh Moo-hyun administration (2003–2008), which focused on "principle and trust" as a vision for government reform and innovation, tax reform was used as one of several instruments to promote trust in government. Two particular measures receive attention: (i) the 1999 organizational and operational reform to improve efficiency, effectiveness, and customer orientation; and (ii) the 2002 Home Tax Service, which became the provider of e-tax administration, enhanced tax audit transparency and objectivity, and introduced a "Cash Receipt system" to keep track of business transactions. The author demonstrates that, owing to the reform, previously hidden transactions are now exposed and taxpayer satisfaction is on the rise. He concludes that the increased efficiency and transparency of the current process, in which government interacts with citizens, have helped to increase trust in government services.

In Chapter 9, Prijono Tjiptoherijanto and Meredith Rowen provide an overview of comprehensive changes implemented during and since the Reformation Era in Indonesia, which began in 1998. Constitutional change, increased democratization, decentralization, public sector reform, and anti-corruption measures receive special attention. Each of these processes is examined in terms of its overall impact on governance and, correspondingly, on trust in government at the national and sub-national levels. The authors see improvements in trust in government, while making a case for additional reforms in specific areas, including the establishment of a special institution for human resource management in order to ensure effective, accessible, and efficient public services.

In Chapter 10, Sukehiro Hasegawa examines the roles and performance of UN missions in Timor-Leste. He argues that trust in post-conflict countries such as Timor-Leste is dependent on the ability of the government institutions to maintain security and stability in the country, deliver public services, maintain the transparency and accountability of governmental operations, and protect human rights and the rule of law.

In the final chapter, Vesselin Popovski presents the main conclusions from the regional reviews and country studies. Together, these chapters result in a greater understanding of the nexus between trust and improvements in governance within the context of the region, as well as the methods that governments and governance partners can use to improve both trust and governance for the benefit of citizens within the larger Asia-Pacific region.

Notes

1. Social trust refers to the confidence that is bestowed on large groups of people, impersonal organizations, institutions, and systems. When social trust is high, citizens have more confidence in one another as members of a community and can pool their efforts to achieve common and mutually beneficial objectives. Political trust exists when citizens perceive the system and political incumbents to be responsive and when citizens appraise the government, its institutions, policy formation and implementation, and/or the individual political leaders as efficient and fair. Political and social trust have a complementary relationship, which is explored in greater detail within this publication. Social trust has a strong positive effect on trust in government. Political trust, in turn, contributes to greater political harmony and a civic culture of bipartisanship and mutual understanding of political differences.

REFERENCES

Almond, Gabriel A. and Sidney Verba (1963) *The Civic Culture: Political Attitudes and Democracy in Five Nations.* Princeton, NJ: Princeton University Press.

Axelrod, Robert (1984) *The Evolution of Cooperation.* New York: Basic Books.

Chaudhury, Nazmul and Shantayanan Devarajan (2006) "Human Development and Service Delivery in Asia," *Development Policy Review* 24:1.

Cheema, G. Shabbir (2005) *Building Democratic Institutions: Governance Reform in Developing Countries*. Westport, CT: Kumarian Press.

Cheema, G. Shabbir and Dennis A. Rondinelli (eds) (2007) *Decentralizing Governance: Emerging Concepts and Practices*. Washington DC: Brookings Institution Press.

Clark, Allen (2008) "Urban Transformation in Asia: Policy Implications for Decentralization," Report of the East-West Center Seminar on Urbanization in Asia.

De Tocqueville, Alexis (1984) *Democracy in America*, edited and abridged by Richard D. Heffner. New York: Penguin Books.

Fukuyama, Francis (1995) *Trust: The Social Virtues and the Creation of Prosperity*. London: Penguin.

Levi, Magarete (1998) *Of Rule and Revenue*. Berkeley: University of California Press.

Putnam, Robert D. (1993) *Making Democracy Work: Civic Traditions in Modern Italy*. Princeton, NJ: Princeton University.

Putnam, Robert D. (1995) "Tuning in, Tuning out: The Strange Disappearance of Social Capital in America," *Political Science & Politics* 28, pp. 664–683.

Putnam, Robert D. (2000) *Bowling Alone: The Collapse and Revival of American Community*. New York: Simon & Schuster.

Reynolds, Paul (2005) "Survey Reveals Global Dissatisfaction," *BBC News*, September 15, <http://news.bbc.co.uk/1/hi/world/europe/4245282.stm> (accessed 24 February 2010).

Rondinelli, Dennis A. and G. Shabbir Cheema (eds) (2003) *Reinventing Government for the Twenty First Century: State Capacity in a Globalizing Society*. Bloomfield, CT: Kumarian Press.

Rondinelli, Dennis A. and John M. Heffron (2009) *Leadership for Development: What Globalization Demands of Leaders Fighting for Change*. Westport, CT: Kumarian Press.

Rosenstone, Steven and John Hansen (1993) *Mobilization, Participation and Democracy in America*. New York: Macmillan.

Rothstein, Bo (2001) "Social Capital in the Social Democratic Welfare State," *Political and Society* 29:2, pp. 207–241.

Rothstein, Bo and Dietlind Stolle (2003) "Social Capital, Impartiality and the Welfare State: An Institutional Approach," in M. Hooghe and D. Stolle (eds) *Generating Social Capital: Civil Society and Institutions in Comparative Perspective*. New York: Palgrave, pp. 191–210.

Stolle, Dietlind (2001) "An Analysis of the Importance of Institutions, Families, Personal Experiences and Group Membership," in Paul Dekker and Eric M. Uslaner (eds) *Social Capital and Participation in Everyday Life*. London: Routledge.

UN-HABITAT [United Nations Human Settlements Programme] (2009) *Planning Sustainable Cities: Global Report on Human Settlements 2009*. London: Earthscan.

UN Millennium Project (2005) *Investing in Development: A Practical Plan to Achieve the Millennium Development Goals*. Report to the UN Secretary-General. New York: Earthscan.

United Cities and Local Governments (2007) "Changing Cities are Driving Our World," *Final Declaration of the Congress of Jeju, the "Island of World Peace"*. Jeju, Republic of Korea, October 31. Available at <http://www.cities-localgovernments.org/uclg/upload/template/templatedocs/UCLG_Final_Declaration_ENG.pdf> (accessed 22 January 2010).

United Nations (2007a) *Report of the 7th Global Forum on Reinventing Government*. New York: United Nations.

United Nations (2007b) *The Challenge of Restoring Governance in Crisis and Post-Conflict Countries*. New York: United Nations.

Wright, Teresa (2007) "Road Blocks on the Way to Democratic Change in Contemporary China," *East West Center Observer*, Fall.

2

Building trust in government: Linking theory with practice

Peride K. Blind

One simple question occupying the mind of the ordinary citizen today is the following: Whom should I be wary of if not the government that wields great power with great temptations to abuse it (Bentham 1999)? This should not come as a surprise when democracies themselves are conceived, and correctly so, as regimes of regulated and institutionalized political conflict (Braithwaite 1998; Dunn 1988; Sztompka 1999; Thompson 2004). In both the developed and the developing world, citizens asking themselves this very same question play a political game of delegation of power with uncertain outcomes. This is mainly because the motivations and actions of political leaders cannot be known in advance with certainty (Przeworski 1991). Trust, in this regard, emerges as one of the most important ingredients upon which the legitimacy and sustainability of political systems are built and maintained.

If a certain degree of suspicion on the part of the citizenry is a necessary condition for a healthy democracy, why is trust so important for good governance? How can individual political representatives and political institutions such as governments and their respective branches foster and develop trust in a way and to a degree that assures a modicum of good governance? How does trust relate to the new social, political, and economic requirements imposed by globalization and why is it crucial, now more than ever, to cultivate and maintain trust? This chapter tries to shed light on these questions, and investigates the place and importance of trust in today's globalized societies and governments. It does that by first embarking on a close examination of the theoretical definitions of

Building trust in government: Innovations in governance reform in Asia, Cheema and Popovski (eds), United Nations University Press, 2010, ISBN 978-92-808-1189-6

the multifaceted concept of trust. It then draws on empirical examples and survey results to show the various determinants of trust, as well as how and why trust has emerged as a crucial issue facing present-day governments. Thirdly, the chapter attempts to establish the actual and potential causal links between different types of trust and effective governance. Finally, the chapter presents a comparative illustration of innovative trust-building mechanisms devised and put in place by governments at different levels of governance, as presented at the Ministerial Roundtable at the 7th Global Forum on Reinventing Government held in Vienna in 2007.

Definitions and categories of trust

Trust is a complex interpersonal and organizational construct (Duck 1997; Kramer and Tyler 1995). "Trust occurs when parties holding certain favourable perceptions of each other allow this relationship to reach the expected outcomes" (Wheeless and Grotz 1977: 251). A trusting person, group, or institution will be "freed from worry and the need to monitor the other party's behaviour, partially or entirely" (Levi and Stoker 2000: 496). In that sense, trust is an efficient means for lowering transaction costs in any social, economic, and political relationship (Fukuyama 1995). Trust is also more than that. It is the underpinning of all human contact and institutional interaction (Misztal 1996; Tonkiss et al. 2000;).

Trust in general has two main variants.[1] Trust assessed in political terms is called *political trust*.[2] Political trust happens when citizens appraise the government and its institutions, policy-making in general, and/or the individual political leaders as promise keeping, efficient, fair, and honest. Political trust, in other words, is the "judgment of the citizenry that the system and the political incumbents are responsive, and will do what is right even in the absence of constant scrutiny" (Miller and Listhaug 1990: 358). As such, "political trust constitutes a central indicator of public's underlying feeling about its polity" (Newton and Norris 2000: 53) and comes into play every time a new policy is announced (Ocampo 2006).

Political trust can be directed toward the political system and its organizations as well as the individual political incumbents. The first category of political trust is referred to as *macro-level* or *organizational trust*. This refers to an issue-oriented perspective whereby citizens become trustful or distrustful of government "because they are satisfied or dissatisfied with policy alternatives" (Miller 1974: 951). Organizational political trust can be further subdivided into the components of *diffuse* or *system-based trust* and *specific* or *institution-based trust*. Diffuse political trust refers to citizens' evaluation of the performance of the overall political system and the regime. Specific political trust, in contrast, is directed toward certain political institutions, such as the Congress or the local police force.

In addition to macro-level or organizational trust, there is a second category of political trust called *micro-level* or *individual political trust*. This is when trust is directed toward individual political leaders. Individual political trust involves a person-oriented perspective whereby citizens become trustful or distrustful of government "because of their approval or disapproval of certain political leaders" (Citrin 1974: 974–975).

Organizational and individual political trust is a categorization based on the object toward which trust is directed. Political trust also has variants based on the different types of motivations people have when trusting their political institutions or leaders.[3] Thus, political trust can be accorded based on either rational or psychological models of reasoning, or a combination of both (Leach and Sabatier 2005). *Rational political trust* involves an interest-based calculation in which citizens evaluate whether the government and/or the political leaders are acting in accordance with their partisan agenda. This is also what Warren (2006) refers to as *first-order* or *encapsulated trust*. In first-order trust, trust exists for A when he or she delegates to B control over C in which A has an interest. A has a good reason to trust B when A knows that his/her interests are encapsulated in B's interests. By the same token, "B becomes trustworthy to the extent that he attends to A's interests" (Warren 1999: 24–26). Citizens who follow the tenets of rational political trust, therefore, tend to trust the political party or the political leaders with whom they identify.[4]

Political trust transcends partisan calculations. Work by Hetherington (2005) maintains that trust in government, by itself and independently of partisanship, has now become a significant predictor of support for government policies. Likewise, Warren (2006) maintains that first-order or encapsulated political trust based on the maximization of self-interest is not sufficient for genuine political trust to transpire. According to Warren (2006), rational political trust depends upon another and equally, if not more, important type of political trust called *psychological* or *second-order political trust*. Psychological political trust involves an assessment of the moral values and attributes associated with a particular government, political institution, and/or individual political leaders. As such, it refers to the perspective that people might have on the trustworthiness of their political representatives. In political trust based on psychological reasoning, people search for sincerity and truthfulness in the personality, public appearances, speeches, and behavior of their political leaders.

Although an analytical categorization of political trust in terms of the nature of its *targets*, i.e. organizations and/or individuals, and its *motivations*, i.e. rational and/or psychological, is useful for didactic purposes, different variants of political trust are mutually inclusive and may tend to work together. Lack of trust toward specific incumbents, for instance, can transform itself into a distrust of different political institutions and, ultimately, of the political system as a whole. People (or trustees), in trusting their representatives and political institutions, combine tenets of both rational and psychological political trust thereby trying to strike an acceptable balance between the maximization of their interest and their perception of the ethical qualities of the political entities. The legitimacy and durability of democratic systems, in other words, depend in large part on the extent to which the electorate trusts the government to do what is right and perceived as *fair* (Easton 1965) as well as what is *efficient* (Citrin and Green 1986; Feldman 1983; Hetherington 1998; Keele 2005; Lawrence 1997).[5]

Political trust does not emerge, nor does it operate, in a vacuum. Social trust, which refers to citizens' confidence in each other as members of a community, is inseparable from the notion of political trust. According to Putnam's eminent theory of social capital, civic engagement in a community and the interpersonal trust among its members contribute to the rising of overall social trust in a given society (1995, 2000). Face-to-face contact with members of the community in societal associations not only allows people to get to know each other better in personal terms, but also permits them to extend the positive feeling derived from this civic experience to strangers in society and in government. It is a well-known fact that citizens who are not involved in civic activities tend to view the government and its institutions in more negative terms. Social capital, as such, has a significant and strong effect on trust in government apart from, and along with, government performance (Keele 2004: 16). The categories and types of trust are summarized in Figure 2.1.[6]

Although social trust and political trust are not mutually exclusive, there is, in the literature, controversy about the presence and direction of the causality between the two. Is it social capital and the forging of social trust that then breed political trust, or is it the other way around? Can trustworthy governments foster social capital and create trustful and active civic communities? What are some of the tools to unite social and political trust in order to bring about efficient and durable political systems? Different theoretical schools have offered different answers to these questions. Modernization theorists, such as Almond and Verba (1963) and Finifter (1970), have maintained that increasing social trust is associated with increasing political participation, especially in the form of voting. Increased participation, in turn, has been a generally accepted sign of political trust and democratization. Sociologists, on the other hand, have associated increasing social distrust, and not trust, with more active political involvement and, eventually, enhanced political trust

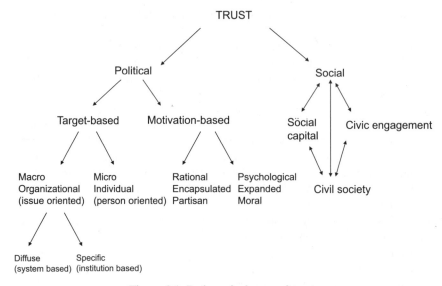

Figure 2.1 Pedagogical map of trust.

(Gamson 1968). Tarrow (2000), for instance, has gone so far as to affirm that contentious politics, in the form of increased social protests and new social movements, constitutes a sign of working trust in industrialized democracies and thus is healthy.[7]

Social capital can be defined as a "lubricant of interactions among people" since it facilitates collective and collaborative action (Arrow 1974: 23). Nevertheless, this should not be taken to mean that social capital or social trust can readily transform themselves into political trust in every society and at all times. Veenstra (2002), for instance, shows that in Canada participation in a range of civil society organizations increases social trust but not political trust. This and similar findings bring a group of scholars called the *new institutionalists* to maintain that it is not social capital that produces political trust but a trustworthy government, which then generates interpersonal trust. New institutionalists insist that it is the state, and the political trust embodied within it, that then promotes social trust along with a productive economy, a peaceful and a cooperative society, and, ultimately, democratic governance (Fukuyama 1995; Levi 1997).[8] Indeed, governments today employ a multitude of political, economic, and social tools to empower citizens and foment social trust, including decentralization, the use of technology for better access to information and services, efficient economic policy-making, and undertakings that directly combat political distrust, such as anti-corruption laws, context-specific crime-fighting mechanisms, and innovative reforms in public institutions. At the same time, however, societies in which people trust each other are more receptive to, and better able to harness, these institutional reforms.

The interplay of social and political trust is even more crucial for crisis and post-crisis countries. Whether the crisis in question is economic, political, or social in its origins, this group of countries conforms to unique parameters of rule-making and institution-building. The literature on the effectiveness of post-crisis reforms does not include an adequate scrutiny of underlying governmental deficiencies. Instead, it focuses on effective economic policy-making, particularly if the crisis involves financial and fiscal problems, as it almost always does. According to Gallo et al. (2006), however, in addition to effective management of economic policy, the political situation and the rebuilding of the political structure are crucial post-crisis variables that political and social leaders should heed. A political structure characterized by corrupt dealings, fragmented power, and a lack of consensus hampers the making of credible economic policies. Consequently, trust becomes embedded in every single action and deed undertaken by leaders in crisis and post-crisis countries.

In crisis and post-crisis countries, strategic bargaining among members of the elite is the first and most important undertaking for achieving the sought-after peace and stability. As such, effective mediation styles, such as facilitation and the formulation and management of issues, are important factors in of crisis abatement (Beardsley et al. 2006). Yet even the processes of strategic bargaining involve the variable of trust in the background. Groups of elite members interacting with each other with the aim of forming new institutions are already starting to build interpersonal trust. They institute sweeping policy changes, they reform the legal framework, and they restructure the sociopolitical models in post-crisis contexts. Whereas the forming of new institutions is relatively easier, their effective functioning and the legitimacy they enjoy are harder to achieve. The building of trust, therefore, must become an implicit part of every project of constitution-making and institution-building from the very beginning.[9]

In addition to the unique case of crisis and post-crisis countries, different perspectives on the relationship between social trust and political trust emerge from the experiences of the developed and the developing world. Whereas increased civic engagement brings enhanced social and political working trust in the industrialized world, Brehm and Rahn (1997) find a negative relationship between civic engagement and political trust in the developing world. Newton (1999), on the other hand, finds an insignificant relationship. Espinal and Hartlyn (2006) demonstrate that, in the case of the Dominican Republic, increased civic engagement decreases political trust because it exposes citizens to the illegitimate and corrupt practices of government institutions on a daily basis. Hazan (2006) arrives at the same conclusion with respect to the case of Morocco. Harutyunyan (2006) directs our attention to the important caveat of social polarization in his account of Armenia, where deficits of social and political trust go hand in hand with low scores for democracy.

The above account of the variety of associations between social and political trust in different countries, regions, and time periods brings the following conclusion. A certain degree of social distrust may generate increased political involvement on the part of some people, in some circumstances, and with respect to only some kinds of political activity. As a result, a country-based institutionalist perspective fares better in investigating the complex nexus between social and political trust (Levi and Stoker 2000). At the same time, "high dissatisfaction with democracy and extremely low levels of trust almost unequivocally go together" (Norris 1999: 228–233). This implies that, although it is healthy for citizens to suspect that their political representatives might not act in line with the wishes of their constituencies, prolonged periods of social and political distrust on the part of the majority of the population can produce deleterious consequences for governments and governance.

Trends in trust: Quantitative perspectives

Since the mid-1960s, public trust in government and political institutions has been decreasing in all of the advanced industrialized democracies (Dalton 2004; Dalton and Wattenberg 2000). Although the pattern and the pace of the decrease vary across countries, the downward trend is ubiquitous. Except for the Netherlands, which actually showed increased trust in the government from the 1970s until the mid-1990s, all of the other advanced industrialized democracies recorded a decline in the level of trust enjoyed by their respective governments. Austrians pointed to the collapse of a collectivist consensus as the main culprit in declining trust in government. Canadians blamed the continuing tensions over nationalism and separatism in the country. Germans attributed their malaise to the strains of unification, while the Japanese condemned successive political scandals and the long economic recession of the 1990s (Dalton 2005). Even the Swedes and the Norwegians, generally associated with a high degree of trust in politics, became distrustful of their political institutions in the 1990s (Christensen and Laegreid 2003).

There is a myriad of surveys undertaken by governmental and nongovernmental organizations in order to measure levels of trust in the developed world. The World Economic Forum, the World Values Survey, Eurobarometer, AsiaBarometer, Latinobarometro, the Australian Government Information Management Office (AGIMO), Accenture, MORI, the BBC and Gallup International, the United Nations Public Administration Network (UNPAN), the United Nations Development Programme (UNDP), Transparency International, and many other national and international organizations have conducted surveys confirming the decline in trust in various parts of the world.[10] These surveys have found a consistent and universal decline in trust in a range of political institutions since January 2004.

Global dissatisfaction with the government was found to be 65 percent in Western Europe, 73 percent in Eastern and Central Europe, 60 percent in North America, 61 percent in Africa, 65 percent in Asia Pacific, and 69 percent in Latin America in 2005 (Reynolds 2005). A review of the data suggests that the situation did not change significantly in 2006, when trust levels rarely rose above 50 percent (Cheema 2006). Whereas trust in institutions seems to be higher in East Asia and the European Union, it plummets when it comes to Latin America. Although trust in the institutions of the European Union is high, trust in the institutions of the enlarged European Union is not. As in Europe, trust in political institutions, and particularly in government, remains fairly low in East Asia.

In South Asia, there are high- and low-trust countries. Overall trust in political institutions is 64 percent in India, 43 percent in Pakistan and 55 percent in Nepal.

It should be noted that, although a multi-regional or sub-regional comparison of degree of trust in institutions is important, it depicts only one point in time in history. Equally important is a longitudinal analysis such as the one undertaken by Dalton (2005), who finds that trust in political institutions and political leaders is consistently declining except in the case of the Netherlands.[11] Citizens of the developed world think that their deputies do not care about the needs of their respective constituencies or the public good. Politicians as a group are perceived as less trustworthy over time in various countries of the developed world. In Austria, Britain, Finland, Norway, and Sweden, people think more and more that all that politicians care about are votes. In Canada, Denmark, Germany, France, Italy, New Zealand, and Australia, people think that the representatives are losing touch with, and do not care about, the public. This cross-regional trend of falling trust in government institutions and representatives pertains to the time period ranging from the 1970s to the mid-1990s. Why is that the case and why should this be seen as a problem?

Determinants of trust: Qualitative perspectives

Some of the symptoms of this so-called "democratic malaise" of declining of trust in advanced industrialized democracies (Tanguay 1999: 325–326) are declining voter turnout (Gray and Caul 2000; Eagles 1999), lack of interested among youth in politics (Adsett 2003), and decreasing levels of civic involvement (Saul 1995; Putnam 2000). Although symptoms do not constitute explanations for declining trust, many factors can be cited as potential reasons. Periods of poor economic performance and citizens' perception that the government is incapable of dealing with the fiscal and financial challenges are one reason (Mansbridge 1997; Newton and Norris 2000). The political economy literature agrees that higher levels of trust are associated with wealthier areas. Reciprocally, lower degrees of trust go hand in hand with poorer areas (Leigh 2006). People have greater trust in governments that can bring about economic growth, create jobs, provide access to education, and deliver services in an easy and transparent manner (Fiorina 1978; Mackuen et al. 1992).

Nye (1997) argues that citizens' negative evaluation of the national economy and their negative perceptions of their government's ability to respond to economic challenges engender even more distrust in an age of globalization. Competitive pressures and the economic dislocations of globalization, growing economic inequality, and increasing numbers of marginalized people in both the developed and the developing world have indeed fueled the loss of political trust in governments' ability and willingness to act in a timely and adequate manner (Alesina and Wacziarg 2000). As a result, trust in people has declined. On the other hand, there is also evidence that economic globalization and in particular the variables of openness of markets and trade integration have positively affected citizens' trust in their governments (Berggren and Jordahl 2006: 154). Economic causes, particularly economic inequality, are not the only propelling forces of the decline in trust worldwide. Political and social parameters are also at play. Successive political scandals, rampant corruption, and the sometimes overrated focus of the media on these issues have also contributed their fair share to the decline of trust in government institutions and political leaders.

Corruption emerges as one of the most important political factors contributing to the decline of levels of trust in the government in both the developed and the developing world.[12] Job (2005) finds that, if individuals perceive corruption in politics, then their trust in local institutions is adversely affected. Since trust in local government institutions is the strongest predictor of trust in remote political institutions, such as the national Congress and/or the Presidency, corruption becomes an important indirect determinant of political trust.[13] The impact of corruption on trust varies not only according to national versus local levels of governance, but also at the transnational level of analysis. Thus, although Espinal and Hartlyn (2006) maintain that security and corruption are much more important for trust in government in the developing than the developed world, political performance on issues of security and corruption is universally associated with increasing trust (Lipset and Schneider 1987; Mishler and Rose 1997, 2001; Turner and Martz 1997).

There seem to be two important caveats about the relationship between trust and corruption with respect to the legitimacy of political systems and good governance. First, it is not enough for political leaders and institutions to fight corruption; they should also avoid appearing corrupt (Warren 2006). Second people might trust their government even if there is some degree of perceived and/or real corruption. This occurs when social capital is strong and people are trustful of each other and of strangers in general (Job 2005). In both cases, however, establishing trust requires an open society where citizens are able to debate and question government policies and can have a sense of making a difference in decision-making processes. That said, although corrupt and authoritarian regimes destroy trust, open and democratic rule does not necessary generate trust either. A democratic governance system is a necessary but not a sufficient element in generating or maintaining trust.

The appearance of corruption is an important issue in political trust. If a political official is honest but appears to be corrupt, he/she will be considered corrupt. Prophylactic laws, or *regulations on appearance*, which have emerged and developed since the 1960s, have made the appearance of corruption an offence in itself, punishable by censure or loss of position, even when the appearance cannot be traced to an underlying improper act. Such laws focus primarily on finances, and put limits on the amounts and sources of campaign contributions, honoraria, and gifts. In such matters, "officials are liable not just for their behaviour but also for how their conduct appears to the public" (Warren 2006: 3).

In addition to and apart from appearance regulations, *appearance standards* have also transpired as the "informal norms of ensuring a relationship of accountability between citizens and their political representatives" (Hellman 2001; Thompson 1995: 125–126). Appearance standards have placed an extra burden on political leaders in ensuring transparency and rules of conduct that will be perceived as honest and trustworthy by society at large. Easy access to information, tools of e-governance, efficient delivery of services, face-to-face contact, and creative and efficient ways of dealing with issues of distrust by converting them into issues of trust are some of the tools used by political leaders to avoid the appearance of corruption (Torres et al. 2006; Warren 2006).[14]

There is a slight difference in the burden placed on *political leaders* compared with *public servants* in regulating the appearance of corruption. According to Warren (2006), the obligations and duties of political representatives are less specific and more conflictual in nature than are those of civil servants and the judiciary. The political nature of the office of political delegates makes them automatically susceptible to charges of corruption. This is mainly because political representatives have a duty to maintain communication with their particular constituents, which makes them prone to being perceived as corrupt officials serving a few powerful interests. Conversely, civil servants are less likely to be perceived as corrupt because the idea of public trust implies that citizens place their trust in civil servants to represent the public interest in established areas of administration. In fact, "suspicions of corruption surround national parliaments much more so than the executive and the judiciary" (Warren 2006: 4). Both political representatives and civil servants, however, must avoid acting in a way that gives rise to a reasonable belief of wrongdoing. "When they fail to do so, they do not merely appear to do wrong; they do wrong" (Hellman 2001: 668).

The second caveat about the relationship between corruption and political trust is the existence and degree of social capital present in the society. This also refers to the group of social factors that affect the outcome of political trust in the government. Accordingly, social and demographic factors, such as the level of literacy and education, gender, and age, are important determinants of social and political trust (Christensen and Laegreid 2003), albeit not universally. Espinal and Hartlyn (2006), for instance, find that age has a non-linear impact on political trust in the developing world: older generations who experienced authoritarian institutions tend to be more tolerant of corrupt but democratic governments. In the developing world, middle-income groups are structurally most likely to be frustrated and distrustful of governments (Lozano 2002). This is because the poor enter into clientelistic relations with the state and the wealthy achieve privileged access to state power; this arrangement leaves the dwindling middle class more and more isolated, hence distrustful. These results are in sharp contrast with survey results from the industrialized world, where the sociodemographic characteristics of societies are normally negatively associated with political trust. Political trust, in other words, decreases as one gets older and/or one's socioeconomic status rises in advanced industrialized countries (Inglehart 1997).

Along with sociodemographic variables such as age and income level, the holistic concepts of social capital and civic engagement are also important social factors influencing the degree of political trust in the government. Veenstra (2002), for instance, finds that participation in civil society is significantly related to social trust but weakly related to political trust in the context of Canada. He explains this dichotomy by referring to the type and nature of civic engagement. The gist of the explanation is that superficial participation in the form of paying annual fees in networks of association does not teach people about trust. He instead recommends meaningful dialogue and regular face-to-face involvement in cooperative civil society organizations. Job (2005), on the other hand, finds a direct relation between social capital, defined in sociological terms, and political trust in the Australian case. She concludes that, if people are trusting of their familiar circle and their close community, they will extend their trust to their local and national representatives and government, even when the latter do poorly at times.

Although the context-specific nature of political trust is irrefutable, one important convergence emerges across cases with respect to social and political trust in the era of globalization. That is the changed expectations of citizens vis-à-vis their governments and their political representatives. This refers to the possible emergence of a *new civic culture* with an emphasis on new ethical and practical concerns. The new civic culture cherishes trust for itself and not as a means to other ends. It cares more about moral or second-order trust than about partisan or first-order trust: it demands sincerity and truthfulness in the words and deeds of representatives (Warren 2006: 7). The new civic culture puts more emphasis on relational trust than on rational trust (Job 2005). It wants to be able to monitor government performance much more closely than before (Torres et al. 2006). The apparent emergence of the new civic culture worldwide, but particularly in the developed world, prompts Krahn and Harrison (2006) to argue that governments today would be better off applying programs and policies that enhance trust in government directly, such as reforms aimed at rendering politics more transparent and dispersing the power of political decision-making to foster accountability, rather than proposing reforms in relation to economic efficiency or neo-populist solutions such as recalls or referendums that promote trust indirectly.

Why all of a sudden are citizens putting more emphasis on ethical and psychological norms than on the partisan and rational attributes of political trust? What is driving societies to value second-order trust more than first-order trust? In short, why is there a sudden preference of morality over capability? The answer to these questions lies in the forces of globalization facing governments of today, more so than the individual institutional characteristics of countries. A decline in trust is happening across countries with diverse institutional structures, historical legacies, and cultural underpinnings. Although the attributes and the relationship of social and political trust are country specific, the possible explanations for, as well as the potential solutions to, the decline in trust in government might very well be grounded in the new requirements imposed by globalization (Dalton 2005).

Causal links between trust and governance in the global age: How can trust help build good and effective governance?

Globalization is a complex concept that refers to a series of social, political, economic, and technological changes spurred by increasing interaction among the people, companies, and governments of the world.[15] Globalization has led to a redefinition of the functions and the role of the state. The state now has to be a strategic planner instead of a provider of goods and services. It has to create and preserve an "even playing field for private enterprise and individual initiative instead of managing the field" (Bertucci and Alberti 2003: 23). The new state also has to pursue fiscal conservatism and create wealth by offering a favorable economic environment for foreign and domestic capital. The new state has to adopt the core values of integrity, professionalism, and respect for diversity while being fully proficient in communications, technology, and economic competition. It must be endowed with political legitimacy and accountability. Although the new state should be tough when it comes to capturing markets and attracting investments, it should also care about softer variables such as norms, values, rules, and symbols. The new state, in other words, has to be a "competent state" (Cheema 2005: 152). The competent state, by definition, strives to generate and maintain what might be called a *trust culture* (Sztompka 1999; Lewicki and Tomlinson 2003). A trust culture is one in which citizens feel that they have a more or less equal and potential chance of making a difference in political decision-making. This is where good governance comes in as the indispensable corollary of the trust culture.

Governance can be defined as the specific ways in which a society organizes itself in order to make decisions, mediate differences, and exercise legal rights. The three main actors of governance are the state, civil society, and the private sector. In this tripartite division of labour, the *state* creates an enabling political, economic, and legal environment; *civil society* facilitates political and social interaction; and the *private sector* generates jobs, goods, and services (UNDP 1997a). *Good governance* is simply the harmonious interaction of these three actors. More broadly, good governance describes an open and efficient way of conducting public affairs, managing public resources, and guaranteeing the realization of human rights. Good governance accomplishes these goals in a manner essentially free of abuse and corruption and with due regard to rule of law.[16] Good governance, as such, is synonymous with *democratic* governance because it is participatory, transparent, and accountable (UNDP 1997b).

Trust, in both its social and its political forms, is the sine qua non of democratic governance. Democratic governance and trust feed into each

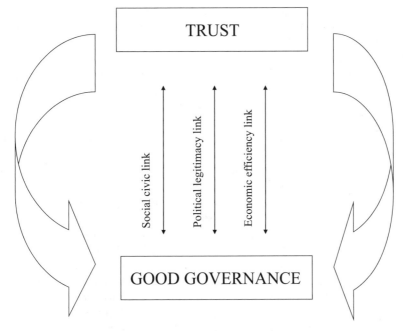

Figure 2.2 Links between trust and good governance.

other: trust breeds democratic governance, and vice versa. Hetherington (2005) refers to political trust as the main motor of good governance. A high level of trust in government and political incumbents benefits all citizens, especially minorities and people who are at a relative disadvantage in socioeconomic and/or political terms. The three main causal mechanisms that operate between trust and good governance are: (1) the *social civic* causal mechanism, (2) the *economic efficiency* causal mechanism, and (3) the *political legitimacy* causal mechanism. Although these three links between trust and good governance are nowhere exclusionary, they provide us with good analytical tools to assimilate and simplify the otherwise extremely complex phenomenon of globalization and its ramifications (Figure 2.2).

The social civic link

Although democratic governance breeds trust, trust is a prerequisite for democratic governance in the first place. In order for public administration to function smoothly and effectively, it must rely on public support and trust. Democratic governance cannot flourish in a society where there is a dearth of social trust. The social civic link between trust and good governance involves principally the building and maintaining of a vibrant civil society. In a society where people distrust each other and choose not to engage in meaningful activities in networks of societal associations, there is a high likelihood of the government and its representatives being accorded low political legitimacy. The formation and maintenance of successful and effective partnerships between the government and other institutions depend on social trust as well as on a strong civil society in constant interaction with the government and the private sector (Jones 2006). A strong civil society mediates effectively between the citizenry and the government. As such, it constitutes an important arena for the intermediation of interests.

The positive impact of civil society participation on good governance can easily be destroyed by corruption. The negative effects of corruption are undeniable when it comes to good governance: corruption saps social trust and constrains the development of local and national economies, with deleterious consequences for sustainable political, economic, and social development. The South African case has clearly demonstrated the complexity and the importance of fighting corruption in order to promote good governance. Insufficient coordination of anti-corruption work within the South African public service and among the various sectors of society is one of the main challenges facing the South African government today (Pillay 2004). Morocco, where a Truth and Reconciliation Commission has pushed for political reforms to fight corruption, is also a good example of the importance of effective coordination between the political and social realms in building trust towards good governance (Hazan 2006).

One innovative way to promote trust is e-government. Computer-based interactions can potentially reach those citizens who would otherwise be reluctant to express or listen to different viewpoints (Redburn and Buss 2004: 163). The enhanced technological tools at the disposal of countries today can be used to devise virtual models of participation where citizens can interact and share opinions freely and openly on the Internet. Enhanced computer technology can also allow citizens to contact their political representatives more easily and hold them accountable for their deeds and actions. E-government has pushed many holders of public office to post regular and detailed information about their performance on the Internet. This, in turn, has contributed to increased transparency and accountability. E-participation and e-government, therefore, not only reduce the information asymmetry between the governors and the governed, but also enhance transparency by inviting greater citizen participation and oversight of policy affairs (Kalu 2006).

The economic efficiency link

Increasing social and political trust through the implementation of sound economic policies is also crucial for good and effective governance. "A competent state needs to provide for open, efficient, and competitive markets" (Rondinelli 2003: 33). States need to create an institutional structure and credibility for market economies to function effectively. Like the process of building trust, the building of institutions to achieve economic competitiveness takes time. Both processes, however, feed into each other: increasing social and political trust facilitates the process of economic restructuring, and sound economic policy-making and institution-building, in turn, enhance social and political trust. The political science literature on economic development concludes that although economic growth is a necessary condition for good governance, it is not a sufficient one: sound economic policy-making increases political trust for only a short period, after which citizens demand more substantial political and social reforms, such as an equitable society and accountable institutions. That said, economic stress and poor governance almost unequivocally go together (Przeworski et al. 1997).

Increasing trust via effective economic policy-making brings good governance only if the economic efficiency link takes into account the social variable, i.e. the social inequality and marginalization associated with globalization. A competent state can increase political and social trust as well as economic efficiency only by implementing safety-nets and social programs that target the poorest and the unskilled. There is an ongoing debate between scholars who argue that economic globalization has strengthened the welfare state (Moon and Yang 2002) and those who maintain that it has actually destroyed it (Faux and Mishel 2000). Either way, the crosscutting attributes of the economic and social realms in building trust toward good and effective governance can hardly be ignored.

The political legitimacy link

Building political trust toward good governance, by definition, implies the political legitimacy link between trust and good governance. Legitimacy embodies the consent that citizens accord to the ruling government and/ or state institutions. If citizens think that a government rightfully holds and exercises power, then that government enjoys political legitimacy. Among the major determinants of legitimacy are social trust, economic effectiveness, and good political governance, along with democratic rights (Gilley 2006). Legitimacy is readily achieved if citizens trust in the government and their representatives. As such, political trust leads to good governance by contributing to the building of political legitimacy. Political legitimacy, in turn, further stimulates and extends political trust, thereby contributing to the democratization of governance.

One way to promote trust through the strengthening of political legitimacy is to bring communities closer to their governments and their governments to them.[17] Local governance and decentralization emerge as the perfect tools for doing this. Local governance means that members of local communities take responsibility and act for their future. Effective and democratic local governance requires the cooperation of all relevant stakeholders, such as local community members, schools, the police force, and local businesses, in tackling the problems at hand. It requires members of the community to watch out for each other and to launch initiatives such as keeping children off the streets, taking care of the elderly, and organizing community events to foster trust (Bovaird and Loeffler 2005). In this process, decentralization can buttress local governance by bringing local government officials closer to the community, and vice versa. Decentralization, by restructuring authority and empowering local governments, can promote partnership between the governors and the governed. As such, it constitutes another essential ingredient in sound governance (Farazmand 2004).

What decentralization and local governance can achieve at the local level is done through free, fair, and regular elections and parliamentary processes at the national level. Elections and parliamentary processes endowed with these characteristics are particularly important for the building of trust and good governance. Without regular, free, and fair elections, it would be quite impossible to talk about good governance. Elections confer and sustain political legitimacy because they symbolize the overall choice of the public. Elections also contribute to the building of trust and good governance by allowing for direct participation and the possibility of individual citizens being heard (Cheema 2005: 25). That said, elections alone are not sufficient for trust and good governance to emerge. In fact, political systems with relatively fair, free, and regular elections but devoid of legitimate parliamentary processes abound. Levitsky and Way (2002) call these systems "competitive authoritarian regimes."

Transparent and efficient parliamentary processes must complement fair, free, and regular elections in order for trust to spread in social and political relations. Legitimate parliamentary processes refer to the democratic functioning of parliaments. In cases where incumbents consistently sidestep the parliament in decision-making, one cannot talk about the meaningful representation of the public interest. By the same token, trust is hampered in political systems where hostile parliaments repeatedly block any policy-making attempt by the executive power. A harmonious and cooperative relationship between the parliament and the executive is therefore necessary for the building of trust, as is citizens' perception of the effective functioning and legitimacy of the parliament.

An independent judiciary is another pillar of trust in societies. The judiciary, as the guardian of all the established laws, has a fundamental role in the establishment and preservation of the rule of law. The idea of the rule of law implies that the exercise of public power must be backed by stable laws applied in an equal manner to all citizens. The rule of law therefore constitutes the perfect barrier against the arbitrary use of power (Finn 2004). In societies where the judiciary is perceived to be corrupt and inefficient, the rule of law is impaired and, as a result, distrust reigns. In such contexts, citizens might resort to violent and/or unlawful means in order to resolve their problems with each other and/or with the governing institutions. Crime might soar as result of these activities, with deleterious consequences for the stability of the overall political system.

The rule of law, an independent judiciary, free, fair, and regular elections, legitimate parliamentary processes, a healthy civil society, combating corruption and the appearance of corruption, local governance and decentralization, and, finally, e-governance all contribute to the enhanced transparency and accountability of the political system. Transparency and accountability are the principal requisites of both trust and good governance. There can be no trust or good governance without transparent and accountable underpinnings. In order for any political action to foster trust, and ultimately promote good governance, it has to be transparent, i.e. open and based on the principle that the architects can be held responsible for their actions, ergo the principle of accountability.

Despite transparency and accountability being universal conditions for fostering trust and promoting good governance, trust and governance remain context-dependent phenomena. Correspondingly, a behaviour that generates trust in one society might do the exact opposite in another. Trust can also vary according to *zeitgeist* or fashions: during certain periods, trust in government is taken for granted; at other times, the opposite is true (Czarniawska and Sevon 1996). Furthermore, trust may vary according to external political forces or based on the internal features of the system. Finally, a minimal degree of healthy distrust by citizens of their representatives might work as an efficient check to actually promote and sustain trust. In fact, consistently and exceedingly high levels of trust in government should always be questioned because this might conceal support for political illiberal alternatives, and even authoritarianism (Batto 2005). That is why it becomes crucial to carefully analyse the type of institutions to which trust is accorded,[18] while process-tracing the nature of and reasons for trust in specific context settings and policy issues.

There still remains, however, the question of how political leaders can create and preserve trust. The 7th Global Forum on Reinventing Government organized by the United Nations Department of Economic and Social Affairs in cooperation with its Institutional Partners Group in Vienna, Austria, in June 2007 provided the perfect venue for leaders and civil servants worldwide to review the complex concept of trust as well as the emerging issues associated with it. The next section provides a summary of the findings and conclusions of the Ministerial Round Table of this Forum and a recapitulation of the principal mechanisms and tools presented there for building and maintaining trust in government.

Innovations in building trust in government: The Ministerial Round Table of the 7th Global Forum on Reinventing Government

The relationship between trust and good governance is circular: while trust in government and its representatives encourages good governance, good governance in turn engenders and strengthens trust in all of its variants. A close examination of the theoretical underpinnings and empirical applications of the notion of social and political trust with respect to good governance shows that political leaders can forge and keep trust by implementing the following strategies:

- Showing genuine concern for the public good by maintaining consistency between words and deeds. This is "moral trust," with the emphasis on ethics and morality.
- Striving to represent the interests of their constituencies effectively, albeit with the embedded objective of serving the public good. This is "economic trust," with the emphasis on economic efficiency and partisanship.
- Implementing political reforms that will increase political trust directly and social trust indirectly, such as decentralization and innovation in public management. This is "political trust," with the emphasis on political legitimacy. Avoiding corruption and scandals is the sine qua non of maintaining political trust.
- Introducing social reforms that will strengthen civil society representation in tandem with political reforms. This is "social trust," with the emphasis on the catalyzing effects of social capital.
- Adopting technological innovations to make government more efficient, inclusive, and accessible to the citizenry, such as e-government and e-participation. This is "technological trust," with the emphasis on technological innovation, accountability, and equity.

- Simplifying the rules and procedures in public administration so that both citizens and civil servants minimize the obstacles of excessive form-filling and signature-acquiring. This is "administrative trust," with the emphasis on performance management and service delivery.

The Ministerial Round Table of the 7th Global Forum on Reinventing Government[19] also corroborated the urgency of proceeding full-speed with simultaneous and targeted trust-building and trust-keeping strategies and mechanisms on all fronts. The Round Table concluded that, in applying these strategies, political leaders must understand that building trust takes time, and a series of repeated games need to take place between the citizenry and the government before trust can flourish. Individuals, in other words, are more likely to trust one another after having interacted for several times together rather than on a first one-shot basis (Ostrom and Walker 2003). Good politicians, bureaucrats, and citizens learn how to behave appropriately and react intuitively with time and through interactions with the different subsets of society that they are representing (Christensen and Laegreid 2003). Politicians thus need to have resolve and patience in applying the above strategies in generating trust and in preserving it.

The Round Table also concluded that instituting and maintaining any kind of trust depends on institutionalizing the rules and norms that make trust relations more likely and enduring. That is when institutions and institution-building come into the picture. Legislated rules and regulations need to be institutionalized and systematized so that they are no longer *enforced rules* but *internalized values*. Institution-building does not only work rationally in terms of a means/ends analysis. Institution-building also makes sense sociologically: institutions promote ethics and trust as ends in themselves.

The Ministerial Round Table put special emphasis on e-government as a key and crosscutting tool in both streamlining and modernizing public administrations worldwide and on institutionalizing open and democratic governance. E-government benefits governments in numerous ways: e-procurement increases efficiency and transparency and helps curb corruption, while on-line applications for public sector employment result in trust and transparency for job applicants and efficiency gains for the government. With time, innovation, and experience, citizens may even participate electronically on a regular basis in the democratic process of government, thus transposing *e-government* into *e-governance*.

In addition to taking advantage of information and communication technologies (ICT) and other means of telecommunication, almost all of the countries that took part in the Ministerial Round Table adopted, at least to a certain extent, some form of performance management and evaluation techniques. Performance management refers to the measuring and assessing of the outcomes of organizations as a way to improve their activities. Therefore, it has now become more important than ever for governments to gauge their citizens' perceptions of different government institutions, policies, and services. Once citizens' perceptions and expectations are determined via the use of extensive public opinion surveys, governments can then take on the task of devising the fastest and most efficient ways of accomplishing these objectives in line with citizen expectations. Such an approach is intrinsically bottom-up and includes various means and rounds of consultation among different actors, and between them and citizens. With performance management, citizens realize that their opinions are valued and that their views are taken into account by their government, which they begin to perceive as caring and working for self-improvement and for the public good.

Among the innovative programs and tools for building and maintaining trust in government, participant governments in the Ministerial Round Table showcased a myriad of undertakings. In the domain of developing social trust, Tunisia created Citizen Listening Bureaus all around the country. Botswana introduced radio programs on accountability structures and capacity-building. Kenya set up neighborhood associations to increase security. Jordan published and distributed to citizens a "Directory of Services" pertaining to each governmental institution. In combining social with technological trust, the Kingdom of Morocco's Idaratouk project offered Moroccans three convenient channels for information: a free telephone line to seek redress and seek information, television programs on public ethics, and a public service website of the government.[20] Luxembourg's e-information, e-participation, and e-decision-making programs provide citizens with easy access to information, tools to interact with the government, and direct consultation opportunities with government representatives at all levels.

In fostering economic trust through the innovative use of ICT, Chile created "ChileCompra," where all activities related to public procurement can be effected online in efficient, transparent, and accountable ways. Kenya introduced the Citizen Service Delivery Charter to enforce effective delivery of quality services to citizens in line with their needs and responses. Azerbaijan heralded the ninth Millennium Development Goal (MDG), namely "Civil Service Reform for Long-Term Reduction of Poverty," as the first and principal legislative act of building trust.

In streamlining public administration and generating administrative trust, Korea, as part of its Innovation Capital Programme, introduced the ON-NARA Business Process System, which enables the computerized processing of all decision-making activities within administrative organizations. Accordingly, Korea's Local Administration Integration Information System (LAIIS) portal links local governments with each other, and with citizens, allowing the latter the opportunity to view and compare information from 260 indexes of local development. Fiji reduced the number of its ministries from 21 to 16 to streamline functions and processes.

In maintaining political trust with an eye to social peace and accountability, the government of Korea launched a website to empower citizens to file civil petitions and submit recommendations to the administrative agency of their choice.[21] The Immigration Clearance Service (Ministry of Justice, MOJ) was another digitalized service that has considerably reduced the waiting time for immigration clearance. Chile created a National Commission for Public Ethics (La Comisión Nacional de Ética Pública) and the Internal Auditing Council of the Government (Consejo de Auditoría Interna de Gobierno). Fiji set up the Fiji Independent Commission Against Corruption (FICAC). Azerbaijan established the Civil Service Management Council and Anti-Corruption Commission. Saudi Arabia founded the General Auditing Bureau and the Supreme Economic Council pursuant to various laws and decrees on financial transparency and development. Botswana formed the Citizen Empowerment Development Agency. China introduced a responsibility system in administrative enforcement of law. Chile legislated a law on transparency and *probidad* to prevent the phenomenon of the revolving door, among other things. The Kingdom of Morocco legislated Intilaka and Idaratouk, which both aimed at the simplification of procedures, the rationalization of structures, and the expansion of channels of citizen access to information.

Conclusions: Trust as a complex notion and multifarious practice

The analysis in this chapter has shown at best that trust is a complex social construct, which can be defined and categorized in many ways. Whether understood as a rational self-interest calculation or as a psychological belief in fairness and sincerity, the trust factor is omnipresent in every society and at all times. It concerns the government and its institutions, and extends beyond to the political system as a whole and down to the individual citizen as the political animal par excellence.

The analysis has also shown that there are numerous ways of generating and maintaining trust, the main ones being the rule of law, an independent judiciary, free, fair, and regular elections, legitimate parliamentary processes, a healthy civil society, combating corruption and the appearance of corruption, local governance and decentralization, and e-governance. These trust-building and trust-maintaining mechanisms may, in turn, rely on various mechanisms, including performance management and evaluation, e-government and other ICT tools, as well as innovative participatory governance mechanisms such as those outlined and demonstrated by the participant countries in the Ministerial Round Table of the 7th Global Forum on Reinventing Government.

Finally, the analysis has also made clear the intrinsic link between trust in all its forms and effective and legitimate governance. Generating and maintaining trust by default contributes to democratic governance, and vice versa. The difference between the two becomes merely a nuance in perception, the prism of trust putting more emphasis on the soft variables of reputation and the longevity of legitimacy. Democratic governance thus becomes enduring when and if trust is explicitly heeded and maintaining a trust culture becomes the rule rather than the exception. The key becomes finding the optimal level of trust in a given context and period for both performance and legitimacy to coexist and prosper (Clark and Lee 2001).

Acknowledgements

An earlier version of this article was published by the United Nations Department of Economic and Social Affairs' Division for Public Administration and Development Management in November 2006.

Notes

1. Some scholars make a distinction between the concepts of "confidence" and "trust," associating the former with a passive emotion accorded to the overall sociopolitical system, and conceptualizing the latter as a group of more dynamic beliefs and commitments accorded to people (Luhmann 2000; Noteboom 2002; Paxton 1999; Seligman 1997; Sztompka 1999). To avoid conceptual stretching and for purposes of parsimony, this chapter uses these two terms interchangeably.
2. The introductory chapter by Dr G. Shabbir Cheema also goes into the variants of trust where political and social trust are included. This chapter aims to go deeper into the definitions while presenting relevant case studies where these types of trust transpire, or fail to do so.
3. Some scholars question the very meaning of political trust based on whether it is directed toward the incumbent leaders or the political regime. Bean (2001), for instance, concludes that, in the Australian context, political trust is understood and perceived as incumbent-based only. A country-specific analysis of the concept of political trust would thus be beneficial for a thorough understanding of the notion.
4. It is interesting to note here that the results of the National Election Surveys (NES) conducted in the United States between 1964 and 2002 have shown that trust changes in accordance with partisan control of the presidency and the Congress (Keele 2005).
5. Job (2005) affirms the coexistence of rational and relational bases of political trust in the Australian political context. Klandermans et al. (2001) show that, in the case of South Africa, political trust depends largely on whether the government can effectively decrease poverty and inequality in the deeply divided South African society. Chanley

et al. (2000: 254) also demonstrate that skillful handling of the economy, along with miti-gation of concerns about crime, will contribute to an increase in political trust in the United States.

6. For a slightly different take on categories of trust, see Rose-Ackerman (2001a: 415–444; and 2001b). The disjunction between "interpersonal trust among citizens" and "citizen trust in government" is well documented in the cases of Central and Eastern Europe. For more, see the outcomes of Collegium Budapest research in 2001, among which are Kornai and Rose-Ackerman (2004) and Kornai et al. (2004). However, even in these publications, the chances for increased democracy are seen in terms of increased social trust, i.e. in committed citizens, whose everyday actions are deemed to be crucial for the success of transitions.

7. *New social movements* refer to the increasing number of non-ideological, culturalist, environmentalist, and anti-globalization protests staged by citizens who are relatively younger, more educated, and wealthier (Tarrow 1994).

8. *New institutionalism* is a paradigm of political science that emphasizes the relative autonomy of political institutions, particularly the state (March and Olsen 1984).

9. See Cherry (2006) for an account of how perceptions and trust proved crucial in the case of Korea following the 1997 financial crisis.

10. For more information on these surveys, see Cheema (2006).

11. A separate case-study analysis of the Netherlands is necessary in order to understand the possible causes of this difference. It is interesting, however, to note that the Nether-lands was also the country where the highest performance and improvement in e-government took place in the 1990s (Accenture 2006: 36).

12. Corruption, like trust, is a complex notion. Political corruption refers to the misuse of public office for private gain. The variants of political corruption can range from minor patronage to do and return favors to institutionalized bribery and kleptocracy, i.e. rule by thieves. Corruption, in all of its variants, is one of the greatest obstacles to develop-ment and legitimacy (see World Bank n.d.). Some of the most straightforward tools for combating corruption are ensuring freedom of the press, transparency, and gender equality (Kaufmann 2005), as well as maintaining economic growth (Kaufmann 2004; Leigh 2006).

13. The finding that trust placed in local representatives and institutions is generally higher than that in national institutions is also context dependent. Botan and Taylor (2005) show that in the case of Bosnia the opposite is true: Bosnians trust their local officials the least. This anomaly is explained by the behavior of these officials prior to and during the civil war.

14. Political leaders have at times criticized the appearance regulations and standards on corruption for the reason that they empower their critics, who might themselves be cor-rupt. Nevertheless, such rules and norms have been efficient in conveying a clean gov-ernment image (Morgan and Reynolds 1997).

15. Globalization is also cultural and intellectual since it involves extensive flows of ideas and symbols across borders (Friedman 2002: 17)

16. The rule of law implies that government authority must be exercised in accordance with the written laws and in an equal manner in relation to every citizen, regardless of any differences, such as gender or social, economic or political status. For more, see Linz and Stepan (1997: 18–20).

17. The caveat here is, of course, that the right balance is found between the freedom to question government and its actions and the scope for collaboration to forge state–society links. In this regard, see Chapter 3, in which Pam Suk Kim argues that, in con-texts of widespread corruption, increased participation by citizens can actually decrease trust.

18. In this volume, see Chapter 4 for a differentiation analysis of trust in order institutions versus representative institutions.
19. Chaired by the Honourable Dr Libertina Amathila, Deputy Prime Minister of Namibia, the Ministerial Round Table welcomed around 40 ministers and ministerial-level government representatives. Among the participating countries that made statements and/or presentations on their government's innovative reforms toward the building of trust were Chile, Syria, Kingdom of Saudi Arabia, Jordan, Kingdom of Morocco, Luxembourg, Azerbaijan, Kenya, Botswana, People's Republic of China, Republic of Korea, Lebanon, Tunisia, Thailand, Uruguay, and Bolivia. The Ministerial Round Table took place in Vienna, Austria, on June 27, 2007.
20. See <http://www.service-public.ma> (accessed 25 January 2010).
21. See <http://www.epeople.go.kr> (accessed 25 January 2010).

REFERENCES

Accenture (2006) *Leadership in Customer Service: Building the Trust.* Minneapolis, MN: Accenture.

Adsett, Margaret (2003) "Change in Political Era and Demographic Weight as Explanations of Youth 'Disenfranchisement' in Federal Elections in Canada 1965–2000," *Journal of Youth Studies* 6:3, pp. 47–64.

Alesina, A., and R. Wacziarg (2000) "The Economies of Civic Trust," in S. Pharr and R. Putnam (eds) *Disaffected Democracies: What's Troubling the Trilateral Countries?* Princeton, NJ: Princeton University Press, pp. 149–173.

Almond, G. A., and S. Verba (1963) *The Civic Culture: Political Attitudes and Democracy in Five Nations.* Princeton. NJ: Princeton University Press.

Arrow, K. (1974) The Limits of Organization. New York: Norton.

Batto, Nathan F. (2005) "The Adverse Consequences of Trust in Government," Conference Paper presented at the Midwest Political Science Association, Chicago, April.

Bean, C. (2001) "Party Politics, Political leaders and Trust in Government in Australia," *Political Science* 53:1, pp. 17–27.

Beardsley, K. C., D. M. Quinn, B. Biswas, and J. Wilkenfeld (2006) "Mediation Style and Crisis Outcomes," *Journal of Conflict Resolution* 50:1, pp. 58–86.

Bentham, Jeremy (1999) *The Collected Works of Jeremy Bentham: Political Tactics,* ed. Michael James Cyprian Blamires and Catherine Pease-Watkin. Oxford: Clarendon Press.

Berggren, Niclas, and Henrik Jordahl (2006) "Free to Trust: Economic Freedom and Social Capital," *Kyklos* 59:2.

Bertucci, G., and A. Alberti (2003) "Globalization and the Role of the State: Challenges and Perspectives," in D. A. Rondinelli and S. Cheema (eds) *Reinventing Government for the Twenty-First Century: State Capacity in a Globalizing Society.* Bloomfield, CT: Kumarian Press, pp. 17–33.

Blamires, M. J. C., and C. Pease-Watkin (eds) (1999) *The Collected Works of Jeremy Bentham: Political Tactics.* Oxford: Clarendon Press.

Botan, C. H., and M. Taylor (2005) "Role of Trust in Channels of Strategic Communication for Building Civil Society," *Journal of Communication* 55:4, pp. 685–702.

Bovaird, T., and E. Loeffler (2005) "Communities, Trust and Organizational Responses to Local Governance Failure," in S. Watson and A. Watson (eds) *Trust, Risk and Uncertainty*. New York: Palgrave, pp. 143–163.

Braithwaite, J. (1998) "Institutionalizing Distrust, Enculturating Trust," in J. Braithwaite and M. Levi (eds) *Trust and Governance*. New York: Russell Sage Foundation, pp. 343–375.

Brehm, J., and W. Rahn (1997) "Individual Level Evidence for the Causes and Consequences of Social Capital," *American Journal of Political Science* 41:3, pp. 999–1023.

Chanley, V., T. J. Rudolph, and W. M. Rahn (2000) "The Origins and Consequences of Public Trust in Government: A Time-Series Analysis," *Public Opinion Quarterly* 64, pp. 239–56.

Cheema, S. G. (2005) *Building Democratic Institutions: Governance Reform in Developing Countries*. Bloomfield, CT: Kumarian Press.

Cheema, S. G. (2006) "Building Trust in Government," Introduction to the Theme and Sessions, The Regional Forum on Reinventing Government in Asia, Seoul, Republic of Korea, September 6–8. Available at: <http://unpan1.un.org/intradoc/groups/public/documents/un/unpan024163.pdf> (accessed 26 January 2010).

Cherry, Judith (2006) "Killing Five Birds with One Stone: Inward Foreign Direct Investment in Post-Crisis Korea," *Pacific Affairs* 79:1, pp. 9–27.

Christensen, T., and P. Laegreid (2003) "Trust in Government: The Significance of Attitudes Towards Democracy, Public Sector and Public Sector Reforms," Working Paper 7, Stein Rokkan Center for Social Studies and Bergen University Research Foundation, April, pp. 1–30.

Citrin, J. (1974) "Comment: The Political Relevance of Trust in Government," *American Political Science Review* 68:3, pp. 973–988.

Citrin, J., and D. P. Green (1986) "Presidential Leadership and the Resurgence of Trust in Government," *British Journal of Political Science* 16:4, pp. 431–453.

Clark, Jeff R., and Dwight R. Lee (2001) "The Optimal Trust in Government," *Eastern Economic Journal* 27:1, Winter, pp. 19–34.

Czarniawska, B., and G. Sevon (eds) (1996) *Translating Organizational Change*. New York: De Gruyter.

Dalton, Russell J. (2004) *Democratic Challenges, Democratic Choices: The Erosion of Political Support in Advanced Industrial Democracies*. Oxford: Oxford University Press.

Dalton, Russell J. (2005) "The Social Transformation of Trust in Government," *International Review of Sociology* 15:1, pp. 133–54.

Dalton, Russell J., and M. Wattenberg (eds) (2000) *Parties Without Partisans: Political Change in Advanced Industrial Democracies*. Oxford: Oxford University Press.

Duck, S. (1997) *The Handbook of Personal Relationships: Theory, Research and Interventions*. New York: Wiley.

Dunn, J. (1988) "Trust and Political Agency," in D. Gambetta (ed.) *Trust: The Making and the Breaking of the Cooperative Bond*. Oxford: Basil Blackwell, pp. 73–93.

Eagles, M. (1999) "Elections," in J. Bickerton and Alain-G. Gagnon (eds) *Canadian Politics*. Peterborough: Broadview Press.

Easton, D. (1965) *A Systems Analysis of Political Life*. New York: Wiley.

Espinal, R., and J. Hartlyn (2006) "Performance Still Matters Explaining Trust in Government in the Dominican Republic," *Comparative Political Studies* 39:2, pp. 200–223.

Farazmand, A. (2004) "Building Partnerships for Sound Governance," in A. Farazmand (ed.) *Sound Governance: Policy and Administrative Innovations*. Westport, CT: Praeger, pp. 77–99.

Faux, J., and A. Mishel (2000) "Inequality and the Global Economy," in W. Hutton and A. Giddens (eds) *Global Capitalism*. New York: New Press.

Feldman, S. (1983) "The Measurement and Meaning of Political Trust," *Political Methodology* 9, pp. 341–54.

Finifter, A. W. (1970) "Dimensions of Political Alienation," *American Political Science Review* 64:2, pp. 389–410.

Finn, J. E. (2004) "The Rule of Law and Judicial Independence in Newly Democratic Regimes," *Good Society Journal* 13:3, pp. 12–16.

Fiorina, M. P. (1978) Economic Retrospective Voting in American National Elections: A Micro-Analysis," *American Journal of Political Science* 22:2, pp. 426–443.

Friedman, S. (2002) "Democracy, Inequality, and the Reconstitution of Politics," in J. S. Tulchin with A. Brown (eds) *Democratic Governance and Social Inequality*. Boulder, CO, and London: Lynne Rienner, pp. 13–41.

Fukuyama, F. (1995) *The Social Virtues and the Creation of Prosperity*. New York: Free Press.

Gallo, A., J. P. Stegmann, and J. W. Steagall (2006) "The Role of Political Institutions in the Resolution of Economic Crises: The Case of Argentina 2001–05," *Oxford Development Studies* 34:2, pp. 93–217.

Gamson, W. A. (1968) *Power and Discontent*. Homewood, IL: Dorsey.

Gilley, B. (2006) "The Determinants of State Legitimacy," *International Political Science Review* 27:1, pp. 47–71.

Gray, M., and M. Caul (2000) "Declining Voter Turnout in Advanced Industrial Democracies: 1950 to 1997: The Effects of Declining Group Mobilization," *Comparative Political Studies* 33, pp. 1091–1121.

Harutyunyan, A. (2006) "Dual Citizenship Debates in Armenia: In Pursuit of National Identity since Independence," *Demokratizatsiya*, March 22, pp. 283–302.

Hazan, P. (2006) "Morocco: Betting on a Truth and Reconciliation Commission," United States Institute of Peace Paper, Washington DC, July 1–16.

Hellman, Deborah (2001) "Judging by Appearances: Professional Ethics, Expressive Government, and the Moral Significance of How Things Seem," *Maryland Law Review* 60:3, pp. 653–687.

Hetherington, M. J. (1998) "The Political Relevance of Political Trust," *American Political Science Review* 92:4, pp. 791–808.

Hetherington, M. J. (2005) *Why Trust Matters: Declining Political Trust and the Demise of American Liberalism*. Princeton, NJ: Princeton University Press.

Inglehart, R. (1997) *Modernization and Postmodernization: Cultural, Economic, and Political Change in 43 Societies*. Princeton, NJ: Princeton University Press.

Job, Jenny (2005) "How Is Trust in Government Created? It Begins at Home, but Ends in the Parliament," *Australian Review of Public Affairs* 6:1, pp. 1–23.

Jones, J. M. (2006) "Trust in Government: Declining, Near Lows for the Past Decade; Less than Half Express Trust and Confidence in Executive Branch," Gallup Poll News Service, Princeton, NJ, September 26.

Kalu, K. N. (2006) "Citizenship, Administrative Responsibility, and Participation in Governance: One More Look," in N. Kakabadse and A. Kakabadse (eds) *Governance, Strategy and Policy: Seven Critical Essays*. New York: Palgrave, pp. 73–94.

Kaufmann, D. (2005) "Myths and Realities of Governance and Corruption," World Economic Forum, November. Available at <http://www.worldbank.org/wbi/governance/wp-governance.html> (accessed 26 January 2010).

Kaufmann, D. (2004) "Corruption, Governance and Security: Challenges for the Rich Countries and the World." World Bank Report, Washington DC: World Bank Institute, October. Available at <http://www.worldbank.org/wbi/governance//wp-governance.html> (accessed 26 January 2010).

Keele, Luke (2004) "Social Capital, Government Performance, and the Dynamics of Trust in Government," October 14. Available at <http://polmeth.wustl.edu/retrieve.php?id=463> (accessed 25 January 2010).

Keele, Luke (2005) "The Authorities Really Do Matter: Party Control and Trust in Government," *Journal of Politics* 67:3, pp. 873–886.

Klandermans, Bert, Marlene Reofs, and Johan Olivier (2001) "Grievance Formation in a Country in Transition: South Africa 1994–1998," *Social Psychology Quarterly* 64:1, pp. 41–54.

Kornai, Janos, and Susan Rose-Ackerman (eds) (2004) *Building a Trustworthy State in Post-Socialist Transition*. New York: Palgrave.

Kornai, Janos, Bo Rothstein, and Susan Rose-Ackerman (eds) (2004) *Creating Social Trust in Post-Socialist Transitions*. New York: Palgrave.

Krahn, H., and T. Harrison (2006) "Democracy, Political Institutions, and Trust: The Limits of Current Electoral Reform Proposals," *Canadian Journal of Sociology* 31:2, pp. 165–182.

Kramer, R. M., and T. R. Tyler (1995) *Trust in Organizations: Frontiers of Theory and Research*. Thousand Oaks, CA: Sage.

Lawrence, J. (1997) "Is It Really the Economy, Stupid?" in J. S. Nye, P. D. Zelikow, and D. C. King (eds) *Why People Don't Trust Government*. Cambridge, MA: Harvard University Press, pp. 111–132.

Leach, W. D., and P. A. Sabatier (2005) "To Trust an Adversary: Integrating Rational and Psychological Models of Collaborative Policymaking," *American Political Science Review* 99:4, pp. 491–503.

Leigh, A. (2006) "Trust, Inequality and Ethnic Heterogeneity," *The Economic Record* 82:258, pp. 268–280.

Levi, M. (1997) *Consent, Dissent and Patriotism*. New York: Cambridge University Press.

Levi, M., and L. Stoker (2000) "Political Trust and Trustworthiness," *Annual Review of Political Science* 3:1, pp. 475–507.

Levitsky, S., and L. A. Way. (2002) "The Rise of Competitive Authoritarianism," *Journal of Democracy* 13:2, pp. 51–66.

Lewicki, R. J., and E. C. Tomlinson (2003) "Trust and Trust Building," in G. Burgess and H. Burgess (eds) *Beyond Intractability*. Conflict Research Consortium, University of Colorado, Boulder, CO, posted December 2003. Available at <http://www.beyondintractability.org/essay/trust_building/> (accessed 25 January 2010).

Linz, J. J., and A. Stepan (1997) "Toward Consolidated Democracies," in L. Diamond et al. (eds) *Consolidating the Third Wave Democracies: Themes and Perspectives*. Baltimore, MD, and London: Johns Hopkins University Press, pp. 14–34.

Lipset, S., and W. Schneider (eds) (1987) *The Confidence Gap: Business, Labor and Government in the Public Mind*. Baltimore, MD: Johns Hopkins University Press.

Lozano, W. (2002) *Después de los Caudillos* [After the Caudillos]. Santo Domingo, Dominican Republic: FLACSO.

Luhmann, N. (2000) "Familiarity, Confidence, Trust: Problems and Alternatives," in D. Gambetta (ed.) *Trust: Making and Breaking Cooperative Relations*. Oxford: University of Oxford Press, pp. 94–107.

Mackuen, M. B., R. S. Erikson, and J. A. Stimson (1992) "Peasants or Bankers? The American Electorate and the US Economy," *American Political Science Review* 86:3, pp. 597–611.

Mansbridge, J. (1997) "Social and Cultural Causes of Dissatisfaction with US Government," in J. S. Nye, P. D. Zelikow, and D. C. King (eds) *Why People Don't Trust Government*. Cambridge, MA: Harvard University Press, pp. 133–153.

March, J. G., and J. P. Olsen (1984) "The New Institutionalism: Organizational Factors in Political Life," *American Political Science Review* 78:3, pp. 734–749.

Miller, A. H. (1974) "Political Issues and Trust in Government, 1964–1970," *American Political Science Review* 68:3, pp. 951–972.

Miller, A. H., and O. Listhaug (1990) "Political Parties and Confidence in Government: A Comparison of Norway, Sweden and the United States," *British Journal of Political Science* 20:3, pp. 357–386.

Mishler, W., and R. Rose (1997) "Trust, Distrust, and Skepticism: Popular Evaluations of Civil and Political Institutions in Post-Communist Societies," *Journal of Politics* 59:2, pp. 418–51.

Mishler, W., and R. Rose (2001) "What Are the Origins of Political Trust: Testing Institutional and Cultural Theories in Post-Communist Societies," *Comparative Political Studies* 34:1, pp. 30–62.

Misztal, B. A. (1996) *Trust in Modern Societies: The Search for the Bases of Social Order*. Cambridge: Polity Press.

Moon, C. I., and J. J. Yang (2002) "Globalization, Social Inequality, and Democratic Governance in South Korea," in J. S. Tulchin, with A. Brown (eds) *Demo-*

cratic Governance and Social Inequality. Boulder, CO, and London: Lynne Rienner, pp. 131–165.

Morgan, P. W., and G. H. Reynolds (1997) *The Appearance of Impropriety: How the Ethics Wars Have Undermined American Government, Business and Society*. New York: Free Press.

Newton, K. (1999) "Social and Political Trust in Established Democracies," in Pippa Norris (ed.) *Critical Citizens: Global Support for Democratic Government*. Oxford: Oxford University Press, pp. 169–187.

Newton, K., and P. Norris (2000) "Confidence in Public Institutions: Faith, Culture, or Performance?" in S. J. Pharr and R. D. Putnam (eds) *Disaffected Democracies: What's Troubling the Trilateral Democracies?* Princeton, NJ: Princeton University Press, pp. 52–73.

Norris, P. (1999) "Institutional Explanations for Political Support," in P. Norris (ed.) *Critical Citizens: Global Support for Democratic Government*. Oxford: Oxford University Press, pp. 217–235.

Noteboom, B. (2002) *Trust: Forms, Foundations, Functions, Failures and Figures*. Cheltenham: Edward Elgar.

Nye, J. (1997) "Introduction: The Decline of Confidence in Government," in J. S. Nye, P. D. Zelikow and D. C. King (eds) *Why People Don't Trust Government*. Cambridge. MA: Harvard University Press, pp. 1–19.

Ocampo, J. A. (2006) "Congratulatory Message," The Regional Forum on Reinventing Government in Asia, Seoul, Republic of Korea, 6–8 September.

Ostrom, E., and J. Walker (eds) (2003) *Trust and Reciprocity: Interdisciplinary Lessons from Experimental Research*. New York: Russell Sage Foundation.

Paxton, P. (1999) "Is Social Capital Declining in the United States? A Multiple Indicator Assessment," *American Journal of Sociology* 105:1, pp. 88–127.

Pillay, S. (2004) "Corruption – The Challenge to Good Governance: A South African Perspective," *International Journal of Public Sector Management* 17:6–7, pp. 586–605.

Przeworski, A. (1991) *Democracy and the Market: Political and Economic Reforms in Eastern Europe and Latin America*. Cambridge: Cambridge University Press.

Przeworski, A., M. Alvarez, J. A. Cheibub and F. Limongi (1997) "What Makes Democracies Endure?" in L. Diamond et al. (eds) *Consolidating the Third Wave Democracies: Themes and Perspectives*. Baltimore, MD, and London: Johns Hopkins University Press, pp. 295–312.

Putnam, R. (1995) "Bowling Alone: America's Declining Social Capital," *Journal of Democracy* 6:1, pp. 65–78.

Putnam, R. (2000) *Bowling Alone: The Collapse and Revival of American Community*. New York: Simon & Schuster.

Redburn, F. S., and T. F. Buss (2004) "Modernizing Democracy: Citizen Participation in the Information Revolution," in A. Farazmand (ed.) *Sound Governance: Policy and Administrative Innovations*. Westport, CT: Praeger.

Reynolds, Paul (2005) "Survey Reveals Global Dissatisfaction," *BBC News*, September 15, <http://news.bbc.co.uk/1/hi/world/europe/4245282.stm> (accessed 24 February 2010).

Rondinelli, D. A. (2003) "Promoting National Competitiveness in a Globalizing Economy," in D. A. Rondinelli and S. Cheema (eds) *Reinventing Government for the Twenty-First Century: State Capacity in a Globalizing Society*. Bloomfield, CT: Kumarian Press, pp. 33–61.

Rose-Ackerman, Susan (2001a) "Trust and Honesty in Post-Socialist Societies," *Kyklos* 54:2–3, pp. 415–444.

Rose-Ackerman, Susan (2001b) "Trust Honesty and Corruption: Reflection on the StateBuilding Process," *European Archives of Sociology* 42:3.

Saul, J. R. (1995) *The Unconscious Civilization*. Toronto: Anansi.

Seligman, A. (1997) *The Problem of Trust*. Princeton, NJ: Princeton University Press.

Sztompka, P. (1999) *Trust: A Sociological Theory*. Cambridge: Cambridge University Press.

Tanguay, Brian (1999) "Canada's Party System in the 1990s: Breakdown or Renewal?" in J. Bicketerton and A. G. Gagnon (eds) *Canadian Politics*. Peterborough: Broadview Press.

Tarrow, S. (1994) *Power in Movement: Social Movements, Collective Action, and Politics*. Cambridge: Cambridge University Press.

Tarrow, S. (2000) "Mad Cows and Activists: Contentious Politics in the Trilateral Democracies," in S. Pharr and R. Putnam (eds) *Disaffected Democracies: What Is Troubling the Trilateral Democracies?* Princeton, NJ: Princeton University Press, pp. 270–289.

Thompson, D. F. (1995) *Ethics in Congress: From Individual to Institutional Corruption*. Washington DC: The Brookings Institution.

Thompson, D. F. (2004) *Restoring Responsibility: Ethics in Government, Business and Healthcare*. Cambridge: Cambridge University Press.

Tonkiss, F., A. Passey, N. Fenton and L. C. Hems (2000) *Trust and Civil Society*. London: Macmillan.

Torres, L. Vicente Pina, and Basilio Acerete (2006) "E-Governance Developments in EU Cities: Reshaping Government's Relationship with Citizens," *Governance: An International Journal of Policy, Administration, and Institutions* 19:2, pp. 277–302.

Turner, F. C., and J. D. Martz (1997) "Institutional Confidence and Democratic Consolidation in Latin America," *Studies in Comparative International Development* 32:3, pp. 65–84.

UNDP [United Nations Development Programme] and Management Development and Governance Division Bureau for Policy and Programme Support (1997a) "Reconceptualizing Governance," Discussion Paper 2, New York, January.

UNDP [United Nations Development Programme] and Management Development and Governance Division Bureau for Policy and Programme Support (1997b) "Corruption and Good Governance in a Globalised Society," Discussion Paper 3, New York, July.

Veenstra, G. (2002) "Explicating Social Capital: Trust and Participation in the Civil Space," *Canadian Journal of Sociology* 27:4, pp. 547–572.

Warren, M. E. (ed.) (1999) *Democracy and Trust*. Cambridge: Cambridge University Press.

Warren, M. E. (2006) "Democracy and Deceit. Regulating Appearances of Corruption," *American Journal of Political Science* 50:1, pp. 160–174.

Wheeless, L. R., and J. Grotz (1977) "The Measurement of Trust and Its Relationship to Self-Disclosure," *Human Communication Research* 3:3, pp. 250–257.

World Bank (n.d.) "Governance and Anti-Corruption," <http://www.worldbank.org/wbi/governance/pubs.html> (accessed 18 January 2010).

3

Building trust in government in Northeast Asia

Pan Suk Kim

Introduction

Over recent decades, trust has become a major concern for many scholars and officials, many of whom think that the declining trend in the public's trust in government has become a global phenomenon (Cook 2001; Etzioni and Diprete 1979; Fukuyama 1995; Hardin 2006; National Opinion Research Center 2000; OECD 2000a, 2000b; Putnam 1995; Seligman 1997).[1] According to the American National Election Studies (ANES 2005), for example, although there have been some fluctuations, the US citizenry has little confidence in government and the degree of trust has declined over time. Consequently, much of the current wave of work on trust in the advanced countries has been directed at understanding apparent changes in trust over time (Putnam 1995, 2000; Pharr and Putnam 2000; Hardin 2006).

Why is trust in government declining? Some say that the people have changed and the social organization of our lives has changed such that people are more skeptical of government (Barber 1983; Barnes and Gill 2000; Etzioni and Diprete 1979; Hardin 2006; Nye et al. 1997; Ostrom and Walker 2002; Sztompka 1999). Others say that styles of politicians have changed and the underlying political issues have shifted in ways that reduce confidence in government (Bianco 1994; Cook 2001; Hardin 2006; Manin 1997). Berman (1997) also asserts that cynicism toward government is largely a function of trust and social capital.

Building trust in government: Innovations in governance reform in Asia, Cheema and Popovski (eds), United Nations University Press, 2010, ISBN 978-92-808-1189-6

The low trust of citizens in government is not just a problem in Western countries. It is also a serious problem in North and East Asia. For example, the level of public trust in government has gradually declined in Japan (Office of the Prime Minister, various years) and South Korea (KDI 2006). Therefore, it is timely to examine major factors related to public trust in North and East Asian countries. There may be numerous factors that have an impact on trust in government in the context, but many of them are beyond the scope of this treatment. From an institutional and public governance perspective, the following key factors were chosen for this study: the quality of the electoral and parliamentary process; decentralization and local governance; service delivery and access; civil society engagement; civil service reform; the judicial system and access to justice; and transparency and corruption. Accordingly, this chapter is organized to examine those issues in North and East Asia, namely, China, Japan, South Korea, Vietnam, and Mongolia.

The next section of this chapter provides a brief review of the socioeconomic and political changes that have taken place in the region over the past few years and the findings of various surveys on trust in government in the region. The following section forms the bulk of the analysis, detailing the context and the impact on trust levels and trust formation of the key factors mentioned above. Finally, the summary and conclusion are presented.

Review of socioeconomic and political changes

Globalization has driven political and socioeconomic change within the region and has indirectly and directly impacted citizens' relationships with their respective governments. It is with this understanding that some of the major shifts in the region are briefly explored, as context for further analysis on changes in trust in government.

China

Among East Asian countries, China's performance has been remarkable in recent years (OECD 2005b; World Bank 2005b; World Economic Forum 2008). China's economy has significantly changed from a centrally planned system to a more market-oriented economy over the past three decades. The restructuring of the economy and resulting efficiency gains have contributed to a rapid increase in gross domestic product (GDP). As of 2009, China stood as the second-largest economy in the world after the United States when adjusted for purchasing power parity, although in per capita terms the country is still at a low level (Central Intelligence

Agency 2009). China's rapidly growing market has attracted large volumes of foreign direct investment in recent years, as transnational corporations have invested heavily in order to benefit from the country's emerging middle class and its higher purchasing power. However, because the country is not addressing its many structural problems and institutional shortcomings quickly enough, their long-term effects may be partly disguised by the booming economy (IMD 2008).

Japan

Japan has a high-quality infrastructure and workforce and efficient markets, but the Japanese economy has not performed well for the last 10 years. The problems of the past decade are the direct consequence of the speculative bubbles in the stock market and the real estate market (Wood 2005). Compounding the impact of the asset bubble and its collapse was a series of economic policy blunders. The last couple of years have a seen a few tentative signs of an economic recovery: land prices in some areas, especially the major city centers, have shown increases; employment has crept back up. However, a number of challenges remain, mainly in the management of public finances and market efficiency (IMD 2008). Furthermore, various changes were evident in the political economy over the course of the decade. The conservative Liberal Democratic Party (LDP) was in power from 1955, except for a short-lived coalition government formed from its opposition parties in 1993. In the August 2009 election for the House of Representatives, however, the liberal Democratic Party of Japan (DPJ) gained political power through the considerable support of the Japanese people.

South Korea

South Korea has been less developed than Japan for the past several decades, but it is now approaching high levels in certain areas, such as macroeconomic management, school enrollment rates, penetration rates for new technologies, and levels of scientific innovation (KDI 2006). South Korea has witnessed significant political liberalization since 1987, including freedom of the press, greater freedoms of expression and assembly, and the restoration of the civil rights of former detainees (EAI 2008; Freedom House 2008; Savada et al. 1990; Woodside 2006). However, South Korea continues to be held back by a number of weaknesses in the area of institutions, both public and private. As for levels of transparency and the impartiality of public sector officials in their dealings with the business community, for example, South Korea has not yet reached global standards (IMD 2008). The Korean economy was hit hard by the financial and currency crisis of 1997, so the Korean government initiated bold reforms in the government, business, banking, and labor sectors. In order to enhance its global competitiveness, the current administration has put a particularly high priority on public sector reform among various presidential agendas.

Mongolia

Mongolia has experienced a transition from a centrally planned economy to a market economy over the past couple of decades. A new constitution was introduced in 1992, and "People's Republic" was dropped from the country's name (ADB 2004; Central Intelligence Agency 2009; USAID 2005). Mongolia has made considerable progress over the last 20 years. Efforts to strengthen the outcome of the struggle for democracy have been undertaken persistently in Mongolia since 1990. The historical outcome of the elections (held on 29 July 1990) was the establishment of a standing parliament named the State Great Khural to be the highest authority of a democratic state. Recent economic performance has been robust, with broad-based growth, declining inflation, a growing budget and balance of payments surpluses, and improving confidence in the banking system.[2] Despite these significant achievements, much remains to be done to achieve the UN Millennium Development Goals.

Vietnam

The Vietnamese government launched a comprehensive renovation process (*doi moi*) following the general development trend and the process of gradual globalization and regionalization since the mid-1980s. The 6th Congress of the Communist Party of Vietnam in December 1986 self-criticized its mistakes in past years, carefully assessing its achievements, analyzing drawbacks, and setting forth a comprehensive renovation policy (Abuza, 2001; ADB 2007; Central Intelligence Agency 2009; Lamb 2002; Tonnesson 2000). Top priority was given to economic reform for creating a multi-sector market economy regulated by the government, and at the same time consolidating the legal environment and renovating the party's and the state's structure. Since then the Vietnamese economy has become open and has made the transition from a centralized planned economy, heavily based on imports, to a market-oriented one. With the renovation process, Vietnam, step by step, has overcome many difficulties and obstacles to achieve great results. The political situation has remained stable, thus actively facilitating the *doi moi* process. However, reforms in the public sector are still slow and incremental based on a piecemeal approach.

Public confidence and major governance issues

As a result of globalization (increasing global connectivity, integration and interdependence in the economic, sociopolitical, technological, cultural, and ecological spheres), greater economic interdependence, increased cultural influence, rapid information exchange through information communication technology (ICT), and geopolitical challenges are salient in the region (Kim and Jho 2005). Like many other countries in different regions, the role of the state changed from central planning to facilitation and arbitration. Although the situation in China and Vietnam is somewhat different, the state in general is no longer merely planning and controlling but is putting in place regulations to facilitate the work of producers and undertakes necessary settlements whenever required. Moreover, government policies can no longer be implemented in isolation at the local or national level. All policies now are influenced by increasingly constrained global economic, political, and cultural factors, which influence sociopolitical aspects, the flow of information on economic resources, and therefore, the well-being of nations.

On the government side, there can be seen a diminishing role for the head of state in many countries. For example, the role of the president in South Korea is certainly shrinking. The imperial presidency has been replaced by an institutional presidency, with a correspondingly weaker role for the state (EAI 2008; Kim 2004; Kim and Hong 2006; Kim and Kim 1997). South Korea used to be an administrative state, but lately it has been slimming down substantially. The role of traditionally powerful agencies (i.e. the military, intelligence agencies, and law enforcement) is also diminishing, declining, or repositioning from the public setting. At the same time, there is an increasing role for the private sector as well as an increasing role for citizens and civil society, plus normalization or an increasing role for the judiciary and the legislative bodies. Whereas in the past, particularly in the 1970s, the legislative bodies just acted as a rubber stamp for executive policy, now they are quite proactive and an important part of policy-making.

Table 3.1 summarizes the degree of confidence in various organizations such as the government, parliament, political parties, the civil service, the justice system, the police, the press, environment protection management, and major companies in four countries (China, Japan, South Korea, and Vietnam). Mongolia was not included in the survey. These scores were adopted from the World Values Survey.[3]

There are various surveys on public governance. For example, the Worldwide Governance Indicators (WGIs) is a research project initiated by Daniel Kaufmann and his associates (2009). These authors define governance as the traditions and institutions by which authority in a country

Table 3.1 Comparison of public confidence in the public sector

Organization	Degree of confidence	China	Japan	South Korea	Vietnam
Government	A great deal	40.0	1.6	2.6	79.9
	Quite a lot	52.7	29.5	43.1	18.4
	Not very much	6.2	50.2	43.9	1.7
	None at all	1.1	18.8	10.5	0.0
Parliament	A great deal	39.9	1.2	1.4	78.4
	Quite a lot	52.5	22.0	24.8	20.4
	Not very much	6.5	55.4	50.6	1.2
	None at all	1.1	21.3	23.3	0.0
Political parties	A great deal	33.2	1.4	1.1	62.9
	Quite a lot	54.6	16.9	23.1	30.9
	Not very much	10.2	56.5	49.4	5.8
	None at all	2.0	25.2	26.4	0.4
Civil service	A great deal	28.8	1.4	6.9	49.0
	Quite a lot	57.0	31.4	55.9	40.3
	Not very much	12.8	51.4	29.5	9.8
	None at all	1.4	15.8	7.7	0.9
Justice system	A great deal	24.4	17.2	2.7	62.2
	Quite a lot	58.1	64.8	48.2	28.2
	Not very much	14.6	15.5	40.1	9.2
	None at all	2.9	2.5	9.0	0.5
Police	A great deal	23.9	8.6	6.6	63.5
	Quite a lot	56.2	58.3	52.0	27.7
	Not very much	17.1	28.6	35.4	8.4
	None at all	2.8	4.5	5.9	0.3
Press	A great deal	17.7	7.6	6.2	54.4
	Quite a lot	54.5	67.0	58.1	34.8
	Not very much	23.5	23.4	31.8	10.8
	None at all	4.3	2.0	3.9	0.3
Environment protection management	A great deal	17.6	4.8	10.1	48.3
	Quite a lot	60.9	52.1	61.6	41.3
	Not very much	18.4	37.1	22.3	9.8
	None at all	3.2	6.0	5.9	0.7
Major companies	A great deal	9.8	2.0	3.2	29.6
	Quite a lot	46.3	39.2	47.0	37.3
	Not very much	39.2	48.4	42.8	30.2
	None at all	4.7	10.4	7.0	2.9

Source: World Values Survey Association (n.d.).

is exercised. The WGIs measure six broad dimensions of governance, including: (1) voice and accountability, (2) political stability and absence of violence, (3) government effectiveness, (4) regulatory quality, (5) rule of law, and (6) control of corruption (see Table 3.2). On all six dimensions, Japan has the highest WGI rating among the five countries, followed by South Korea. On government effectiveness, both Japan and South Korea

Table 3.2 Worldwide Governance Indicators (WGIs) in five Asian countries, 2008

Country	Control of corruption	Voice and accountability	Rule of law	Regulatory quality	Political stability and absence of violence	Government effectiveness
China	41.1	5.8	45.0	46.4	33.5	63.5
Japan	85.5	76.0	89.5	86.5	79.4	89.1
Korea (South)	69.6	65.4	74.2	72.9	59.8	86.3
Mongolia	32.4	55.3	34.9	43.5	57.9	27.5
Vietnam	25.1	6.7	41.6	32.4	56.5	45.5

Source: Kaufmann et al. (2009).

have similar scores, although Japan's is slightly higher than Korea's. Among the other three countries (China, Mongolia, and Vietnam), China's scores on government effectiveness and control of corruption are clearly higher than those of Mongolia and Vietnam, but China's level on voice and accountability as well as on political stability and the absence of violence is the lowest among the five countries. In the areas of rule of law and regulatory quality, three countries (China, Mongolia, and Vietnam) show a similar level. On voice and accountability, Mongolia significantly exceeds the scores of China and Vietnam, whereas Vietnam's government effectiveness is better than Mongolia's.

The case of China

According to the World Values Survey, the degree of public confidence in the Chinese government and parliament is relatively high (see Table 3.1). In fact, the overall degree of confidence in the socialist countries including China and Vietnam was higher than that in other non-socialist countries such as Japan and South Korea. It is not clear why the degree of confidence is higher in China and Vietnam than in other neighboring non-socialist countries. The level of positive responses was generally high, so that interpreting these results requires a careful review.

To aid meaningful interpretation, this chapter pays attention to the negative side of survey responses as an alternative angle. When we review the negative responses, we find substantial differences: the level of negative responses on the civil service, justice, and the police was higher than the level on government and parliament. Such differences may indicate that the level of dissatisfaction with service delivery is substantial. In addition, Table 3.1 shows that the level of confidence in environment protection management was relatively high. However, the level of confidence in major companies was not high in comparison with governmental organizations (Table 3.1).

In China, the unicameral National People's Congress (NPC) is the highest organ of state power. It elects the president for a legal term of five years and it appoints the prime minister with the consent of the president.[4] The NPC is elected in an indirect manner (Li 1998; Lieberthal 2004; Shi 1999). Members of the NPC (2,987 seats) are elected by municipal, regional, and provincial people's congresses and by the People's Liberation Army to serve five-year terms. Interestingly, the 1998 Organic Law of Village Committees provided for competitive local elections, meaning that there are to be more candidates than seats. In several localities, a substantial proportion of the newly elected local deputies are not members of the Communist Party of China (CPC) (Nohlen et al. 2001: 350). China has had village elections since 1988 and a sprinkling of such experiments at higher-level party organs since then (Jeffries 2001). Though no major policy shifts are expected on intra-party democracy in China, the Chinese leadership has stated that the CPC considers that introducing more direct elections at the grassroots and the government level would "gradually expand direct elections in the selection of leading members in grass-roots party organs,"[5] shifting away from the traditional practice of assigning officials across the hierarchy.

China has four sub-national levels of state administration (OECD 2005b; Zhong 2003): (1) provincial – 31 units, comprising 22 provinces,[6] five autonomous regions, and four big cities (Beijing, Shanghai, Tianjin, and Chongqing); (2) prefecture – 333 units (most provinces are entirely subdivided into prefecture-level cities, whose governments administer large areas of mostly rural character, divided into counties, and city districts, but 51 prefectures have a different structure); (3) county – 2,861 units, comprising 1,642 counties, 374 county-level cities, and 845 districts in higher-level cities; and (4) township – about 44,000 units (18,100 mostly rural townships, 20,200 towns, and 5,750 street communities in cities).[7]

Beginning in the 1980s, local governments started assuming increasing responsibilities for economic development. Because local governments kept an increasing share of locally collected taxes, an unexpected consequence of localism was that local authorities sought to protect their industries, which were important sources of fiscal revenues. At the 14th National Party Congress of the Communist Party of China (CPC) in 1992, Chinese leaders acknowledged the need for recentralization in order to correct the excesses of the decentralization of the 1980s. However, local governments at county and township levels are still saddled with unusually heavy expenditure responsibilities in areas such as education and health. This has led to a large gap between available financial resources and expenditure responsibilities (OECD 2005b).

Chinese civil society organizations (CSOs) are growing in number and engaging in valuable educational work and issue advocacy. The growth of these organizations suggests the gradual emergence of a more pluralistic Chinese society. As of 2009, there were more than 415,000 officially registered CSOs.[8] Moreover, thousands of grassroots or community-based organizations are registered as businesses or not even registered. They play an active role in many fields such as environmental protection, the provision of basic health and education services, poverty reduction and rural development, and assistance to vulnerable groups. Many non-governmental organizations (NGOs) are making a significant contribution to China's social and economic development by engaging in public benefit activities in the environment, health, education, scientific research, cultural services, poverty relief, legal aid, social welfare, and services to disadvantaged groups such as orphans, the elderly, and the disabled. NGOs constitute an important part of an emerging civil society in China.[9] Although the Chinese government recognizes the value of civil society organizations that provide social services, the Chinese authorities fear that these private organizations might emerge as a source of political opposition among disgruntled members of society (Gries and Rosen 2004; Xia 2000). Over the past decade, more diverse Chinese civil societies have emerged. However, their future development depends on removing regulatory obstacles and building organizational and management capacity.

Regarding civil service reform in China, two major developments are notable: (1) the Provisional Regulations on Civil Servants, promulgated in 1993; and (2) the Civil Servant Law, enacted in 2005.[10] In the area of public sector reform, the so-called "China factor" is significant.[11] Since 1993, the Chinese government has taken significant steps to reform the country's civil service system, which is still evolving. Civil service reform involves four main dimensions: a transition from cadre management to a civil service system, staffing reform, wage reform, and staff development reform. The transition from cadre management is a process of administrative downsizing and singling out of qualified staff from the public sector to join the civil service created in 1993. Competitive examinations are used to recruit civil servants with the right job-related knowledge, skills, and education level. A brain drain in some sectors of the civil service was so serious that wage reform was introduced. Staff development reform focuses on performance appraisal and training (Burns 2003, 2007; Chou 2007). However, China's civil service system is far from being homogeneous. Central ministries are staffed by many competent and committed employees and conform in many respects to the performance paradigm articulated above, but outside the center the quality of the public service varies considerably (OECD 2005b; Tong et al. 1999).

When the drive to establish a functioning legal system began, most of the changes were promulgated in the economic arena. Over the years, legal reform became a government priority. Legislation designed to modernize and professionalize the nation's lawyers, judges, and prisons was enacted. The 1994 Administrative Procedure Law allows citizens to sue officials for abuse of authority or malfeasance. In addition, the criminal law and the criminal procedures laws were amended to introduce significant reforms (US Department of State 2006). In addition, the constitution was amended in 2004 to include the protection of individual human rights and of legally obtained private property. The Property Law of the People's Republic of China was adopted by the National People's Congress in 2007 and went into effect on October 1, 2007. The law covers the creation, transfer, and ownership of property in the mainland of China and is part of an ongoing effort by China to gradually develop a civil code.

Transparency International's Corruption Perceptions Index shows that China ranked 72nd among 180 countries in 2008 and 70th among 163 countries in 2006.[12] Transparency International's Bribe Payers Index shows that China ranked 21st among 22 countries.[13] Corruption poses one of the most serious threats to China's future economic development and political stability. Corruption also undermines the legitimacy of the ruling Communist Party, fuels social unrest, contributes directly to the rise in socioeconomic inequality, and undermines China's environmental security. Illicit activities such as bribery, kickbacks, theft, and the mis-spending of public funds cost at least 3 percent of GDP (OECD 2005b; Pei 2007; World Bank 2005b). Corruption looms as one of the biggest political and economic challenges that face China in the twenty-first century. The Chinese government has taken numerous measures to fight corruption. These include forbidding the government, the police, and the military to take part in business enterprises; implementing different accounting channels for revenues and for expenditures; and implementing a system of "accountant accreditation." In 2007, China established the National Bureau of Corruption Prevention (NBCP) in Beijing, a major deterrent to corruption activities (*China Daily*, September 13, 2007).[14] The new bureau reports directly to the State Council (China's cabinet). However, the establishment of the NBCP is not enough. The transparency and accountability system must be improved and the mass media should play a more active role in monitoring governmental affairs.

The case of Japan

According to the World Values Survey, the degree of public confidence in the Japanese public sector is generally low (see Table 3.1). However, there are some differences among public agencies. For example, the Japanese justice system received the highest degree of public confidence, followed by the police. Overall confidence in parliament, political parties, and the civil service was slightly lower than in government. The press received a relatively high degree of confidence, whereas the degree of public confidence in major companies was relatively low. Regarding environment protection management, the public confidence level was somewhat mixed: positive views were higher than negative ones, but the difference was not substantial (Table 3.1).

There was a major change in Japanese politics in 2009. After the August 2009 election, the Democratic Party of Japan (DPJ, founded in 1998 through the merger of several opposition parties)[15] became the ruling party in the House of Representatives, defeating the long-dominant

Liberal Democratic Party (LDP). The weak performance by LDP leaders on various policies and reform measures led to their party's defeat in the same 2009 election.[16] The DPJ's victory will change the power structure in a country ruled almost uninterruptedly by the LDP for 54 years, since 1955. However, it is not known whether the DPJ's historic win will signal the dawn of a stable two-party system.

The DPJ's success in the 2009 election, winning 308 of the 480 seats in the lower chamber, meant that it could shed its label as an opposition force and set course for the first power change through an election since the LDP was founded in 1955. As a result of the 2009 election, the percentage of women in the House of Representatives rose to double digits for the first time, reaching 11.25 percent.

In Japan, local government is structured along two-tier lines: prefectures (comparable to provinces) and municipalities (comparable to cities and towns). Prefectures serve wider areas and municipalities provide local services (Nakamura 2006). Many towns and villages amalgamated following the central government's introduction of legislation promoting municipal mergers. As of September 2009, the total number of municipalities was 1,774, whereas in March 1999 it was 3,232. This led to improvements in their administrative and financial capabilities, and helped to promote the growth of local autonomy and the urbanization that followed, as Japan entered its boom years (CLAIR 2006). Although the prefectures and municipalities enjoy considerable levels of autonomy in the fields of administration, Japan is a unitary state with no reference to federal structures in its constitution.

Perhaps the most striking feature of Japan's civil society over the past century has been the degree to which the state has taken an activist stance toward civic life, infiltrating it and seeking to steer it with a wide range of distinct policy tools targeted by group or sector. State laws and regulations have prevented many independent civic groups from gaining legal status and access to resources and tax exemptions (Hirata 2002; Schwartz and Pharr 2003). One means of exerting influence over civil society is through the types of group the state favors. The state promotes small community groups, such as neighborhood associations that provide services to local citizens, through the provision of financial incentives. Since the framing of the Civil Code over a century ago, the Japanese regulatory framework for civil society has promoted the creation of many small local groups, most notably the neighborhood associations, and a few large professional groups. At the same time, the state has actively discouraged the formation and operation of independent advocacy groups (Hirata 2002; Schwartz and Pharr 2003). The state accommodates non-state actors only when this serves its interest. In Japan, social capital has been promoted whereas pluralist interest groups have been discouraged.

This has resulted in a dual civil society: many people belong to civil society groups, but few work for them (Pekkanen 2006). After a century, however, the first major change to this regulatory framework came about in the form of the 1998 Law to Promote Specified Nonprofit Activities (NPO Law). The future will likely hold elements of change and continuity, both in good measure. The 1998 NPO Law, the 2001 Intermediary Legal Persons Law, and 2001 and 2002 tax reforms are part of self-perpetuating changes that will alter the regulatory framework in Japan.

In Japan, the current call for civil service reform has emerged partly as a result of two negative perceptions held by the electorate regarding government bureaucrats (Nakamura 2005). First, Japan's central bureaucracy has a tradition of elitism, dating from the nineteenth century, in which the best and the brightest in the country are encouraged to serve in one of the select corps of the national government. The recruitment system reflects this tradition, ensuring that only these highly talented people become government bureaucrats. Recently, however, a number of shortcomings in this elite bureaucracy have come to light. There have been several incidents in which privileged officials have been revealed to be involved in scandals. *Amakudari* (descent from heaven) – the institutionalized practice whereby senior bureaucrats retire to high-profile positions in the private and public sectors – has been heavily criticized by the public. Second, Japan's central government bureaucrats have traditionally wielded substantial powers in law-making and national finance. On average, they create the majority of the bills that are approved by the national legislature. Accordingly, it is expected that the new administration will attempt to update the Japanese civil service system, but this may not be easy owing to inertia and resistance by government employees.

Transparency International's Corruption Perceptions Index shows that Japan ranked 18th among 180 countries in 2008 and 17th among 163 countries in 2006.[17] Transparency International's Bribe Payers Index shows that Japan ranked 5th among 22 countries.[18] In Japan, some contend that there is far less corruption now than there was in the past and they predict that corruption is almost certain to continue to decline in importance in years to come. Others argue that corruption will continue to flourish in Japan because its cultural roots are deeply imbedded in government and society (Curtis 1999; Johnson 2000, 2001; Mitchell 1996). Although some critics doubt that corruption in the bureaucracy has declined, the record shows a substantial improvement over the years (see the survey results from Transparency International).

The case of South Korea

According to the World Values Survey, the degree of public confidence in the South Korean government is generally low (see Table 3.1). However, there are some differences among public agencies. For example, the Korean justice system and police received a high degree of public confidence. Interestingly, the Korean civil service had the highest degree of public confidence among public agencies. Overall confidence in parliament and political parties was low, so that it is fair to say that public distrust in national politics is high in South Korea. The press received a relatively high degree of confidence, as did environment protection. As a matter of fact, civil society in South Korea is generally active. There are many advocacy NGOs in South Korea and their sociopolitical influence is substantial. The degree of public confidence in major companies was also relatively high, although a substantial level of negativity remains. In recent years, major Korean conglomerates have performed well, and therefore it is speculated that public confidence in major Korean companies including Samsung, LG, and Hyundai has improved over the years.

In South Korea, a strong Presidency has been converted into an institutional Presidency, and the role of both the legislative body (the National Assembly) and the judiciary has been strengthened (Kim 2000, 2004; Oh 1999). Recently, irregularities in the elections have been substantially reduced owing to heavy penalties. In the National Assembly (a unicameral legislature with four-year terms), there are currently 299 seats. Of those seats, 245 are distributed by plurality in single-member constituencies and 54 are distributed by proportional representation to closed and blocked party lists in one national constituency. The most recent general elections were held on April 9, 2008.

The power to investigate state affairs has strengthened over the years. During the authoritarian regimes, the role of the National Assembly was quite limited because leaders of the National Assembly were influenced by the president. Since the 1990s, when South Korea became a full-scale democracy, the power of the National Assembly and its members has substantially improved. The National Assembly now holds the power to recommend the removal of the prime minister or a cabinet minister. The consent of the National Assembly is required for the appointment of the prime minister, the chairman of the Board of Audit and Inspection, and all Supreme Court justices (not just the Chief Justice).

Local autonomy was introduced in 1949 by President Rhee Syng-man (1948–1960), but was eliminated by the military coup in 1961. In 1991, local autonomy was re-established with elections for council members, started as part of a move towards democracy in South Korea. Today, each local authority has a local council and the head of each local authority is elected by its constituents every four years. Between the central and the local governments are 16 provincial-level governments – 9 *do* (provincial governments), Seoul capital city, and 6 *kwangyuk-si* (metropolitan city governments). Cities and counties are under the auspices of provincial governments, whereas urban autonomous districts form the sub-units of metropolitan cities, with the exception of a few counties in agricultural areas that belong to metropolitan cities as a result of geographical consolidation (Kim and Kim 2003). Financially, local governments still rely heavily on the central government for several reasons, including a lack of balance in the distribution of revenue sources between central and local governments and, more fundamentally, the poor tax base in many of the local governments.

In recent history, South Korean citizens' movements have contributed greatly to the development of civil society and democratic order through the expansion of citizens' participation in the public sector. By presenting possible alternatives they are shaping the popular consensus to meet the needs of the times, constructively monitoring and criticizing the existing sociopolitical systems, and applying pressure for the sound development of almost all areas of Korean society by mobilizing mass media attention and ICT applications (Kim and Jho 2005). There are three major advocacy NGOs in South Korea. The Citizens' Coalition for Economic Justice (CCEJ) was established in 1989. After that, the People's Solidarity for Participatory Democracy (PSPD) and the Korean Federation for Environmental Movement (KFEM) were established. These three NGOs, the so-called "Big Three NGOs," which are recognized nationwide, are relatively stable in terms of financial resources, but many other NGOs are in severe financial difficulties because they lack membership fees and external donations but their hands are full (Kim and Hong 2006; Kim and Moon 2003; NGO Times 2006).

The South Korean central government carried out a bold civil service reform from the late 1990s. In particular, the Kim Dae-jung administration (1998–2003) named the public sector as one of four areas – together with the financial, corporate, and labor sectors – targeted for aggressive reform to cope with the financial crisis of 1997, which immediately preceded his inauguration, and to enhance the nation's competitiveness (Kim 2000). His administration attempted to initiate urgent reforms that would reshape the government's role and improve the efficiency of the public sector. The administration seemed sure that reforms in the four sectors would solve the country's economic crisis. In order to achieve urgent national objectives in the public sector the government introduced market mechanisms (downsizing, privatization, openness, and competition), performance-based management (pay for performance), customer satisfaction (service quality improvement), deregulation, and e-government. In particular, the initiatives on openness and competition and on performance-based management are considered to be critical for reforming and revitalizing the long-standing closed civil service system

(Hood and Peters 2003; Kim 2000, 2002; Kim and Hong 2006). The Roh Moo-hyun administration (2003–2008) also heavily promoted public sector reform. On July 1, 2006, a Senior Civil Service was introduced into the South Korean central government. The members of the Senior Civil Service are required to go through a competitive assessment process and they have to compete for vacant senior posts internally and externally.[19] During the Lee Myung-bak administration (2008–2013), however, the pace of administrative reform, including civil service reform, has somewhat slowed down, in order to concentrate on economic recovery.

Law in South Korea has historically been viewed as merely a tool of authoritarian rule, but since the transition to democracy it now serves a more important and visible role (Ginsburg 2004). Recently, many government actions have turned out to be unconstitutional and the general public has been very pleased with the Constitutional Court's decisions.[20] Consequently, the degree of public trust in the Constitutional Court is in general much higher than in governmental agencies (EAI 2008). This phenomenon is a new development in South Korea, but it is the result of the development of society as a whole, as well as the maturation of Korea's legal community and civil society, not simply because of the current regime's failures.

Transparency International's Corruption Perceptions Index shows that South Korea ranked 40th among 180 countries in 2008 and 42nd among 163 countries in 2006.[21] The Bribe Payers Index shows that South Korea ranked 14th among 22 countries.[22] Various anti-corruption initiatives have been tried by different administrations, but substantial changes appeared only during the early 1990s. During the Kim Young-sam administration (1993–1998), the Real Name Financial Transactions System was instituted by the Presidential Emergency Order for National Finance and Economy in 1993. In banning the use of anonymous financial accounts it was a significant step toward financial transparency. In 1997, the Act on Real Name Financial Transactions and Guarantee of Secrecy was enacted in order to solve partial defects, such as inconveniences in financial transactions following the verification of real names and anxieties about tax investigations under the Presidential Emergency Order. However, much more salient transformations took place during the Kim Dae-jung administration in modern South Korean history. In 1999, the Office of the Prime Minister announced some comprehensive programs. Accordingly, the Anti-Corruption Act was enacted in 2001 and the Korea Independent Commission against Corruption (KICAC) was established in 2002. In 2008, KICAC was merged with other two agencies (the Ombudsman of Korea and the Administrative Appeals Commission) and became the Anti-Corruption and Civil Rights Commission (ACRC).

The case of Mongolia

Mongolia did not participate in the World Values Survey, and therefore it was not possible to review the degree of confidence in major Mongolian public agencies.

Mongolia is a parliamentary republic. At national level, Mongolia elects a head of state (the president) and a legislature. The president is directly elected for a four-year term by the people, with a limit of two terms. The legislative body, the State Great Khural, has one chamber (it is a unicameral parliamentary system) with 76 seats and members are elected every four years by general elections. The State Great Khural is powerful in the Mongolian government, with the president being largely symbolic (although he can block the parliament's decisions) and the prime minister being confirmed by the parliament. Past parliamentary sessions have been turbulent, characterized by a series of political crises, resulting in several changes of cabinet, long periods without the selection of a prime minister, and a deadlock within the parliament on critical legislation. Mongolia currently has a number of political parties, the biggest ones being the Mongolian People's Revolutionary Party and the Democratic Party. In 2006, the Law on Central Elections Agency was passed by the parliament.[23] As a result of the new legislation, the General Election Commission has been assigned new functions for voter education and advocacy for election-related laws, among others things.

Mongolia is divided into 21 provinces (*aimags*), which are subdivided into counties/districts (*sums*; sometimes called *summons* or *somons*) and the big municipality of Ulaanbaatar (The capital Ulaanbaatar is administered separately as a district).[24] Lately, the Mongolian government has focused on the following key issues: (1) the respective roles and responsibilities of the different levels of government should be clarified; (2) transparent tax-sharing and/or expenditure transfer mechanisms should be re-established by central and local governments; and (3) the extent to which new accounting and computing systems will reach down to the various levels of local government should be assessed (IMF 2008).

Mongolia's civil society has been actively engaged in public management reform and maintains that the country could achieve a more successful transition if leaders and citizens efficiently combined their efforts to accomplish development results (ADB 2004; Center for Citizens' Alliance 2006). A significant number of NGOs are involved in addressing the following issues: the lack of accountability of public leaders, and unpredictable and frequent changes in public management mechanisms such as organizational structure, the legal process, and the administrative environment. One well-known organization, the Open Society Forum (OSF), aims to support the active participation of informed citizens in developing public policies as well as monitoring and implementing the progress of these programs. OSF was established in June 2004 as a result of the transformation of the Mongolian Foundation for Open Society.[25] The OSF's goals are to provide both physical and virtual space for policy research and analysis, broad public access to information resources on policies, law, and regulations, and a venue for public engagement in the policy formulation and implementation monitoring process (Dambadarjaa 2007). The Civil Society Index assessment revealed that the civil society arena in Mongolia is increasingly diverse and vibrant, with a growing number of non-governmental organizations, grassroots groups, and social movements (Center for Citizens' Alliance 2006).

Major public administration and civil service reforms undertaken in the early 1990s centered on establishing legal and policy frameworks for the state structure. During 1993–2000, the focus shifted to the creation of a professional civil service capable of implementing state policies. Since 2000, strengthening institutional capacities and efficiency has become a major challenge for the civil service of Mongolia. Despite the reforms, the size of the civil service in Mongolia remains large, its composition skewed in favor of support staff, and wage scales highly compressed. After a long delay in implementing the medium-term Civil Service Reform Strategy (CSRS) adopted in early 2004, the government finally approved an action plan for the CSRS in July 2007. The action plan envisages a number of specific actions in line with several strategic objectives. These actions include: (1) introducing open, competitive selection processes for senior civil servants, (2) establishing a civil service human resource management information system, and (3) modernizing the remuneration system for civil servants by making it more responsive to labor market conditions and more performance based. The Mongolian government has also adopted a comprehensive public sector reform strategy relying on a new contract-based system to achieve enhanced accountability, governance, fiscal management, and professionalism (ADB 2004; IMF 2008).

The Supreme Court serves as an appeals court for the people's court and the provincial courts but rarely overturns verdicts of lower courts. Judges are nominated by the General Council of Courts and approved by the president. A new constitution was introduced in 1992. Since then, the constitution and numerous new laws have allowed Mongolia to reform its legal system extensively, and Mongolia has put in place the basic legal structure required for a market economy and the rule of law to operate. Although major revisions of key laws were made over the years, significant gaps remain in the legal framework. Draft laws and government regulations are being made publicly available, but overall a lack of thoroughness in drafting is evident, and accessibility to laws and regulations is inconsistent. Although Mongolia's legal and judicial systems still bear traces of the socialist system from which they emerged, wide-ranging legal and judicial reform is evident. The judicial system is strained, but the civil law system seems to function reasonably well and the government has tried to strengthen enforcement mechanisms. Nonetheless, serious concerns remain about the state of the entire criminal law system (ADB 2004).

Transparency International's Corruption Perceptions Index shows that Mongolia ranked 102nd among 180 countries in 2008 and 99th among 163 countries in 2006.[26] These indicators imply that corruption still remains salient in Mongolia. Both petty and grand corruption should be of serious concern to Mongolians, but grand corruption should be considered to be more serious because it solidifies linkages between economic and political power that can negatively impact or ultimately derail democracy and development, as it has in other post-communist countries.

Several interrelated factors contribute to the growing corruption problem in Mongolia, the most significant of which are: (1) a profound blurring of the lines between the public and the private sectors brought about by endemic and systemic conflicts of interest at nearly all levels; (2) a lack of transparency and access to information that surrounds many government functions and undermines nearly all aspects of accountability by contributing to ineffective media and hindering citizen participation in policy discussions and government oversight; (3) an inadequate civil service system that gives rise to a highly politicized public administration and the existence of a spoils system; and (4) limited political will and leadership to actually implement required reforms in accordance with the law, complicated by conflictive and overlapping laws that further inhibit effective policy implementation (USAID 2005).

The case of Vietnam

According to the World Values Survey, the degree of confidence in the Vietnamese government and parliament is significantly high (see Table 3.1). As in the case of China, such high levels of positive responses must be carefully analyzed. If we review the negative side of the survey responses, substantial differences were found among public agencies: the level of negative responses for the civil service, justice, and the police was higher than the level for government and parliament. Such differences indicate that the level of dissatisfaction with service delivery is substantial. Major companies received the highest level of negative views. Economic development could have affected citizens' views in various ways, but negative views of major companies were still salient in Vietnam (Table 3.1).

Vietnam is a socialist country under the leadership of the Communist Party of Vietnam. According to the amended 1992 constitution, the Communist Party is the force leading the state and society. The party organizational system is established in line with the state administrative apparatus from central level to provincial, city, district, and communal levels, as well as in administrative bodies, schools, enterprises, political, social, and professional organizations, army units, and police forces. The National Assembly is the supreme organ of state and the only body with constitutional and legislative power.[27] In the past, it served as a rubber stamp for decisions already reached by the Communist Party. Recently, it has begun to adopt a more independent position on issues of direct concern to the Vietnamese populace. The president is elected by the National Assembly from among its members for a five-year term, and the prime minister is appointed by the president from among the members of the National Assembly. Cabinet members are appointed by the president based on a proposal by the prime minister and should be confirmed by National Assembly.

Vietnam is divided into 58 provinces and 5 cities directly under the central government (these cities have the same level as provinces). The provinces are further divided into provincial municipalities and counties, and then subdivided into towns or communes. At each level (province, city, district, town, and commune), voters elect people's councils with legislative powers, in accordance with universal suffrage. These councils in turn elect a people's committee from among their members to serve as an executive body. In some respects, people's councils and people's committees resemble local governments in many countries. They have the right to question decisions taken by other governmental organs at their level, but their decisions and actions are subject to review by higher organs of government power. Moreover, decisions by local government organs are normally undertaken in accordance with the instructions of Communist Party committees at that level, although party influence has somewhat declined since the inception of the economic renovation program in 1986 (Abuza 2001; Lamb 2002).

In Vietnam, civil society's influence on policy-making is mostly indirect (Norlund 2006). A few years ago it was not possible to mention the term "civil society" because it was generally accepted to be a sensitive subject; now people can discuss it. According to a summary of research by the World Alliance for Civic Participation (CIVICUS) and the Vietnam Institute of Development Studies (VIDS) (Norlund 2006), there are about 2,000 sundry NGOs in Vietnam, many of them engaged in charity and volunteer work and that were trusted by the citizenry. Vietnam holds membership of 63 international organizations and maintains relations with over 650 NGOs worldwide (Vietnam Ministry of Foreign Affairs

2007). Cooperation among the groups is still weak and they have a limited impact. The study by CIVICUS and VIDS reports that there were originally mass organizations under the auspices of the party, but they have become more independent in the last 10 years of market-oriented reforms that have driven rapid growth (World Bank 2004). It highlights their strengths and weaknesses and relationships with the ruling Communist Party and the increasingly influential National Assembly legislature. It seems that the doors are opening for advocacy these days (Dalton et al. 2002; Sabharwal and Huong 2005). The state and the market where people associate to advance common interests were involved in many of Vietnam's legal reforms. Vietnam is open to business competition, but there is no political competition at present.

The government and the Communist Party of Vietnam (CPV) have given strong signals in recent years of intentions to reform the public administration system. The Public Administration Reform Master Program, approved in September 2001 following extensive deliberations at the highest levels of the leadership, including the CPV, envisages the reform of the entire public administration system. The agenda for reform and renovation is far-reaching and bold in vision. It includes: (1) replacing cumbersome administrative procedures with more simplified and transparent ones; (2) reducing red tape and corruption; (3) streamlining (downsizing) and better defining the mandates and functions of institutions; (4) reforming provincial and other sub-national administrations and redefining their relations with the center; (5) rationalizing the organizational structure of ministries (Asian Development Bank 2007; World Bank 2004). In 2008, the Vietnamese government promulgated a civil service law for the first time in its history, and, as a result, a broad range of civil service reform (recruitment, selection, promotion, training, etc.) is taking place in Vietnam.

The Vietnamese judicial system is based on communist legal theory and has been influenced by the French civil law system. The Chief Justice of the Supreme People's Court is elected for a five-year term by the National Assembly on the recommendation of the president. The Supreme People's Court of Vietnam is the highest court of appeal in the nation. Beneath the Supreme People's Court stand the provincial municipal courts and the local courts. Military courts are also a powerful branch of the judiciary with special jurisdiction in matters of national security. During the last decade, Vietnam has undergone a massive legislative transformation. Emerging from decades of rule through administrative fiat, reforms now aim to shift economic regulation from government edicts to universally applicable legislative norms and macroeconomic levers. The state is now belatedly reconfiguring legal institutions to suit the post-*doi moi* environment. Since it has the potential to change both state imple-

mentation and social perceptions of law, this kind of institutional transformation should form the focus of further research (Australian Agency
for International Development 2000).

Transparency International's Corruption Perceptions Index shows that
Vietnam ranked 121st among 180 countries in 2008 and 111th among 163
countries in 2006.[28] In recent years, many international development
partners have encouraged the Vietnamese authorities to promote anti-
corruption measures. Consequently, Vietnam has been involved in a massive anti-graft campaign. Relevant agencies have prosecuted many people
involved in economic crimes in this period, including thousands of smug-
glers and traffickers and corrupt officials. Many violations have been
found in "wet" areas, including the infrastructure construction sector,
from the stages of designing and approving projects to the stages of allo-
cating loans, bidding, providing consultancy services, supervising, oversee-
ing, and payment (*Xinhua News Agency*, June 9, 2005). Consequently,
Vietnam's legislature passed a long-awaited anti-corruption law in 2005
that requires officials and their relatives to declare their assets every year.
A high-level national Anti-Corruption Committee headed by the Vietnamese prime minister was also established.

Conclusion

The public sector increasingly recognizes that good governance requires
the highest standards of accountability, transparency, public integrity,
openness, efficiency, effectiveness, equity, and participation (Braithwaite
and Levi 1998; Kim and Jho 2005; OECD 2005a; Weber and Carter 2003).
This can be illustrated by the pervasive effects these factors have on government performance, the use of public resources, general morale in public services, the legitimacy of the state, and the rule of law. In general,
Japan and South Korea have made substantial progress in their democratic governance and economy over time. Both governments have paid
serious attention to new challenges such as globalization and informatization. Nonetheless, they still have salient problems to tackle. Among
these problems are their middle ranking in global competitiveness (Japan
ranked 17th and South Korea 27th in 2009),[29] a lack of competence, and
rigid systems of employment (IMD 2009). Furthermore, electoral and political scandals including corruption are still salient problems in both
countries. Trust in parliament and political parties in both countries is
still low, as shown in the World Values Survey and other surveys. Therefore, a key challenge for Japan and South Korea is how to develop their
own creative approach to national development and public governance,

because imitation of the Western model is no longer applicable to their development.

The economic performance of both China and Vietnam has been remarkable in recent years (IMD 2008, 2009; World Bank 2004, 2005a, 2005b). For example, the volume of foreign direct investment is increasing significantly in both countries. China's global competitiveness exceeded South Korea's, placing it 20th in 2009,[30] but Vietnam's competitiveness is far behind that of China, Japan, and South Korea (IMD 2009). Moreover, both China and Vietnam have made a serious commitment to modernize their civil service and legal systems. Both China and Vietnam promulgated a civil service law – China in 2005 and Vietnam in 2008. As socialist states, however, the Communist Party in both countries monopolizes both politics and administration. Although the shoots of pluralism or diversity are growing at a local level, national politics and administration are still under the heavy influence of the Communist Party. Furthermore, civil society engagement in both countries is still evolving, although general social modernization in both countries and the *doi moi* reforms in Vietnam are stimulating the development of an independent civil society. To some degree, many civil groups in both countries are state mobilized, although there are growing signs of independence and a diversity of views within groups. China has become a member of the Group of Twenty (G-20) and plays an important role in world politics, but a key challenge for China is how to deal with uneven development.

The Mongolian people abolished the totalitarian regime in 1990, rejected the planned economy, and began a comprehensive transition toward a new political system (ADB 2004). The aim was to develop a country that respects human rights, democratic values, the market economy, and the rule of law. From a narrow perspective, this led to the comprehensive reform of the legislative system and structure. This reform did not take place all at once, but rather was an ongoing and gradual process. In March 1990, one-party rule was abolished. Political pluralism was recognized and the shift towards a multi-party system commenced. In sum, many political, administrative, economic, and legal systems are rapidly changing in Mongolia. However, competent human resources are seriously lacking, and the new systems are still facing stalemate.

Overall, East Asian countries are making substantial progress through dynamic public sector reforms (Sampford et al. 2002). In addition, economic well-being is improving gradually, although the degree might be different in each country. However, these public sector reforms can be damaged by, for example, the role of parliament and political parties, political scandals, and corruption. East Asian countries have made a significant commitment to promoting public sector reform in recent years, regardless of their political ideology. For example, South Korea actively participated in the Global Forum on Reinventing Government and presidents since the early 1990s have made government reform a top priority. Even China and Vietnam, as socialist states, are seriously carrying out public service reforms. Mongolia threw out its old socialist systems and began to establish new systems. As a result, it is expected that the quality of public service will substantially improve over time, but it is not clear whether the general perception of the government by the general public will substantially change.

The general public see the issue of the quality of public services as one of several key factors in government. As long as the public have a high degree of cynicism and distrust in politics (parliament, political parties, president or prime minister, etc.), their perception of government may not change significantly. Most governments now recognize the value and the role of civil society in nation-building and they have even officially made civil society a participant in their nation's development processes. However, there are still some governments that consider civil society as a potential threat, and limit its organizational activities (Dalton and Shin 2003). Therefore, it is fair to say that political reform is one of the most urgent and critical tasks for North and East Asian countries in the near future in order to regain public trust in government.

Governability depends on governance, and governance is important for the development of trust and confidence. It follows that there is a need to move from governance for the sake of governance to governance as a means of greater growth and development. In addition, prescriptions for governance must change to jointly identified sustainable development strategies (Fukuyama 1995; Hardin 2006; OECD 2000a; Putnam 2002). Moreover, a transformation from separate sectoral work to a fairly holistic, multi-sectoral approach to governance is required. There should also be a change from the ideal world of best practice to the real world of best fit. Finally, in developing countries, the donor-driven approach does not always work well so there needs to be an effort towards indigenization and ownership-building in developing countries. Therefore, developing countries may need to utilize a realistic governance approach, not simply imitate what the advanced countries do (Grindle 2004; Rodrik 2008). In other words, each developing country needs to find its own solution based on the individual importance of its needs and situations.

Notes

1. Trust is a complex construct, and well-documented researches (Blind 2006) on trust can be found via the website of the United Nations Department of Economic and Social Affairs at <http://www.unpan.org/directory/conference/guest/browseoneconference.asp?conference_id=2030> (accessed 26 January 2010).

2. For more details, see the Official Website of the Government Organizations of Mongolia at: <http://www.pmis.gov.mn/gov_eng.htm> (accessed 26 January 2010).
3. For more details, see World Values Survey Association (n.d.).
4. For more details, see the National People's Congress website at: <http://www.china.org.cn/english/27743.htm> (accessed 26 January 2010); or the Chinese Central Government's website at: <http://english.gov.cn/> (accessed 26 January 2010).
5. For more details, see Huang (2009).
6. Taiwan is regarded as one of China's provinces in the People's Republic of China. For more details, visit the Chinese Central Government's official web portal at: <http://english.gov.cn/links/content_25073.htm#2> (accessed 26 January 2010).
7. For more details, see the following websites: <http://chinasite.com/Regions/regions.html> and <http://english.gov.cn/links/content_25073.htm#1> (accessed 26 January 2010).
8. The World Bank has been working to strengthen its engagement with civil society in China since the mid-1990s. For more details, see the World Bank's website at <http://web.worldbank.org> (accessed 26 January 2010).
9. For more details, visit the World Bank's webpage on NGOs in China: "The World Bank and Civil Society in China", <http://go.worldbank.org/8IPDHI01D0> (accessed 19 January 2010).
10. These two legal documents significantly affected the development of the civil service in other socialist countries, including Vietnam and Laos. I call this "the China Factor" in civil service reform in socialist countries.
11. When China adopts a particular type of reform, this does subsequently affect neighboring socialist countries, including Vietnam and Lao PDR.
12. For more details, see <http://www.transparency.org> (accessed 26 January 2010).
13. For more details, see <http://www.transparency.org/policy_research/surveys_indices/bpi> (accessed 26 January 2010).
14. For more details, see <http://www.chinadaily.com.cn/china/2007-09/13/content_6104202.htm> (accessed 26 January 2010).
15. For more details, see the DPJ's website at: <http://www.dpj.or.jp> (accessed 26 January 2010).
16. For more details, see the LDP's website at: <http://www.jimin.jp> (accessed 26 January 2010).
17. For more details, see <http://www.transparency.org> (accessed 26 January 2010).
18. For more details, see <http://www.transparency.org/policy_research/surveys_indices/bpi> (accessed 26 January 2010).
19. For more details, see the Korean Civil Service Commission's website at: <http://www.csc.go.kr/eng/> (accessed 26 January 2010).
20. As of December 2004, the Constitutional Court had declared 418 articles of laws (statutes, presidential decrees, etc.) unconstitutional and revoked about 214 governmental actions. On May 14, 2004, the Constitutional Court dismissed the National Assembly's presidential impeachment request and ruled that President Roh's powers should be restored so that President Roh Moo-hyun could resume his presidential duties, which had been suspended for 63 days. For more information, visit the Constitutional Court's homepage at: <http://www.english/ccourt.go.kr/> (accessed 26 January 2010).
21. For more details, see <http://www.transparency.org> (accessed 26 January 2010).
22. For more details, see <http://www.transparency.org/policy_research/surveys_indices/bpi> (accessed 26 January 2010).
23. The following laws were approved by the Parliament: (1) the Law on Parliamentary Elections in December 2005; (2) the Law on Central Elections Agency in January 2006; and the Law on Local Elections in January 2007. For more details, see the UNDP

Mongolia's website at: <http://www.undp.mn/dghr-erm.html> (accessed 4 February 2010).
24. For more details, visit the Official Website of the Government Organizations of Mongolia at: <http://www.pmis.gov.mn/pro_eng.htm> (accessed 26 January 2010).
25. For more details, see OSF's website at: <http://www.openforum.mn/en/index.php> (accessed 26 January 2010).
26. For more details, see <http://www.transparency.org> (accessed 26 January 2010).
27. For more details, see the National Assembly's website at: <http://www.na.gov.vn/htx/english/C1330/> (accessed 26 January 2010).
28. For more details, see <http://www.transparency.org> (accessed 26 January 2010).
29. For more details, see the Institute for Management Development's "World Competitiveness Scoreboard 2009" at: <http://www.imd.ch/research/publications/wcy/upload/scoreboard.pdf> (accessed 26 January 2010).
30. Ibid.

REFERENCES

Abuza, Zachary (2001) *Renovating Politics in Contemporary Vietnam.* Boulder, CO: Lynne Rienner.

ADB [Asian Development Bank] (2004) *Governance: Progress and Challenges in Mongolia.* Manila: Asian Development Bank.

ADB [Asian Development Bank] (2007) "Public Administration: Viet Nam," <http://www.adb.org/Governance/good_gov_pa.asp> (accessed 26 January 2010).

ANES [American National Election Studies] (2005) "The ANES Guide to Public Opinion and Electoral Behavior: Trust in Government Index 1958–2004." Available at <http://www.electionstudies.org/nesguide/toptable/tab5a_5.htm> (accessed 18 January 2010).

Australian Agency for International Development (2000) "Vietnam: Legal and Judicial Development," Working Paper 3. Canberra, Australia: Australian Agency for International Development.

Barber, Bernard (1983) *The Logic and Limits of Trust.* Brunswick, NJ: Rutgers University Press.

Barnes, D., and D. Gill (2000) *Declining Government Performance: Why Citizens Don't Trust Government.* New Zealand: State Services Commission.

Berman, Evan M. (1997) "Dealing with Cynical Citizens," *Public Administration Review* 57:2, pp. 446–458.

Bianco, William T. (1994) *Trust: Representatives and Constituents.* Ann Arbor, MI: University of Michigan Press.

Blind, Peri K. (2006) "Building Trust in Government in the Twenty-First Century: Review of Literature and Emerging Issues," paper prepared for the 7th Global Forum on Reinventing Government, Vienna, Austria, 26–29 June 2007. Available at: <http://unpan1.un.org/intradoc/groups/public/documents/un/unpan025062.pdf> (accessed 4 February 2010).

Braithwaite, Valerie, and Margaret Levi (eds) (1998) *Trust and Governance.* New York: Russell Sage Foundation.

Burns, John (2003) "Downsizing the Chinese State: Retrenching the Government in the 1990s," *The China Quarterly* 175, pp. 775–802.

Burns, John (2007) "Civil Service Reform in China," *OECD Journal on Budgeting* 7:1, pp. 1–15.

Center for Citizens' Alliance (2006) "State of Civil Society in Mongolia: Civil Society Index Country Report 2004–2005." Available at: <http://www.un-mongolia.mn/icnrd5/pdf/CSI_Executive_Summary.pdf> (accessed 4 February 2010).

Central Intelligence Agency (2009) "The World Factbook: East & Southeast Asia," <https://www.cia.gov/library/publications/the-world-factbook/region/region_eas.html> (accessed 4 February 2010).

Chou, Kwok Ping (2007) "China's Civil Service Reform: Success and Failure," EAI Background Brief 338, pp. 1–16.

CLAIR [Council of Local Authorities for International Relations] (2006) *Local Government in Japan*. Tokyo: Council of Local Authorities for International Relations. Available at: <http://www.clair.or.jp/e/forum/other.html> (accessed 4 February 2010).

Cook, Karen S. (ed.) (2001) *Trust in Society*. New York: Russell Sage Foundation.

Curtis, Gerald L. (1999) *The Logic of Japanese Politics: Leaders, Institutions, and the Limits of Change*. New York: Columbia University Press.

Dalton, Russell, and Doh Chull Shin (2003) "Democratic Aspirations and Democratic Ideals: Citizen Orientations toward Democracy in East Asia." Available under "Publications" on the World Values Survey's website: <http://www.worldvaluessurvey.com/> (accessed 26 January 2010).

Dalton, Russell, Pham Minh Hac, Pham Thanh Nghi, and Nhu-Ngoc Ong (2002) "Social Relations and Social Capital in Vietnam: Findings from the 2001 World Values Survey," *Comparative Sociology* 1:3, pp. 369–386.

Dambadarjaa, Jargalsaikhan (2007) "Mongolia: The Role of Civil Society in MfDR – Open Society," in *Emerging Good Practice in Managing for Development Results: Sourcebook*, 2nd edn. Managing for Development Results, pp. 147–153. Available at: <http://www.mfdr.org/Sourcebook/2ndEdition/5-1MongoliaCivilSociety.pdf> (accessed 19 January 2010).

EAI [East Asia Institute] (2008) *Survey on Influence and Trust in Korea*. Seoul: East Asia Institute.

Etzioni, Amitai, and Diprete, Thomas (1979) "The Decline in Confidence in America: The Prime Factor a Research Note," *Journal of Applied Behavioral Science* 15:4, pp. 520–526.

Freedom House (2008) *Freedom of the Press 2008: A Global Survey of Media Independence*. Washington DC: Freedom House.

Fukuyama, Francis (1995) *Trust: The Social Virtues and the Creation of Prosperity*. New York: Free Press.

Ginsburg, Tom (2004) *Legal Reform in Korea*. London: Routledge Curzon.

Gries, Peter Hays, and Stanley Rosen (eds) (2004) *State and Society in 21st Century China*. London: Routledge Curzon.

Grindle, Merilee S. (2004) "Good Enough Governance: Poverty Reduction and Reform in Developing Countries," *Governance* 17:4, pp. 525–548.

Hardin, Russell (2006) *Trust*. Cambridge: Polity Press.

Hirata, Keiko (2002) *Civil Society in Japan: The Growing Role of NGOs in Tokyo's Aid and Development Policy*. New York: Palgrave.

Hood, Christopher, and B. Guy Peters (2003) *Reward for High Public Office: Asian and Pacific Rim States*. London: Routledge.

Huang, Cary (2009) "Direct Polls for Party Officials on the Way," *South China Morning Post*, September 29.

IMD [Institute for Management Development] (2008) *IMD World Competitiveness Yearbook 2008*. Lausanne, Switzerland: IMD.

IMD (2009) *IMD World Competitiveness Yearbook 2009*. Lausanne, Switzerland: IMD.

IMF [International Monetary Fund] (2008) *Mongolia: Selected Issues and Statistical Appendix*. Washington DC: International Monetary Fund.

Jeffries, I. (2001) *Economics in Transition: A Guide to China, Mongolia, North Korea and Vietnam at the Turn of the Twenty-first Century*. New York: Routledge.

Johnson, David (2000) "Why the Wicked Sleep: The Prosecution of Political Corruption in Postwar Japan," *Asian Perspective* 24:4, pp. 23–43.

Johnson, David (2001) "Bureaucratic Corruption in Japan," Japan Policy Research Institute Working Paper No. 76, University of San Francisco.

Kaufmann, Daniel, Aart Kraay, and Massimo Mastruzzi (2009) "Governance Matters VIII: Aggregate and Individual Governance Indicators, 1996–2008," World Bank Policy Research Working Paper No. 4978. Available at: <http://econ.worldbank.org/external/default/main?pagePK=64165259&theSitePK=469372&piPK=64165421&menuPK=64166093&entityID=000158349_20090629095443> (accessed 26 January 2010).

KDI [Korea Development Institute] (2006) *Comprehensive Report on Social Capital*. Seoul: Korea Development Institute (in Korean).

Kim, Bun W., and Pan Suk Kim (1997) *Korean Public Administration: Managing the Uneven Development*. Seoul: Hollym International.

Kim, Pan Suk (2000) "Administrative Reform in the Korean Central Government," *Public Performance and Management Review* 24:2, pp. 145–160.

Kim, Pan Suk (2002) "Civil Service Reform in Japan and Korea: Toward Competitiveness and Competency," *International Review of Administrative Sciences* 68:3, pp. 389–403.

Kim, Pan Suk (2004) "Presidential Personnel Innovation for Presidential Appointees in Korea: Toward an Institutional Presidency," *Public Administration and Development* 24:3, pp. 235–246.

Kim, Pan Suk, and K. P. Hong (2006) "Searching for Effective HRM Reform Strategy in the Public Sector: Critical Review of WPSR 2005 and Suggestions," *Public Personnel Management* 35:3, pp. 199–215.

Kim, Pan Suk, and J. Y. Kim (2003) "Fiscal Autonomy of Korean Local Governments and Intergovernmental Relations in the 1990s," *Journal of Public Budgeting, Accounting and Financial Management* 15:3, pp. 414–437.

Kim, Pan Suk, and M. J. Moon (2003) "NGOs as Incubator of Participatory Democracy in South Korea: Political, Voluntary, and Policy Participation," *International Journal of Public Administration* 26:5, pp. 549–567.

Kim, Pan Suk, and Whasun Jho (eds) (2005) *Building e-Governance*. Seoul: NCA.

Lamb, David (2002) *Vietnam, Now: A Reporter Returns*. New York: Public Affairs.

Li, J. (1998) "The NPC System and Its Evolution: From Nomenklatura to Selectorate," *Issue and Studies* 34:3, pp. 1–23.

Lieberthal, Kenneth (2004) *Governing China: From Revolution though Reform*, 2nd edn. New York: Norton.

Manin, Bernard (1997) *The Principles of Representative Government*. Cambridge; New York: Cambridge University Press.

Mitchell, Richard H. (1996) *Political Bribery in Japan*. Honolulu: University of Hawaii Press.

Nakamura, Akira (2005) "The Debilitating Power of Japan's Central Government Bureaucrats in Civil Service Reform: Reality or Fallacy?" in Anthony Cheung (ed.) *Public Service Reform in East Asia*. Hong Kong: Chinese University of Hong Kong, pp. 19–37.

Nakamura, Akira (2006) *Civil Society and Local Governance*. Tokyo: EROPA Local Government Center and Local Autonomy College.

National Opinion Research Center (1972–2000) *Rope Center for Public Opinion Research. National Opinion Research Center–General Social Survey Cumulative Data File*. Chicago: University of Chicago NORC.

NGO Times (2006) *Encyclopedia of Korean Associations*. Seoul: NGO Times (in Korean).

Nohlen, Dieter, Florian Grotz, and Christof Hartman (eds) (2001) *Elections in Asia and the Pacific: A Data Handbook*. Oxford: Oxford University Press.

Norlund, Irene (ed.) (2006) *The Emerging Civil Society: An Initial Assessment of Civil Society in Vietnam*. Hanoi: Vietnam Institute of Development Studies, UNDP Vietnam, SNV Vietnam, CIVICUS Civil Society Index, March. Available at: <http://www.snvworld.org/en/countries/vietnam/ourwork/Documents/Civicus%20Civil%20Society%20Index.pdf> (accessed 4 February 2010).

Nye, Joseph S., Philip D. Zelikow, and David C. King (eds) (1997) *Why People Don't Trust Government*. Cambridge, MA: Harvard University Press.

OECD [Organisation for Economic Co-operation and Development] (2000a) *Trust in Government: Ethics Measures in OECD Countries*. Paris: OECD.

OECD (2000b) *Government of the Future*. Paris: OECD.

OECD (2005a) *Modernising Government: The Way Forward*. Paris: OECD.

OECD (2005b) *Governance in China*. Paris: OECD.

Office of the Prime Minister (various years) *Public Opinion Survey Data on Society and State*. Tokyo: Office of the Prime Minister (in Japanese).

Oh, J. K. (1999) *Korean Politics: The Quest for Democratization and Economic Development*. Ithaca, NY: Cornell University Press.

Ostrom, Elinor, and Jimmy Walker (eds) (2002) *Trust and Reciprocity*. New York: Russell Sage Foundation.

Pei, Minxin (2007) "Corruption Threatens China's Future," Carnegie Endowment for International Peace Policy Brief 55.

Pekkanen, Robert (2006) *Japan's Dual Civil Society: Members without Advocates*. Stanford, CA: Stanford University Press.

Pharr, Susan J., and Robert D. Putnam (eds) (2000) *Disaffected Democracies: What's Troubling the Trilateral Countries?* Princeton, NJ: Princeton University Press.

Putnam, Robert D. (1995) "Bowling Alone: America's Declining Social Capital," *Journal of Democracy* 6, pp. 65–78.

Putnam, Robert D. (2000) *Bowling Alone: The Collapse and Revival of American Community.* New York: Simon & Schuster.

Putnam, Robert D. (2002) *Democracies in Flux: The Evolution of Social Capital in Contemporary Society.* Oxford: Oxford University Press.

Rodrik, Dani (2008) "Second Best Institutions," *American Economic Review* 98:2, pp. 100–104.

Sabharwal, Gita, and Than Thi Thien Huong (2005) "Civil Society in Vietnam: Moving from the Margins to the Mainstream," Global Policy Forum reports. Available at: <http://www.globalpolicy.org/ngos/state/2005/07vietnam.htm> (accessed 26 January 2010).

Sampford, Charles, Suzanne Condlin, Margaret Palmer, and Tome Round (eds) (2002) *Asia Pacific Governance: From Crisis to Reform.* Burlington, VT: Ashgate.

Savada, Andrea Matles, and William Shaw (eds) (1990) *South Korea: A Country Study.* Washington DC: GPO for the Library of Congress.

Schwartz, Frank J., and Susan J. Pharr (eds) (2003) *The State of Civil Society in Japan.* Cambridge, MA: Cambridge University Press.

Seligman, Adam B. (1997) *The Problem of Trust.* Princeton, NJ: Princeton University Press.

Shi, T. (1999) "Village Committee Elections in China: Institutionalist Tactics for Democracy," *World Politics* 51:4, pp. 385–412.

Sztompka, Piotr (1999) *Trust: A Sociological Theory.* Cambridge: Cambridge University Press.

Tong, Caroline Haiyan, Jeffrey Straussman, and Walter Broadnax (1999) "Civil Service Reform in the People's Republic of China: Case Studies of Early Implementation," *Public Administration Development* 19, pp. 193–206.

Tonnesson, Stein (2000) "The Layered State of Vietnam," in Kjeld Brodsgaard and Susan Young (eds) *State Capacity in East Asia.* Oxford: Oxford University Press, pp. 237–267.

Transparency International (various years) "Corruption Perceptions Index." Available at <http://www.transparency.org/> (accessed 19 January 2010).

USAID [United States Agency for International Development] (2005) *Assessment of Corruption in Mongolia: Final Report.* Ulaanbaatar: USAID Office in Mongolia.

US Department of State (2006) "Background Note: China." Available at: <http://www.state.gov/r/pa/ei/bgn/> (accessed 26 January 2010).

Vietnam Ministry of Foreign Affairs (2007) "Vietnam and International Organizations," <http://www.mofa.gov.vn/en/ctc_quocte> (accessed 26 January 2010).

Weber, Linda R., and Allison I. Carter (2003) *The Social Construction of Trust.* New York: Kluwer Academic and Plenum Publishers.

Wood, Christopher (2005) *The Bubble Economy: Japan's Extraordinary Speculative Boom of the '80s and the Dramatic Bust of the '90s.* San Luis Obispo, CA: Solstice Publishing.

Woodside, Alexander (2006) *Lost Modernities: China, Vietnam, Korean and the Hazards of World History.* Cambridge, MA: Harvard University Press.

World Bank (2004) *Vietnam Development Report 2005: Governance*. Hanoi: World Bank Office.

World Bank (2005a) *East Asia Decentralizes: Making Local Government Work*. Washington DC: World Bank.

World Bank (2005b) *World Bank Report on PSU Reform in China: Deepening Public Service Unit Reform to Improve Service Delivery*. Washington DC: World Bank.

World Economic Forum (2008) *Global Competitiveness Report 2007–2008*. New York: Palgrave.

World Values Survey Association (n.d.) *World Values Survey 2005–2008*. Online Data Analysis: Confidence. Madrid: World Values Survey Association. Available at <http://www.worldvaluessurvey.org> (accessed 19 January 2010).

Xia, Ming (2000) *The Dual Developmental State: Development Strategy and Institutional Arrangements for China's Transition*. Brookfield, VT: Ashgate.

Xinhua News Agency (2005) "Vietnam to Intensify Fight against Corruption, Smuggling," 9 June 2005. <http://www.business-anti-corruption.com/country-profiles/east-asia-the-pacific/vietnam/sources/> (accessed 14 April 2010).

Zhong, Yang (2003) *Local Government and Politics in China*. Armonk, NY: M. E. Sharpe.

4

Building trust in government in Southeast Asia

Ledivina V. Cariño

This chapter focuses on the level of trust in order and representational institutions in Southeast Asia (SEA). After introducing the key concepts and the geographic area, I proceed to the trust and governance processes associated, first, with order and, second, with representational institutions. Finally I present the key issues and trends found and underscore the challenges to understanding and improving trust in government. The chapter uses existing data on the trust of citizens in their public institutions, and the governance mechanisms related to them. However, such information is not available for all of SEA. Moreover, most studies on governance do not explicitly relate it to trust. Underpinning these limitations is the fact that the region itself is little more than a geographic reality. Thus, situations in one country might not be as applicable to the whole. I have also used only relevant English-language studies of individual countries and the region, thus absorbing the sampling limitations of their cases, issues, and language used.[1]

The concept of trust

The primary object of trust in this chapter is government, a large-scale institution that is impossible to know intimately. Yet it has been trusted by citizens even though they may know only an infinitesimal part of it (the neighborhood cop instead of the police force, a public school teacher rather than the whole Ministry of Education, a senator rather than

Building trust in government: Innovations in governance reform in Asia, Cheema and Popovski (eds), United Nations University Press, 2010, ISBN 978-92-808-1189-6

parliament). Such trust may arise from characteristics of both the truster and the trustee, the citizens as well as the government. Higher income, education, and social status all seem to work against individual trust of government (Albritton and Bureekul 2005). More familiarity about an object of trust may push someone toward distrust.

Trust in government may provide "governance capital" that gets citizens to cooperate with government even when it makes unpopular decisions whose benefits will accrue only in the long run (Bratton et al. 2005). Ikeda et al. (2003) found that social trust[2] is positively correlated with participation, but institutional trust, or confidence in political institutions, is either not related or negatively related to political participation in Japan, Taiwan, and Thailand. This counterintuitive result may empirically evidence familiarity breeding contempt. However, it contradicts findings that "interactions with government are significantly more important than cultural factors in producing trust in government," and that a general trust in other people produces considerable support for democracy (Albritton and Bureekul 2005: 10).

Government may engender trust by lowering personal investments in monitoring the actions of other individuals; by enforcing contracts that give buyers and sellers reason to trust each other; by "restricting the use of coercion to tasks that enhance rather than undermine trust"; and by "eliminating risky personal reliance on another" (e.g. through freeing families of the burden of caring for sick members) (Levi and Braithwaite 1998: 82). Rather than seeking society-centered reasons for low trust and social capital, Rothstein and Stolle (2008) conclude that it is dysfunctional institutions that cause the lack of social capital.

The context of Southeast Asia

All but one of the countries covered by this description are members of the Association of Southeast Asian Nations (ASEAN). Geography and ASEAN are the main commonalities of the countries in the region. ASEAN members have a host of colonial histories (only Thailand escaped colonization). Singapore, Malaysia, Brunei, and Myanmar were under the British; Cambodia, Lao PDR, and Vietnam under the French; Indonesia under the Dutch; and the Philippines under the Spanish and the Americans. Their wars of liberation affected their historical trajectories – the wars of independence of the Filipinos, Indonesians, and Indo-China (Vietnam, Cambodia, and Laos), the relatively peaceful transfer of power in Singapore, Malaysia, Myanmar, and Brunei from Britain, and the Philippines from the United States.

The countries had their share of authoritarian rule under indigenous leaders. Indonesia and the Philippines had long-time dictators ousted by non-violent people's uprisings in the 1980s. Cambodia's recent history includes Vietnamese domination and a bloody civil war that necessitated UN tutelage. Timor-Leste, colonized by Portugal, was occupied by Indonesia in 1975 and got its independence in 2002. Separatist movements and terrorism have rocked Indonesia, the Philippines, and Thailand. The region is not a stranger to wars, and trust here is an important commodity.

The ASEAN ratings in the 2006 human development index (HDI) are positively correlated to the gross domestic product (GDP) of the member countries. The wide variation within ASEAN should not obscure the fact that no country has a low human development rating, even applicant Timor-Leste, with a rank five steps above the highest low HDI rating (United Nations 2006). The average rating of 0.728 is higher than that for all developing countries, and for South Asia, the Arab States, and sub-Saharan Africa.

Although the ranges of GDP per capita and HDI show a close correlation, an analysis of Philippine sub-national data cautions against simple acceptance of that relationship and suggests that the balance of the explanation may lie in, among others, the pro-poor reform of institutions and policies. This is consistent with findings in Vietnam and Thailand (Balisacan and Pernia 2002).

The ranking changes when income inequality is taken into consideration. Using the ratio of incomes of the richest 10 percent to the poorest 10 percent, Indonesia, Laos and Vietnam, tend to be the most equal, while Malaysia, Singapore, and the Philippines are the most unequal. On the Gini index, Southeast Asian countries bunch up in the middle levels, with the ranks closely following the first inequality indicator except for the change of places of the Philippines and Singapore.

Singapore, Malaysia, and Thailand were among the economic tigers of the late twentieth century. High standards of living, low birth rates, and steady improvements in health and education accompanied their booming economies. Their performances inspired even the communist states of Vietnam, Cambodia, and Laos to open up their economies and embrace globalization. Then the financial crisis of 1997 exposed the economic weaknesses and the social costs – among them, growing inequality and unemployment increases despite prosperity. These countries have since bounced back, but the crisis raised questions about the state of their governance (Nunberg 2002; Takashi and Abinales 2005).

Buddhism is dominant in the Greater Mekong Area comprising Thailand, Cambodia, Laos, and Vietnam. The Confucian ethic is evident in Singapore. Indonesia, Malaysia, and Brunei have Muslim majorities,

whereas Thailand and the Philippines have Buddhist and Christian majorities, respectively, with restive Islamic communities. Public policy tends
towards religious tolerance and moderation but the region has been
caught up in some extremist politics and terrorism, which can affect both
peace and trust.

At the start of the century it would have been acceptable to describe
Southeast Asia as home to fledgling democracies. The democratically
elected strongmen of Singapore and Malaysia had passed on the torch to
new leaders, confident of their economic and political legacies. The Philippines and Indonesia had shaken off their dictators and promulgated
new constitutions. The communist states of Vietnam and Laos had embarked on economic reforms, which also opened up their political systems; Cambodia had just completed a type of UN trusteeship. Only
Myanmar seemed impervious to democratic transition. Then along came
Thailand's coup in 2006, ending more than a decade of regular, elective
successions of leadership. That event not only laid bare the political
weaknesses of one country; it also encapsulated the state of governance
in much of Southeast Asia – charismatic leadership, populism, corruption,
politicized militaries, and poorly functioning institutions.

Trust in Southeast Asia

Against the backdrop of the aforementioned governance deficits, one
would have expected a frustrated people unwilling to trust their governments. However, the trust expressed by East Asia in the Global Barometer Survey (GBS) is the highest among the regions of the world (Table
4.1). The East Asian data are from only five countries – three Northeast
Asian (China, Japan, and Korea) and two Southeast Asian (the Philippines and Thailand).

Southeast Asian countries in the Asian Barometer Survey (ABS) and
the World Values Survey (WVS) all evince trust in order institutions

Table 4.1 Trust expressed by regions in the 2001 Global Barometer Survey

	Percent expressing			
	Little or no trust	Neutral	A lot of trust	Don't know
East Asia	42	–	49	9
Latin America	75	–	20	5
Africa	51	–	43	6
Northern Europe	53	21	26	–

Source: Bratton et al. (2005: 64).

Table 4.2 Trust in order and representational institutions: Selected SEA countries, 2001

| | Percent expressing trust in | | | |
| | Type of institution | | Government | |
	Order	Representational	Mean[a]	Direct question[b]
Asian Barometer Survey				
Philippines	52	39	49	47
Thailand	63	51	61	83
SEA	57	45	55	66
World Values Survey				
Indonesia	58	36	50	n.d.
Philippines	63	53	60	n.d.
Vietnam	89	91	90	n.d.
SEA	70	60	67	n.d.

Sources of raw data: Asian Barometer Survey (ABS) 2001 and World Values Survey (WVS) 2001.[1]
Notes: n.d. = no data, not asked of WVS respondents.
[a] Based on mean of answers on individual institutions.
[b] Percent responding positively to: "You can generally trust the people who run our government to do what is right."

Table 4.3 Generalized trust: Selected SEA countries, 2001

	Generalized trust rate[a]
Global Barometer Survey	
Thailand	81
Philippines	9
World Values Survey	
Philippines	8
Indonesia	46
Singapore	17
Vietnam	39

Sources: ABS 2001; WVS 2001, except for Singapore (2002).
[a] Percent responding positively to "Most people can be trusted".

(Table 4.2). These institutions also tend to be more trusted than representational institutions in all countries except Vietnam.[3]

The high trust in SEA public institutions is significant, considering that their level of generalized trust is not high (Table 4.3). To the query: "Generally speaking, would you say that most people can be trusted or that you need to be very careful in dealing with people?", most respondents in all SEA sample countries except Thailand are distrustful.

Why such low levels of generalized trust? Most Asian cultures still have strong insider/outsider divides when dealing with people. Francis Fukuyama (1995) has described members of those cultures as not inclined to spontaneous sociability beyond the family or family-like small circles. Thus, when dealing with large institutions, they tend to deal with people they know. He has found, for instance, that firms in China (as in France, Italy, and South Korea) tend to emerge from family corporations, and as such center on industries where human relationships are not trumped by hierarchy, and companies tend to be small. He contrasts them not only with Germany and the United States, but also with Japan, which, based in large part on its Buddhist tradition, bases its large network organizations on generalized social trust rather than family and kinship. Japanese Buddhism sanctifies economic activity and pushes towards perfectionism in everyday activities, much like an Asian variant of the Protestant Ethic (Fukuyama 1995). This may be the same reason Thailand stands out as the only Southeast Asian country high on generalized social trust.

Ironically, when low-social-trust Asians do deal with outsiders, they do not trust them to be fair, so that they seek patrons or surround the outside relationship with rules and contracts. Again, Fukuyama shows Korean large corporations getting much more government support for their ventures, unlike Japanese and US firms. The governments in those countries imbue the culture with this narrow range of trust and become centralized and hierarchical, with watchers at every turn supervising other watchers.

This lack of generalized trust may not contradict findings of trust in public institutions in three ways. First, people may have found culturally sanctioned ways of dealing with government. Whereas Westerners may regard these entities objectively, Southeast Asians deal with bureaucracies by personalizing them, either by identifying them with staff and officials they know, or by seeking persons in those offices who humanize the contacts. To the rest of the world, fixers are symbols of corruption, but they may not be so regarded by a Southeast Asian entering the strange world of the bureaucracy. For their part, fixers regard their work as legitimate and significant (Amorado 2007).

Mediating institutions and individuals do not have to imply corruption. Non-governmental organizations (NGOs) may also be mediators, either by being the people's advocates to government, by providing the service themselves, or by organizing the community so that trust is engendered outside the family bond. Civil servants, too, may make the bureaucracy less forbidding, with greater service orientation and participatory methods. Gene Brewer (2003) has found government employees to be more active than other citizens in civic affairs. As such they can serve "as catalysts for building social capital in society at large" (Brewer 2003: 1). In other words, human mediators can mitigate the effects of low generalized trust.

Second, people may place trust in government on a Churchillian scale, accepting a lesser evil when a better situation is not available. Most Southeast Asians have lived under such oppressive regimes that the current one, despite its many problems, becomes worthy enough of trust.[4]

The third explanation is connected to the second and draws, this time, from positive psychology. Trust may have been expressed because people *hope* that the legitimacy so proffered can then make the object feel accountable to the trustee. That hope may be ill founded but can still affect outcomes. Citizens may show a kind of collective hope that is "empowering, action-oriented, subject to cold analysis, and authentic through their engagement of the state" (Braithwaite 2004). On the part of the government as the object of trust and hope, the answer is to prove worthy. In many ways, the quest for trustworthiness is the reason for reinventing government.

Trust in order institutions: The executive branch

Southeast Asian nations – from the "Asian miracles" of Singapore, Malaysia, and Thailand to the communist states of Lao PDR, Vietnam, and Cambodia – have introduced reforms such as corporate governance, market orientation, privatization, and deregulation. These have mixed implications for trust in government. On the one hand, these reforms have enabled governments to be more efficient and innovative and better able to deal with globalization. This should have positive implications for trust as they counter waste, unresponsiveness, and corruption. On the other hand, a pro-business orientation could also diminish the sense of connectedness between government and citizens and exacerbate inequality, undermining trust (Haque 1998; Higgott and Nesadurai 2002).

These neo-liberal reforms were blamed when the 1997 financial crisis hit, along with growing inequality and unemployment (Beeson 1998; Haque 1998; Higgott and Nesadurai 2002; Yu 2002). Global Integrity Scorecard (GIS) ratings also show generally poor executive performance.[5] These should have reduced the legitimacy of and support for SEA governments. Yet trust is generally high, suggesting the validity of the lesser-evil and hope hypotheses (Table 4.4).

Consider Vietnam. The weak GIS rating may be due to insufficient and inconsistent finance and budgeting policies and very low salaries.

Table 4.4 Trust in the civil service and government and ratings of general executive performance: Selected SEA countries, stated years

	Indonesia	Philippines	Vietnam
Trust in the respective institution			
Civil service (ABS)	n.d.	58	n.d.
Civil service (WVS)	57	70	74
Government (WVS)	50	48	97
Global Integrity Scorecard 2004[a]			
Executive	weak	strong	n.d.
Privatization	very weak	very strong	n.d.
Global Integrity Scorecard 2006[a]			
Privatization	n.d.	very strong	very weak
Executive accountability	moderate	moderate	very weak
Budget process	very weak	weak	very weak

Sources: Trust – ABS 2001, WVS 2001; performance ratings – Global Integrity (2004a, 2004b, 2006a, 2006b, 2006c).
Notes: n.d. = no data.
[a] Rating of performance for both government offices and policies implemented.

Budgets relate to the size of an agency instead of its performance. Staffing and staff development planning are not yet rationalized. However, the *doi moi* economic reforms and the Communist Party now allow for more openness and consultations than before. Moreover, the 1996 State Budget Law and civil service reforms have led to the development of a coherent financial and personnel management system (Global Integrity 2006a).

Most Indonesians characterize the government as weak in its structure and performance, as borne out in the associated trust levels. The patrimonial politics Suharto exemplified, along with shortcomings of the bureaucracy, have not been entirely removed despite attempts at modernization. The budget process's weakness is the result of very large discretionary accounts and insufficient allocations for programs, generating pressure for corruption, non-performance, and patronage. Privatization has consolidated ownership in a few families, firms allegedly having been sold at manipulated prices or serving as hidden sources of funds for government officials (Beeson 1998).

Trust and performance seem to go in tandem in the Philippines, with its strong showing in privatization, a highly qualified staff, and a bureaucracy in step with modernization trends. It has a rationalization program that could be a textbook case of agency-level decentralization. However, implementation lags behind the modern plans. Trust in the executive branch and the latter's performance also do not correspond to the 20-year polls, which show a downtrend in net satisfaction for all presidents.

Table 4.5 Economy and efficiency of selected SEA governments

	Extent of red tape[a]	Waste in public spending[b]	Competence of officials[c]	Country mean
Indonesia	2.9	3.9	4.4	3.7
Malaysia	1.6	2.8	4.9	3.1
Philippines	2.3	2.3	4.8	3.8
Singapore	1.8	1.1	2.3	1.7
Thailand	3.4	2.7	4.4	3.5
Vietnam	2.2	3.9	3.9	3.3
SEA mean	2.4	3.1	4.1	3.2

Source: World Economic Forum (2001).
Notes:
[a]"How much time does your company's senior management spend working with government agencies/regulations?" (1 = less than 10% of its time, 2 = 10–20%, 3 = 21–30%, 8 = 71–80%).
[b]"The composition of government spending in your country is ..." (7 = wasteful, 1 = provides necessary goods and services not provided by the market).
[c]"The competence of personnel in the public sector is ..." (7 = lower than in the private sector, 1 = higher than in the private sector).

This suggests trust as an expression of hope, not as an appraisal of actual conditions.

The principal contact between citizens and government is through the efficient and effective delivery of goods and services. Efficiency and economy involve the rules, funds, and personnel that are inputs to government services. Quality or effectiveness captures the performance of government.

Three questions from the Global Competitiveness Index (GCI) are related to economy and efficiency: the extent of red tape, waste in government spending, and personnel quality (Table 4.5).[6]

Southeast Asia as a whole has streamlined rules and regulations, and is close to the theoretical middle (3.5) in reining in waste, but it leaves a lot to be desired in the capacity and performance of its human resources. The short time needed to get over red tape probably results from the deregulation that all the countries have instituted. Procurement reform and more judicious spending have also decreased waste.

The quality of government services

The GCI asked business executives about the quality of basic services (Table 4.6). Some might argue that, since they hardly use these services, they are not in a position to judge their quality. However, because they

Table 4.6 The quality of government services in selected SEA countries

	Public schools[a]	Public health agencies[b]	Infrastructure quality[c]	Minimum wage enforcement[d]	Country mean
Indonesia	2.7	4.2	3.0	5.2	3.8
Malaysia	4.2	4.9	5.4	3.9	4.6
Philippines	2.3	4.0	2.4	5.0	3.4
Singapore	6.4	6.5	6.8	4.9	6.1
Thailand	3.9	5.4	4.6	5.2	4.8
Vietnam	3.3	3.8	2.2	4.3	3.4
SEA mean	3.8	4.8	4.1	4.8	4.4

Source: World Economic Forum (2001).
Notes: The higher the rating, the better the quality of government services.
[a]"Public (free) schools in your country are ..." (1 = of poor quality, 7 = equal to the best in the world).
[b]"Public health agencies in your country are able to deal with public outbreaks of disease ..." (1 = barely at all, 7 = very effectively).
[c]"General infrastructure in your country is ..." (1 = poorly developed and inefficient, 7 = among the best in the world).
[d]"The minimum wage set by law in your country is ..." (1 = never enforced, 7 = strongly enforced).

may avoid them precisely because of their poor quality, executives may be a better source of such a rating than those who have no choice but to seek public services.

In general, SEA is above the theoretical middle in the services rated here. Still, except for Singapore, there is much room for improvement.

Equality of access

Government is supposed to serve everyone, particularly those marginalized by poverty, low education, rural residence, and ethnic minority status. Such policies not only would be social justice, but would also affect the stability of the nation and therefore the security of investments. The GCI thus asked business executives to gauge the extent of equality of benefits (Table 4.7).

Social transfers are generally regarded as equally benefitting the rich and the poor, except in Singapore where the perception is a greater benefit for the disadvantaged. A large gap is perceived, except in Singapore and Malaysia, regarding the educational and health facilities accessible to the rich and the poor.

The fourth indicator describes the performance of individuals, not institutions. Nevertheless, it is rated like the others, with Singapore leading the pack and the Philippines and Indonesia, whose educational and

Table 4.7 Equality of access to public institutions in selected SEA countries

	Social transfer recipients[a]	Difference in quality of schools[b]	Difference in quality of healthcare[c]	Favoritism in government decisions[d]	Country mean
Indonesia	3.5	2.1	1.8	2.6	2.5
Malaysia	3.5	3.6	3.5	3.0	3.4
Philippines	3.5	1.8	1.8	2.7	2.4
Singapore	4.1	5.6	5.6	5.1	5.1
Thailand	3.5	2.5	2.5	3.5	3.0
Vietnam	3.5	2.9	2.2	3.0	2.9
SEA mean	3.6	3.1	2.9	3.3	3.2

Source: World Economic Forum (2001).
Notes:
[a]"Government social transfers go primarily to ... " (7 = poor people, 1 = rich people). Original scores were reversed so that the most equal is the highest in all indicators.
[b]"The difference in the quality of schools available to rich and poor children in your country is ..." (1 = large, 7 = small).
[c]"The difference in the quality of healthcare available to rich and poor people in your country is ..." (1 = large, 7 = small).
[d]"When deciding upon policies and contracts, government officials ..." (1 = usually favor well-connected firms and individuals, 7 = are neutral among firms and individuals).

healthcare institutions are at the bottom, also having government officials who display favoritism. It may be that the organizational ethos of favoring the well-connected also infuses the officials implementing policies. These data are significant because they indicate the perceptions of those who probably benefit from the inequality.

With their current inequality levels, more attention to the needs of the disadvantaged is still called for. However, in the public sector reform in Thailand, Malaysia, Indonesia, the Philippines, and Singapore, principles of political neutrality, responsiveness, and equal opportunity have been de-prioritized in favor of competition, efficiency, public–private partnerships, and profitability (Haque 1998).

Increasing access through ICT

Information and communications technology (ICT) has theoretically solved the problem of access, since anyone can communicate with any other practically at will. Nevertheless, the digital divide is related to past disadvantages of lack of wealth and education, or ethnicity and gender. Thus to take advantage of ICT and to ensure it provides better access,

Table 4.8 The existence of ICT policy and laws in selected SEA countries

	ICT policy	Presence of ICT laws	Country mean
Indonesia	3.8	2.7	3.3
Malaysia	5.4	4.8	5.1
Philippines	4.3	4.1	4.2
Singapore	6.4	5.8	6.1
Thailand	4.6	3.3	4.0
Vietnam	3.9	2.6	3.3
SEA mean	4.7	3.9	4.3

Source: World Economic Forum (2001).
Notes:
[a]"Information and communications technologies are an overall government priority" (1 = strongly disagree, 7 = strongly agree).
[b]"Laws relating to electronic commerce, digital signatures, and consumer protection are ..." (1 = non-existent, 7 = well-developed and enforced).

government has to enable its use and propagate its benefits whenever possible.

The GCI tried to determine if government has promulgated ICT policy and programs. ICT policy is gauged by whether or not ICT is a government priority and whether laws have been enacted to regulate electronic commerce and consumer protection (Table 4.8). The regional mean is high, indicating that all countries have recognized the importance of ICT for their economy and society.

To find out how well ICT programs are faring, the GCI uses public access to the Internet and the quality of ICT competition and general ICT availability. The availability of government on-line services and the success of government ICT programs measure government use of ICT (Table 4.9).

Again, the regional mean is above the middle, except for government on-line services. State enabling of competition and ICT service has the best rating; government ICT programs are also deemed successful. Singapore's "Public Service for the 21st Century" (PS21), aimed at "being on time for the future," is probably the model to study (Singapore Public Service Division 2006).

The military and the police

The military is supposed to defend the country against external threats and the police are a civilian force to maintain internal peace and order. That differentiation in roles is not clear in countries with politicized militaries that presume they can govern better than civilian authorities. No

Table 4.9 ICT programs in selected SEA countries

	Public access to Internet[a]	ISP competition[b]	Government on-line services[c]	Success of government ICT programs[d]	Country mean
Indonesia	3.4	4.6	2.0	3.2	3.3
Malaysia	3.4	4.4	3.3	4.2	3.8
Philippines	2.8	4.8	2.3	3.7	3.4
Singapore	5.7	5.9	6.4	6.0	6.0
Thailand	3.4	4.6	3.2	3.9	3.8
Vietnam	2.6	3.1	2.2	3.8	2.9
SEA mean	3.6	4.6	3.2	4.1	3.9

Source: World Economic Forum (2001).
Notes:
[a]"Public access to the Internet through libraries, post offices etc is ..." (1 = very limited, 7 = pervasive – most people have frequent access).
[b]"Is competition among your country's Internet Service Providers sufficient to ensure high quality, infrequent interruptions and low prices?" (1 = no, 7 = yes, equal to world's best).
[c]"On-line government services – e.g. downloadable permit applications, tax payments – in your country are ..." (1 = not available, 7 = commonly available).
[d]"Government programs promoting the use of ICT are ..." (1 = not very successful, 7 = highly successful).

Southeast Asian nation has escaped being under military rule, albeit with varying levels of repression and participation by civil authorities. The military remains a constant presence even under civilian government in areas with separatist movements or rebel strongholds and with the heightened need for security amidst threats and acts of terrorism.

Most respondents expressed trust in both institutions, with the exception of the Philippines relative to the police. However, the military is more trusted than the police in all countries (Table 4.10).

Table 4.10 Trust in the military and the police: Selected SEA countries

	Percent expressing confidence in:	
	Armed forces	Police
World Values Survey		
Indonesia	73	51
Vietnam	95	91
Philippines	74	61
Asian Barometer Survey		
Philippines	54	46
Thailand	76	56

Sources: WVS 2001, ABS 2001.

Table 4.11 Corruption Perceptions Index: Southeast Asia, 2006

Country	Rank		Score
	Overall	SEA	
Singapore	5	1	9.4
Malaysia	44	2	5.0
Thailand	63	3	3.6
Laos	111	5	2.6
Timor-Leste	–	5	2.6
Vietnam	–	5	2.6
Philippines	121	7	2.5
Indonesia	130	8	2.4
Cambodia	151	9	2.1
Myanmar	160	10	1.9

Source: Transparency International (2006).

Accountability, transparency, and anti-corruption

Corruption is a serious SEA problem.[7] In Transparency International's 2006 Corruption Perceptions Index (CPI), Singapore ranks among the world's least corrupt countries, and Malaysia and Thailand are above the median. The rest score below 3, "indicating that corruption in these countries is . . . endemic" (Transparency International 2006) (Table 4.11).

Filipino trust in the civil service and government as well as the moderate-to-strong rating on the Global Integrity Scorecard (GIS) does not jibe with high corruption in the Global Competitiveness Index and Corruption Perceptions Index. The strong showing in the GIS recognizes the legal and institutional apparatuses the Philippines has set up to tackle corruption and accountability (ADB 2006). However, conviction of high officials is rare and public perception of the extent of corruption corresponds with Transparency International's information. Quah (2003) underscores the importance of political will and independent single institutions in the relative progress of Thailand vis-à-vis the Philippines and Indonesia. However, Prime Minister Thaksin's fall showed the ineffectiveness of post-1997 anti-corruption reforms. Meanwhile, political will can be demonstrated by going after the big fish, as Indonesia and Malaysia have done recently.

Vietnamese GIS data align with the CPI and GCI but not with the trust surveys. Bribes for everyday services such as education and healthcare are commonplace. In a Swedish-sponsored study of corruption undertaken by the Communist Party, two-thirds of respondents in Hanoi and Ho Chi Minh City admit to committing bribery to get things done and a third of the civil service admitted to receiving bribes (Global Integrity 2006a). On a positive note, the Party launched an anti-corruption self-criticism campaign in 1999, an Anti-Corruption Law was passed in 2005, and the National Assembly required the disclosure of assets of officials in 2006 (Global Integrity 2006a; ADB 2006). The reforms may have further engendered trust because the citizens perceive *doi moi* as not being foreign instigated (ADB 2001).

Indonesia moved up on the Public Integrity Scorecard between 2004 and 2006, with improvements in administration, the civil service, and anti-corruption. The exposure of "Buloggate"[8] was made at the turn of the century. An Anti-Corruption Commission was in place by 2004. E-procurement was launched in 2006 (ADB 2006). All these actions would have been taken into account only in the post-2004 assessment. Attacks on corruption continued through 2006, although conflicts of interest and a lack of independence mar the relationship of regulatory agencies with the private sector and other clients (Global Integrity 2006b).

Trust in the judiciary

A key problem of governance is providing justice to all citizens. The World Bank's World Business Environment Survey 2000 asked a stratified sample of entrepreneurs from 94 countries and 60,000 firms to describe the impact of their country's investment climate on their firm. They report on their actual experiences, not just their perception of the general country situation. The SEA mean confidence level in the judiciary is 63. This is lower than the mean for all East Asia and Pacific (66), the Middle East (67) and the OECD (74) (Batra et al. 2003).

Trust in the judiciary is reported by most respondents to the Asian Barometer Survey (ABS) and the World Bank Enterprise Survey (WBES), except in Cambodia. These data largely correspond with the GCI judicial independence measure (Table 4.12). Trust in courts is related to how independently the judiciary makes its decisions, one finding here where trust is merited by government performance.

The Global Integrity ratings convey different information from the others. For Indonesia, the very weak rating in 2004 may be attributed to the "astonishing corruption in the judiciary," all the way to the Supreme Court (Ghoshal 2004: 15). The strong showing in 2006 may be traced to the start of judicial reform and the conviction of several high-profile officials on corruption charges in 2005 and 2006. This contrasts with the pre-2004 lack of prosecution of similar individuals (Global Integrity 2006b).

Table 4.12 Trust in the courts and judicial accountability: Selected SEA countries, stated years

	Trust in courts			Global Integrity surveys	
	ABS	WBES	GCI on judicial independence	Judiciary (2004)	Judicial accountability (2006)
Cambodia	n.d.	39	n.d.	n.d.	n.d.
Indonesia	n.d.	59	2.8	very weak	strong
Malaysia	n.d.	n.d.	3.6	n.d.	n.d.
Philippines	50	66	3.7	strong	weak
Singapore	n.d.	n.d.	5.7	n.d.	n.d.
Thailand	58	74	4.7	n.d.	n.d.
Vietnam	n.d.	77	3.7	n.d.	very weak

Sources: Trust in courts – ABS 2001, and World Bank Enterprise Surveys (WBES) 2003 for Cambodia, Indonesia and the Philippines, 2004 for Thailand, and 2005 for Vietnam (see <http://www.enterprisesurveys.org/>); Judicial independence [answer to: "The judiciary in your country is independent and not subject to interference by the government and/or parties to disputes" (1 = not true, 7 = true)] – World Economic Forum (2001); Judiciary and Judicial accountability scores – Global Integrity (2004a, 2004b, 2006a, 2006b, 2006c).

For the Philippines, the higher rating in 2004 may be due to reforms, including the removal of corrupt judges, streamlining the court system, and the resolution of some high-profile cases. However, other cases were unfinished as of 2006, leading to the weak rating that year. The mean of the two ratings may be more credible because the judiciary is indeed trying to reform itself, but insinuations about the continued tenure of "hoodlums in robes" (in the colorful words of President Estrada) and the very slow resolution of cases push the court performance down. Social Weather Stations surveys say citizens do not expect the successful prosecution of corrupt officials, but they have greater trust in the court's ability to protect property rights (Mangahas 2004).

Vietnam's very low GIS rating may be traced to the lack of judicial independence and the arrest and detention of government critics. On the other hand, fraud and corruption charges have been lodged against high-ranking officials since 1999 (Global Integrity 2006a).

Trust in representational institutions

For people to be empowered, they need to have a say in how they are governed. This is why representational institutions are significant for enhancing trust in government.

Table 4.13 Trust indicators and ratings related to elections: Selected SEA countries, stated years

	Indonesia	Philippines		Thailand	Vietnam
Trust (2001)	WVS	ABS	WVS	ABS	WVS
Political parties	35	34	47	47	87
Election commission	n.d.	47	45	61	n.d.
Electoral processes (2004)	moderate	weak		n.d.	n.d.
National elections	very strong	strong		–	–
Election monitoring agency	very strong	strong		–	–
Political party finances	very weak	very weak		–	–
Elections (2006)	weak	very weak		n.d.	very weak
Voting and citizen participation	strong	very strong		–	weak
Election integrity	moderate	moderate		–	very weak
Political financing	very weak	very weak		–	very weak

Sources: Trust data – ABS 2001, WVS 2001; Electoral and Political Processes/ Elections – Global Integrity (2004a, 2004b, 2006a, 2006b, 2006c).

Electoral processes

Representation is supposed to be ensured by citizens' participation in the choice of those elected to parliament. Electoral processes therefore need to be transparent, honest, and efficient to gain the people's trust. Trust in SEA electoral processes and parties tends be low, except in Thailand's election commission and in Vietnamese parties (Table 4.13).

The Philippines has had the longest experience in electoral democracy in the region. However, it is still burdened by the poor quality of its electoral system, the influence of a few families, a lack of party loyalty, and a focus on personalities. The low trust in political parties is understandable given that one does not even know which political party exists at any given time, because each election throws up new "parties" created primarily for a particular candidate(s).

The very low rating of the Philippines on political financing gets at the vote-buying and political corruption nexus; its scores on the other GIS indicators acknowledge that electoral institutions are in place and that elections take place regularly. However, if their quality had been taken into greater account, the ratings would have corresponded more to the level of the trust indicators.

Indonesia's 2004 elections have been called "the most complex and challenging elections to have faced any democracy, let alone a new democracy like Indonesia's." They were held in three phases and had

448,705 candidates in 24 political parties for 15,276 positions (Kuppus-wamy 2004); of an eligible 147 million, 75 percent voted (KPU 2005). The presence of electoral institutions and the regularity of the electoral process are reflected in the GIS indicators. Low trust in political parties may be due to their sheer number, their lack of clear differentiation, and the inability of incumbents to deliver promised economic and social benefits. The disclosure of party finances is generally believed not to be credible, and vote-buying is assumed to be rampant (Global Integrity 2004a).

The Thais' low trust in political parties was because they are "shifting coalitions of interest groups, bound together by some perceived affinity and mutual advantage, but prone to defections and shifting alliances" (ADB 2001).

Vietnam is a one-party state and all senior government positions may be filled only by members of the Communist Party of Vietnam. This explains the low GIS ratings for elections (Global Integrity 2006a). The Vietnamese trust in parties is unproblematic because the referent is clearly the one party respondents know. It may convey approval of the government, or reflect fear of expressing dissent.

Parliamentary processes

Parliamentarians are supposed to make citizens present in spirit ("represent") in their deliberations and decisions. In practice, of course, few citizens think of themselves as the principals of those in parliament, nor do they demand that their representatives make decisions for the public good. This is why Rothstein and Stolle (ADB 2001) posited that trust in representational institutions may find enhancement in partisan/personal accomplishments instead of in fairness. Parliaments are trusted by large respondent groups, but legislative accountability is adjudged weak in all the selected countries (Table 4.14).

Filipinos have been electing their representatives to a law-making body since US colonial rule, interrupted only by Martial Law (1972–1986). The

Table 4.14 Trust in parliament and ratings on the legislature: Selected SEA countries, stated years

	Indonesia	Philippines	Thailand	Vietnam
Trust in parliament (WVS)	40	60	n.d.	94
Trust in parliament (ABS)	n.d.	44	55	n.d.
Legislature (2004)	weak	strong	n.d.	n.d.
Legislative accountability (2006)	weak	weak	n.d.	very weak

Sources: Trust data – ABS 2001, WVS 2001; Legislature and Legislative Accountability – Global Integrity (2004a, 2004b, 2006a, 2006b, 2006c).

Philippine Congress is a functioning institution, hence the strong GIS rating of 2004. Despite political dynasties and continued elite domination, the Congress has managed to enact social reform, economic liberalization, and other landmark laws. However, the quality of its performance and questions of how members get elected and perform are issues of legislative accountability, which the GIS rated as weak in 2006.

Thailand has been a constitutional monarchy since 1932 and had had 50 different governments by 1992, with military coups and elections alternating. From 1992 to 2006, it had a functioning parliament – until the elected Thaksin government, burdened by corruption charges, was overthrown by a coup. At that time, it was working under the 1997 constitution, widely known as the "People's Charter." The 2001 ABS probably not only reflects the trust of the Thais in their parliamentary processes but also embodies the hopes they have invested in it. The survey followed the first election of the Senate in 2000, which ended almost seven decades of political patronage for military and civil service officials (ADB 2001; Pathmanand 2001).

The high trust of the Vietnamese in their parliament may seem misplaced in a one-party state. However, the 1992 constitution had instituted the National Assembly, which performs an oversight role over, and appoints officials for, all state bodies. Moreover, the Communist Party has allowed debate on, and even the rejection of, some draft legislation in the Assembly (ADB 2001). The high trust accorded this fledgling institution may express the hope that it would stay the course.

Indonesia's rating on trust in parliament is low in all the indicators. Parliament has been in place since the collapse of Suharto's New Order in 1998; there have been national and provincial elections, an amended constitution, and basic freedoms of the press, assembly, and association. However, the multi-party system has produced a fragmented parliament that allows neither the president nor the parliament a base from which to make difficult decisions for the country. Aside from the quality of their performance, legislators are also under fire for selling their votes to those who need legislative endorsement (Ghoshal 2004).

Local governments

Decentralization is a growing phenomenon. Work (2002) reported that, as early as 1999, 76 percent of the world's 126 countries had at least one elected sub-national government. SEA is at the forefront of this revolution. Thailand, the Philippines, and Indonesia all have newly strengthened devolution regimes. Decentralization was at the heart of Cambodian rehabilitation. Even Singapore has become more deconcentrated. Information on how these reforms have affected trust in SEA is available for

Table 4.15 Views on local government in the Philippines and Thailand, 2001

Percent expressing:	Philippines	Thailand
Trust in local government	56	64
Trust in national government	n.d.	65
Widespread corruption in:		
Local government	54	19
National government	66	n.d.
National government should have more authority over local decisions	61	81

Source: ABS 2001.

only the Philippines and Thailand (Table 4.15). The majority accord trust to local governments; this is to the same extent as the national government in the case of Thailand. However, answers to related queries do not provide a resounding approval of decentralization. Filipinos perceive a lot of corruption at the local level (though by a smaller group than those complaining of national-level corruption), and also suggest more national oversight over local governments. Thais do not see much corruption in local government, but more of them recommend national oversight over local decisions.

Key issues, trends and challenges

This exploration has yielded some surprises. The first is that Southeast Asians trust their governments and their order institutions to a much greater extent than their representational institutions. This is surprising because it does not jibe with the worldwide trend of either low levels of trust or a decline from some higher point.

The second source of surprise is that trust in government is expressed by people who do not exhibit a generalized trust of others. Like much of the developing world, Southeast Asians proceed from a culture based on close family and personal ties, valuing face-to-face interaction, we-feeling, and distrust of strangers. Their kind of social capital tends to focus on bonds, not bridges. And yet they accord trust to government, no matter how the question is phrased. The availability of mediators, the Churchillian idea of a lesser evil, and trust as a means of expressing hope were offered as possible explanations for according trust to governments when it is not proffered generally to others.

The third reason for surprise is that so much of this trust seems not to be merited. Current levels of governance leave much to be desired. Weaknesses are evident in the performance of institutions for order and impartiality, whether it be in the efficiency and quality of service delivery, equality of citizen access, the use of and access to ICT, the performance of the military and the police, the implementation of anti-corruption processes, or the provision of justice. There are also shortfalls in the performance of representational institutions, but at least the people accord less trust in them and so there is less of a sense of betrayal.

The reasons for expressing trust in undeserving institutions call to mind the same Churchillian and hope hypotheses. Expressing trust may signal the citizens' acceptance of the current situation because it is not as bad as others they have experienced. Most of the region has undergone authoritarian regimes, civil wars, or occupation by an outside army. The current regime – though still lacking in efficiency, quality, accountability, and fairness – may still seem much better in comparison.

Beyond Churchillian relativity, trust may have been given in the hope that it would beget positive outcomes. It could work for citizens when their governments are sincerely trying to serve the public interest and deserve to receive more encouragement for their endeavors. If governments are not responsive, citizens' hope may propel them to action, and lead toward their empowerment. As Braithwaite (2004: 7) reminds us, hope allows us "not only to dream of the extraordinary but also to do the extraordinary."

These findings present a challenge to governments to be more worthy of trust. This concluding section will cite extant models from Southeast Asia that can be built upon to respond to these challenges.

An improvement in service delivery and access is the first concern, because this is the first point of contact between government and the people. It deserves notice that general Southeast Asian ratings on efficiency, quality, and ICT access are above neutral, suggesting the efficacy of public sector reforms. Nevertheless, governance needs to be improved, through, first, the continuous encouragement of innovation. A possible model here is "The Enterprise Challenge" (TEC) in Singapore, which recognizes that innovation is fraught with uncertainty and that agencies must be provided with a safety-net for venturing into the unknown. Thus TEC provides funds for the risk that the agencies will take in trying that innovation (Singapore Public Service Division 2006).

The second challenge is to recognize and keep the people who run the civil service content but challenged. To achieve better-performing human resources, Malaysia offers an "apex mechanism for reform." Distinguished by its comprehensiveness and synergy, the reform package recognizes the following as vital ingredients in the administrative reform loop: awards and recognition, guidelines, promotion and training, advice and consultation, and inspectorate and audit (Hussin 2006).

The third challenge is made necessary by the fact that equality of access to services does not seem to be as highly prized as efficiency, effectiveness, and technological development (Haque 1998; Higgott and

Nesadurai 2002). Thailand's Balanced Scorecard of the Public Sector for 2007, involving effectiveness, quality of service, efficiency of operations, and organizational development, is worthy of emulation. Its quality of service dimension emphasizes customer satisfaction, people participation, and transparency (Pairuchvet 2006). However, one area for reform is an explicit concern for equality and justice such that growth will not result in greater economic disparity.

Corruption remains a scourge in Southeast Asia, but it is not an intractable problem. Swift and severe retribution, especially of big fish, has been Singapore's slogan since the 1970s, and its approach has worked excellently (Rahman 1986). It embodies the political will and institutional focus that are primary ingredients in fighting corruption. Transparency of operations and judicial independence and accountability would also help to root out corruption. This is not to forget the role of individuals imbued with ethics and accountability on both the private and public sides of the transaction.

For its part, Transparency International is pushing for every country to ratify the United Nations Convention against Corruption as an indicator of commitment at the highest level. Meanwhile, the Asian Development Bank (ADB) and the Organisation for Economic Co-operation and Development (OECD) have focused on procurement, which is a major avenue of government corruption. Hopeful signs are shown in self-assessments done by 25 countries in the Asia-Pacific region. For instance, a third of the countries substantially overhauled their rules of procurement or passed new comprehensive laws between 2000 and 2006. In addition, Internet-based, anonymous procedures, rotation of personnel, panel reviews, and integrity pacts are becoming common (ADB 2006).

Transparency International joins the United Nations, the Asian Development Bank and the World Bank, as well as many scholars, in pointing out the role of citizens and their organizations in rooting out this scourge. At the United Nations Regional Forum on Reinventing Government in Asia held in Korea in 2006, the experience of the NGO Concerned Citizens of Abra for Good Government (CCAGG) was presented as a best practice in this regard (Sumangil 2006). CCAGG's approach is effective and also offers lessons on the complex relationship between trust and anti-corruption. What pushed for CCAGG's creation was a distrust of government, inflamed by the obvious corruption and inefficiency shown by the poor record of road construction it had witnessed. Yet for poor rural people to take on powerful experts and to engage in a corruption assessment required a certain level of trust as well: perhaps not in the part of the government that it was criticizing, but in the larger governmental system to which it filed its report. It was also bolstered by social trust (received from the CCAGG membership itself), trust in democracy as a system that permits dissent, and a hope fueled by empowerment and cold analysis.

The other key challenge related to order institutions is to point out the danger of too much trust in the military. The alternative is not to spread distrust of an important public institution. Rather, what is called for is better civic education, so that such democratic principles as a loyal opposition, dissent expressed in dialogue and not through guns, civilian pre-eminence, and respect for minority rights and the basic freedoms are learned and appreciated by all citizens.

For representational institutions, avenues for political and moral reform should deal with the integrity of electoral processes and the performance of legislatures and local governments. Political parties, the electoral process, parliament itself, and, concomitantly, campaign financing must all be improved. The International Foundation for Electoral Systems recommends improving the electoral process, through a code of conduct for political actors, intensive voter education, the use of election observers, and the effective operation of independent election commissions (IFES 2007). The United Nations Development Programme (UNDP) has assisted in direct reforms for political parties in the Philippines through projects incorporating advocacy for improved election laws and a political party summit. As Ghoshal (2004: 19) said, speaking of Indonesia in the 1960s, "parliamentary democracy would not have failed if the political parties took pains to establish their base among the people through party building and interest mobilization." The advice is still relevant today.

Decentralization as a governance process has been accepted by most of the world's nations. However, it is not an unmixed blessing, and civil society as well as national governments should be alert to the possibility that decentralization might nurture local tyrants or produce an imbalance in development. At the same time, it should be recognized that decentralization is a national policy and is not the responsibility of local administration units alone. Instead, the central government has the duty of fostering a national vision, maintaining national standards, providing assistance to disadvantaged units, and checking local tyrants so that decentralization does not become an excuse for leaving poorer, more conflict-ridden, or more elite-dominated local administration units behind. On the other hand, decentralization is also about letting go and allowing local administrations the autonomy, flexibility, and accountability to be confronted by their own citizens. Therefore, general supervision rather than controls is called for, and trust must be accorded to the newly emancipated local governments. Citizens themselves play an important role in encouraging local administrations to be more trustworthy. An example is Indonesia's program that recognizes the major role that decentralization can play in poverty reduction. But rather than bombarding the local level with central rules, it provides for participatory assessments at the regional level to accommodate the views of the poor while fostering local autonomy (Soedjito 2006).

In many of these challenges, civil society engagement has been mentioned. That is as it should be. Trust in government necessitates the involvement of citizens in governance, not as onlookers or passive recipients but as full participants and decision-makers in the process. Yet, despite the trust that Southeast Asians accord to their often undeserving governments, the latter have not responded in kind. A few windows have been opened: the reining in of red tape and the welcome to e-governance might suggest increased trust of citizens by government. The making of the Thai constitution of 1997 also showed a government willing to trust citizens with no less than the basic law. On the whole, however, governments tend to erect barriers between themselves and their citizens. The multiplicity of agencies fighting corruption is a case in point. It shows a government not only distrustful of its citizens but also not trusting its officials and employees.

If trust in government is to be promoted, the radical idea is that government should also make trust in citizens a guiding principle. This will mean not trusting money and hoodlums to deliver election results, but believing that citizens will make rational choices. This will mean less favoritism in making decisions and trusting that the unknown people who present their credentials to you are as qualified as someone known to you. This will mean having fewer document requirements and fewer guards guarding guardians because integrity holds sway. It will make both citizens and government more responsible for their actions. It will still require spot checks by government, evaluations by citizens, and vigilance all around. But the model is promise-keeping exemplified by Brunei's client charter (Yassin 2006) and other citizens' charters around the globe.

Trust begets trust. Southeast Asians have accorded trust to governments that have as yet not shown themselves to be trustworthy. But the citizens have begun the experiment to trust first, so that they may pressure the other party to earn that trust. Can governments take the plunge and accord trust to their citizens too? When they do, they will have entered not just the politics of trust, but also the new politics of hope, to dream of extraordinary things, and thence to do them.

Notes

1. Trust data are from two primary sources: the Global Barometer Survey (GBS) and its Asian arm, the Asian Barometer Survey (ABS), and the World Values Survey (WVS). GBS grew out of the Eurobarometer in the 1970s and has since become a network of

several regions (see <http://www.globalbarometer.net>, accessed 14 April 2010). ABS is based in National Taiwan University, and is used unless discussing results beyond Asia (see <http://www.asianbarometer.org/newenglish/Introduction/ProgramOverview.htm>, accessed 8 April 2010). WVS is based in the University of Michigan and has been investigating sociocultural and political change on a global scale since 1901 (see <http://www.worldvaluessurvey.org/>, accessed 8 April 2010). Governance indices are listed in United Nations Development Programme (2004).

2. "Social trust" is indicated by answers to a four-point scale between "Most people can be trusted" and "One can't be too careful in dealing with them."

3. The Philippines is the only country of overlap of GBS and WVS. Even though WVS respondents tend to be more positive, the trust ranking of Philippine institutions is the same.

4. This point is inspired by Park and Shin (2005). They allude to Winston Churchill's remark that "democracy is the worst form of government, except those other governments that have been tried from time to time." They find that support for democracy is genuine, rather than an acceptance of it as a lesser evil, which is the argument this chapter is making.

5. The Global Integrity Scorecard (GIS) consists of peer-reviewed scores, commentary, and references on 292 integrity indicators. Using local teams of researchers and journalists, GIS considers the existence of anti-corruption mechanisms and practices, their level of effectiveness, and the extent to which citizens can access these mechanisms (see Global Integrity n.d.). The Philippines and Indonesia were included in 2004; Vietnam was added in 2006. Global Integrity is funded by the investment firm Legatum Global Development, the Sunrise Foundation, the Wallace Global Fund, and the World Bank. See Global Integrity (n.d.).

6. The Global Competitiveness Index has been drawn from publicly available data, plus the results of an expert opinion survey of 11,000 business leaders in 125 economies worldwide. The GCI is a product of the World Economic Forum (WEF), which describes itself as "an independent international organization committed to improving the state of the world by engaging leaders in partnerships to shape global, regional and industry agendas." Founded in 1971, it is supervised by the Swiss government. See the WEF website, "History and Achievements," <http://www3.weforum.org/en/about/History%20and%20Achievements/index.html> (accessed 19 January 2010).

7. See, for instance, Quah (2003). Of Cambodia, Oskar Weggel (2006) quotes the World Bank as having said that the three tasks to rehabilitate the economy are "fighting corruption, fighting corruption, fighting corruption."

8. Wahid's masseur and business partner allegedly tricked Bulog, a partially privatized government agency, into transferring funds to secret relief operations in war-torn Aceh province. A special parliamentary commission found the president acting improperly on this and other issues. Wahid was impeached and dismissed. See Global Integrity (2006b).

REFERENCES

ADB [Asian Development Bank] (2001) *Asian Development Outlook 2001*. New York: Oxford University Press. Available at: <http://www.adb.org/Documents/books/ADO/2001/default.asp> (accessed 26 February 2010).

ADB [Asian Development Bank] (2006) "Annual Report: Southeast Asia," <http://www.adb.org/Documents/Reports/Annual_Report/2006/ADB-AR2006-Southeast-Asia.pdf> (accessed 26 February 2010).

Albritton, Robert B., and Thawilwadee Bureekul (2005) "Social and Cultural Supports for Pluralist Democracy in Eight Asian Nations: A Cross-National, Within-Nation Analysis," Working Paper Series No. 3. Taipei: Asian Barometer Project Office, National Taiwan University.

Amorado, Ronnie (2007) *Fixing Society: The Inside World of Fixers in the Philippines*. Davao City: Ateneo de Davao University.

Balisacan, Arsenio, and Ernesto Pernia (2002) "Probing Beneath Cross-national Averages: Poverty, Inequality and Growth in the Philippines," Working Paper Series No. 7. Manila: Asian Development Bank Economic and Research Department.

Batra, G., D. Kaufmann and A. H. W. Stone (2003) *Investment Climate Around the World: Voices of the Firms from the Business Environment Survey*. Washington, DC: World Bank. Available at: <http://web.worldbank.org/WBSITE/EXTERNAL/WBI/EXTWBIGOVANTCOR/0,,contentMDK:20791540~menuPK:1928469~pagePK:64168445~piPK:64168309~theSitePK:1740530~isCURL:Y,00.html> (accessed 26 February 2010).

Beeson, Mark (1998) "Indonesia, the East Asian Crisis and the Commodification of the Nation-State," *New Political Economy* 3:3, pp. 357–375.

Braithwaite, Valerie (2004) "Collective Hope," in Valerie Braithwaite (ed.) *Hope, Power and Governance: The Annals of the American Academy of Political and Social Science* 592, No. 1. Thousand Oaks, London and New Delhi: Sage Publications, pp. 6–13.

Bratton, Michael, Yun-han Chu, Marta Lagos, and Richard Rose (2005) "The People's Voice: Trust in Political Institutions," in *Ten Years of Supporting Democracy Worldwide*. Stockholm: International IDEA 62.

Brewer, Gene A. (2003) "Building Social Capital: Civic Attitudes and Behavior of Public Servants," *Journal of Public Administration Research and Theory* 13:1, pp. 5–26.

Fukuyama, Francis (1995) *Trust: The Social Virtues and the Creation of Prosperity*. New York: The Free Press.

Ghoshal, Baladas (2004) "Democratic Transition and Political Development in Post-Soeharto Indonesia," *Contemporary Southeast Asia* 26:3, pp. 506–529.

Global Integrity (2004a) *Global Integrity. An Investigative Report Tracking Corruption, Openness and Accountability in 25 Countries: Indonesia*. The Center for Public Integrity. Available at: <http://www.globalintegrity.org/reports/2004/docs/2004/2004Indonesia.pdf> (accessed 27 January 2010).

Global Integrity (2004b) *Global Integrity. An Investigative Report Tracking Corruption, Openness and Accountability in 25 Countries: Philippines*. The Center for Public Integrity. Available at: <http://www.globalintegrity.org/reports/2004/docs/2004/2004Philippines.pdf> (accessed 27 January 2010).

Global Integrity (2006a) *Global Integrity. 2006 Country Report: Vietnam*. Available at: <http://www.globalintegrity.org/reports/2006/pdfs/vietnam.pdf> (accessed 27 January 2010).

Global Integrity (2006b) *Global Integrity. 2006 Country Report: Indonesia*. Available at: <http://www.globalintegrity.org/reports/2006/pdfs/indonesia.pdf> (accessed 27 January 2010).

Global Integrity (2006c) *Global Integrity. 2006 Country Report: Philippines*. Available at: <http://www.globalintegrity.org/reports/2006/pdfs/philippines.pdf> (accessed 28 January 2010).

Global Integrity (n.d.) "Global Integrity Report," at <http://report.globalintegrity.org/> (accessed 19 January 2010).

Haque, M. Shamsul (1998) "New Directions in Bureaucratic Change in Southeast Asia: Selected Experiences," *Journal of Political and Military Sociology* 26:1, pp. 97–120.

Higgott, Richard A., and Helen E. S. Nesadurai (2002) "Rethinking the Southeast Asian Development Model: Bringing Ethical and Governance Questions," *ASEAN Economic Bulletin* 19:1, pp. 27–40.

Hussin, Dato Haji Yaacob (2006) "Effective Coordination for Administrative Reform for Malaysia," paper presented at the United Nations Regional Forum on Reinventing Government in Asia, Seoul, Republic of Korea, September.

IFES [International Foundation for Electoral Systems] (2007) "Thai Government Must Earn Back Public's Confidence," May 3, <http://www.ifes.org/features.html?title=Thai%20Government%20Must%20Earn%20Back%20Public%25s%20Confidence> (accessed 28 January 2010).

Ikeda, Ken'ich, Yasuo Yamada, and Masaru Kohno (2003) "Influence of Social Capital on Political Participation in Asian Cultural Context," Working Paper Series No. 10, Taipei: Asian Barometer Project Office, National Taiwan University and Academica Sinica.

KPU [General Election Committee] Indonesia (2005) "Summary of the 5 July and 24 September 2004 Indonesian Presidential Election Results, 2005," <http://www.kpu.go.id/> (accessed 18 May 2007).

Kuppuswamy, C. S. (2004) "Indonesia: Elections 2004," South Asia Analysis Group Paper No. 981, <http://www.southasiaanalysis.org/papers10/paper981.html> (accessed 28 January 2010).

Levi, Margaret and Valerie Braithwaite (1998) *Trust and Governance*. New York: Russell Sage Foundation.

Mangahas, Mahar (2004) "The Philippines: Integrity Assessment," Washington DC: Global Integrity. <http://www.globalintegrity.org/reports/2004/2004/country64b8.html?cc=ph&act=ia> (accessed 19 January 2010).

Nunberg, Barbara (2002) "Civil Service Quality after the Crisis: A View of Five Asian Cases," *Asian Journal of Political Science* 10:2, pp. 1–20.

Pairuchvet, Supannee (2006) "Building Trust in Government: Innovations to Improve Governance – the Thai Experience," paper presented at the United Nations Regional Forum on Reinventing Government in Asia, Seoul, Republic of Korea, September.

Park, Chong-Min, and Doh Chull Shin (2005) "Do East Asians View Democracy as a Lesser Evil? Testing Churchill's Notion of Democracy in East Asia," Working Paper Series No. 30, Taipei: Asian Barometer Project Office, National Taiwan University and Academica Sinica.

Pathmanand, Ukrist (2001) "Globalization and Democratic Development in Thailand: The New Path of the Military, Private Sector and Civil Society," *Contemporary Southeast Asia* 23:1, pp. 24–43.

Quah, Jon S. T. (2003) "Causes and Consequences of Corruption in Southeast Asia: A Comparative Analysis of Indonesia, the Philippines and Thailand," *Asian Journal of Public Administration* 25:2, pp. 235–266.

Rahman, A. T. R. (1986) "Combating Corruption," in Ledivina V. Cariño (ed.) *Bureaucratic Corruption in Asia: Causes, Consequences and Controls*. Manila: College of Public Administration and JVC Press.

Rothstein, B., and D. Stolle (2008) "The State and Social Capital: An Institutional Theory of Generalized Trust," *Comparative Politics* 40:4, pp. 441–459.

Singapore Public Service Division, Prime Minister's Office (2006) "Proud to Serve, Ready for the Future: The Singapore Public Service: Integrity, Service, Excellence," <http://www.ps21.gov.sg/> (accessed 26 February 2010).

Soedjito, Bambang Bintoro (2006) "Decentralized Poverty Reduction Strategy through Minimum Service Standard: Experience from Indonesia," paper presented at the United Nations Regional Forum on Reinventing Government in Asia, Seoul, Republic of Korea, September.

Sumangil, Pura (2006) "Accountability, Transparency and E-Governance: Concepts and Experiences in the Philippines," paper presented at the United Nations Regional Forum on Reinventing Government in Asia, Seoul, Republic of Korea, September.

Takashi, Shiraishi, and Patricio N. Abinales (2005) *After the Crisis: Hegemony, Technocracy and Governance in Southeast Asia*. Victoria, Australia: Trans Pacific Press and Kyoto University Press.

Transparency International (2006) "Corruption Perceptions Index 2006," <http://www.transparency.org/policy_research/surveys_indices/cpi/2006> (accessed 19 January 2010).

United Nations (2006) *Human Development Report 2006. Beyond Scarcity: Power, Poverty and the Global Water Crisis*. New York: Macmillan. Available at: <http://hdr.undp.org/en/reports/global/hdr2006/> (accessed 19 January 2010).

United Nations Development Programme (2004) *Governance Indicators: A Users' Guide*. New York: UNDP. Available at: <http://www.undp.org/governance/docs/policy-guide-IndicatorsUserGuide.pdf> (accessed 19 January 2010).

Weggel, Oskar (2006) "Cambodia in 2005: Year of Reassurance," *Asian Survey* 46:1, pp. 155–161.

Work, Robertson (2002) "Overview of Decentralisation Worldwide: A Stepping Stone to Improved Governance and Human Development," paper presented at the 2nd International Conference on Decentralization "Federalism: The Future of Decentralizing States?" Manila, Philippines, July 25–27. Available at: <http://www.undp.org/governance/docs/DLGUD_Pub_overview-decentralisation-worldwide-paper.pdf> (accessed 26 February 2010).

World Economic Forum (2001) *The Global Competitiveness Report 2001–2002*. See <http://www3.weforum.org/en/initiatives/gcp/Global%20Competitiveness%20Report/PastReports/index.html> (accessed 27 January 2010).

Yassin, Hamid (2006) "Accountability, Transparency and e-Government: Brunei Darussalam," paper presented at the United Nations Regional Forum on Reinventing Government in Asia, Seoul, Republic of Korea, September.

Yu, Samuel C. Y. (2002) "The Political Economy of Regime Transformation: Taiwan and Southeast Asia," *World Affairs* 165:2, pp. 9–79.

5

Building trust in government in South Asia

Sajjad Naseer

Developing countries, especially in South Asia, face a constant dilemma of poor governance that has undermined the proficient and impartial delivery of public services and the efficient implementation of programs. This has contributed to political instability, increasing violence, the emergence of extremist groups, and declining citizen trust in government. This chapter examines the role of governments in South Asian countries in promoting good governance, participation, development, and security – four of the cornerstones of building trust in government. The first section describes the historical context of the role of state. This is followed by a discussion of governance practice in South Asia and its impact on building trust. The last three sections examine the participation, development, and security performance of the countries in the region.

Global and regional context

As in other developing regions of the world, countries in South Asia have experienced a decline in trust in government. As Table 5.1 shows, trust in political parties and the police is particularly low. This lack of trust should be examined in the historical context of the region, i.e. the inability of the state to respond effectively to internal and external pressures for more effectual governance systems and processes to meet the challenges of globalization.

The collapse of the Soviet Union and the paradigm shift towards globalization raised serious concerns about governance and its attendant

Building trust in government: Innovations in governance reform in Asia, Cheema and Popovski (eds), United Nations University Press, 2010, ISBN 978-92-808-1189-6

Table 5.1 Levels of trust in national institutions in South Asia

Country	Political parties	Military	Police	Mean[a]	N
India	46	85	49	47	5,390
Pakistan	35	75	22	20	2,681
Sri Lanka	37	77	57	36	4,616
Mean	39.3	79.0	42.7	34.3	4,229

Notes:
[a]The national mean also includes national and local government, civil service, courts, parliament, and the media.
Source: Based on DeSouza and Uyangoda (2005).

functions, in both the developed and the developing world. The developed world, in most cases living in a post-industrial era, faced little difficulty in negotiating the post-1990 change internally, but the developing countries' capacity was tested to the fullest as they struggled to mediate the globalizing forces. In developing countries, the issue of governance assumed crisis proportions, raising alarm bells, and expressions such as "rogue state," "failing state," and "failed state" were used frequently to indicate the gravity of the emerging situation. Consequently, a body of literature emerged seeking to address the governance crisis. Besides advocating a holistic approach to meet the emerging situations in the developing countries, it was considered imperative to "build trust in the government" as a solution to the governance crisis. If this is the route to improve governance, particularly in the case of South Asia, then it will be appropriate to dwell briefly on the nature of the crisis and to contextualize the issue.

The onset of the Cold War coincided with the decolonization process, which gave birth to a large number of independent states. The colonial structures were largely not dismantled, and they shaped the post-independence landscape. The euphoria of independence, coupled with a sense of nationalism, led the political leadership in these countries to embrace a wide-ranging agenda in a bid to meet the expectations and the aspirations of the people. This was a formidable and challenging task and the inherited structures were not designed to accommodate such significant changes. Additionally, during the attempts to strengthen and consolidate the state, nation-building functions were usurped by state-building activities. The magnitude of the agenda caused errors and failures on the part of the governments.

While the performance of governments was often in decline, the Cold War milieu kept many pressing socioeconomic, ethnic, regional, and religious issues under the carpet. With the end of the Cold War, these "suppressed issues" erupted, and in some cases were accompanied by violence.

As these multiple crises deepened, the globalization paradigm demanded major shifts in the orientation of many governments in South Asia. The exhausted developing country states were pressed hard to embrace the new agenda of a free-market economy, privatization, and deregulation, and were also pushed to democratize by opening up spaces for civil society organizations. The new strategy was intended to enable governments to unburden themselves either through privatization and private/public partnerships or through joint ventures with foreign investors. However, these benefits were limited by the fact that the private sector in most developing countries is weak and did not experience the same evolution as occurred in the developed world during its industrialization phase. Consequently, the unburdening process did not include a clear and comprehensive view of the new role of the state.

Although states often responded to the forces of globalization through this strategy of unburdening, they did so without defining the role of the state or evaluating the capacity of the private sector. The private sector and civil society organizations, which were often in their infancy, found it difficult to cope with the rapid change. The opposition between the private and the public causes confusion and a perceived decrease in the credibility of governments. The issue of the state's ability to provide for basic needs is further aggravating this crisis, because the state's capacity to provide safe drinking water, electricity, security, and so on is fast eroding. The situation is especially problematic owing to the burgeoning levels of poverty over the past decade. These difficult conditions are rationalized as emerging during periods of transition. However, the "transition" shows no signs of abating.

On the agenda for democracy and human rights, there seems to be no visible evidence of improvements or progress. The prediction of a "future wave of democracy" advanced during the early 1990s does not appear to be materializing. The current political situation in Bangladesh and the ongoing judicial crisis in Pakistan are examples, among many other such cases. Democracy, therefore, is playing hide and seek, and different stakeholders have yet to harmonize their interests for the sake of viable democracy.

According to the Mahbub ul Huq Human Development Centre's report for 2006, South Asia's share in the world population is 22 percent, but it contains more than 40 percent of the world's poor. "There are over 867 million people without access to basic sanitation, more than 400 million adults are unable to read or write, and 300 million are undernourished" (MHHDC 2007: 2). Pakistan's Human Rights Commission has stated that South Asian governments have failed miserably to address the needs of the people (Human Rights Commission of Pakistan 2005). Generating trust in government can be accomplished by relying on the democratic governance model. To confront the complexities in the developing world, it would be equally appropriate to see the governance paradigm in the context of three variables: security, development, and participation. This may appear to be a simplified representation. It also dismisses politics in terms of dichotomies such as modern vs. traditional forces or democratic vs. non-democratic political systems. Two issues of paramount importance in this context are developing countries' need to quickly situate and stabilize themselves politically, and their need to increase their income.

Governance practice

United Nations reports have pointed to eight major characteristics of good governance:

> It is participatory, consensus oriented, accountable, transparent, responsive, effective and efficient, equitable and inclusive and follows the rule of law. It assures that corruption is minimized, the views of minorities are taken into account, and that the voices of the most vulnerable in society are heard in decision-making. It is also responsive to the present and future needs of society. (UNESCAP n.d.)

These issues run parallel to factors that governments must successfully mediate, including corruption, terrorism, the media, globalization, the basic necessities of life, and freedom of religion and caste. Successfully addressing these factors is paramount to establishing trust in the government.

The *Human Development in South Asia* report of 2006 points out that all the developing countries of South Asia are facing identical problems of governance. The report notes that certain governance issues in "South Asian countries" continue to recur in different degrees in various projects. These include limited coverage; poor targeting; a high degree of political interferences in identifying beneficiaries; leakage due to corruption and lack of transparency; weak administrative capacity and the lack of monitoring and evaluation mechanisms" (MHHDC 2007: 5). All these factors are central to the performance of governments in South Asian countries. The report also highlights the embedded inequalities in that, in South Asia, "public service delivery is fraught with the failure of governance that tends to hit the poor more than the rich" (MHHDC 2007: 3).

Most of the developing countries in South Asia were former colonies of the British. After gaining their independence, the majority of these countries followed the same system of governance, with minor changes.

The inherited systems included the judiciary, bureaucratic systems, and the police apparatus, which are the basis of governance.

After independence, most of these counties were ruled by either autocratic or monarchial rulers, or had a democratic system. Pakistan has been ruled by an autocratic ruler for more than 27 of its 60 years of history. The abrupt changes in government structure and the frequent intrusions of the army into the affairs of the state have hampered the credibility of the government. These changes have not allowed a democratic system to flourish and function in the country. Monarchs rule Nepal and Bhutan. Nepal has always been a monarchy resistant to social change. Its policy orientation has been particularly deficient in addressing the welfare of the poor (MHHDC 2007: 149). Countries such as India and Sri Lanka have democratic systems. Sri Lanka had been "a flourishing democracy" throughout its history, and the government showed a strong political commitment to develop the country as a "social welfare state" after independence in 1948. "At present, around 7–10 per cent of the GDP of Sri Lanka is used to finance free health and education services, food subsidies, food stamps and subsidized credit" (MHHDC 2007: 149). Despite these features, Sri Lanka was in the grip of a civil war for over two decades. Compared with Sri Lanka, India is facing multifaceted problems of communal violence and sectarian unrest in different parts of the country. Bangladesh is also a democratic country, but the interference of the military is one of the most evident features of state operation. Through the 1990s, governments in Bangladesh worked for the betterment of people, but lately successive governments have failed because of corruption and other misconduct and have given way to military involvement into the political system.

Representative institutions

Participation by both men and women is a key cornerstone of good governance. Participation may be either direct or through legitimate intermediate institutions or representatives. It is important to point out that representative democracy does not necessarily mean that the concerns of the most vulnerable in society will be taken into consideration in decision-making. Participation needs to be informed and organized. This means freedom of association and expression on the one hand, and an organized civil society on the other hand.

The way governments operate and uphold the constitution plays a pivotal role in governance issues. Pakistan, for example, has seen 30 years of dictatorial rule that ran counter to the basic tenets of the constitution of Pakistan. This practice of a narrowing of decision-making, in all its forms, is a serious impediment to good governance. Dr Muzaffar Iqbal writes, "In the Western world, the military might has not acquired political clout of the kind that has been the fate of the rest of the developing world. The control of the west passed from kings to politicians without the immediacy of military intervention. Political establishments were established by lawyers in partnership with wealthy families, and this marriage of convenience has been institutionalized through formal and informal relations between the state and those who control the greatest economic share of these countries." In his preceding comments he also added, "people are squeezed between politicians and generals who have lost their hope of ever asserting any rights" (*The News*, Pakistan, April 13, 2007). This "dysfunction" of the state machinery can be seen in an inability to provide basic services.

In order to regain trust, the government of Pakistan entrusted the National Reconstruction Bureau (NRB) with the task of "restructuring of political and service structures through devolution of power including empowerment of citizens, decentralization of administrative authority, decentralization of professional functions, and distribution of financial resources to the provincial and local governments with checks and balances against misuse of power and authority through the diffusion of power–authority nexus" (Paracha 2003: 8). However, the report issued by the government fails to take into account the socioeconomic and political milieu of Pakistan in which several experiments have collapsed.

The Himalayan kingdom of Bhutan staged mock polls to practice its transformation from absolute monarchy to democracy, prior to real elections in 2008. As the culmination of a plan by former king Jigme Singye Wangchuck, the crown was handed to his Oxford graduate son Jigme Khesar Namgyel Wangchuck in December, to change with the times and relinquish absolute rule (*Dawn*, Lahore, April 20, 2007). This practice shows that countries as underdeveloped as Bhutan are changing their age-old mode of ruling. These practices develop trust in the government as people get a sense of participation.

In India, under the regime of customary *panchayats*, villagers were ruled through informal processes of consultation and decision-making by village factions of landed peasants. The *panchayati raj* was constructed of tiered institutions, at whose village base councilors and their chair would be chosen by adult suffrage and a representative of ordinary villagers. This system was meant not only to stimulate rural development but also to introduce social and economic democracy into the countryside. The Green Revolution in India was an agricultural success that was meant to deliver substantial increases in the agricultural productivity of the poor and "overpopulated" countryside. This kind of in-depth participation of people breeds trust in the government (Stern 2001).

In Nepal there are critical governance issues involving participation that need to be addressed. For instance, most of the programs are designed and implemented at the central level, with very little local participation (MHHDC 2007: 163).

Decentralization and local governance and justice reform

Let us scrutinize the area of decentralization and local governance and of legal and justice reform as two indicators of good governance in India and Pakistan.

Pakistan is the only country in the region that decided to depart from the inherited British tradition of local government in 1955. It reintroduced the system during Ayub Khan's martial law in 1959, when 50 percent of the elected members worked with 50 percent of the nominated members. In four-tiered councils, the upper three were chaired by government functionaries. These elected democrats also served as an electoral college for the election of the president. This system worked under government patronage and regulated control to serve the interests of the regime. This system was discarded in 1969 and Pakistan remained without a local system until 1979. It was General Zia-ul-Haq, the military ruler of Pakistan, who revived local bodies in the interests of grassroots democracy while the country was in the grip of martial law. It was the compulsion of a military ruler to gain some sort of legitimacy with domestic and foreign audiences. The civilian rule of the 1990s saw an absence of local bodies. Under General Musharraf, Pakistan held elections to local bodies through a devolution plan to build democracy from the grassroots, but the brand of democracy at the national level remained military. A third tier of district government has been created but no powers have been devolved to the provinces from the center. It is ironic that local bodies are a provincial subject but are managed and regulated from the center. During the Zia and Musharraf periods, elections to local bodies were held on a non-party basis and the system was managed "officially." Obviously, the political parties criticized and opposed the devolution plan, and in the present situation local bodies are viewed as an instrument for generating "positive results" in the national elections. In fact, their power to rig elections is greatly enhanced because 70 percent of the Pakistani population live in rural areas and monitoring arrangements cannot be adequately spread to ensure free, fair, and transparent elections. The absence of an independent Election Commission and the presence of a biased interim government necessarily limit media freedom and slant coverage in favor of the "King's Party." When local bodies were primarily used by military rulers to gain some semblance of legitimacy, they could not become the part of the political process to produce a culture of local government politics. Local government comes into being at the will and compulsion of military rulers and ceases to exist when they depart. This system of governance still awaits institutionalization in Pakistan.

India, on the other hand, continued with the inherited British system of local government. It successfully framed the constitution in two years and held national elections in 1950. Since then, India has held regular elections to the national and provincial levels. In this political culture of routine elections, the local government continued without interruption. Having implemented land reforms in the early 1950s, the local government was not under the influence of the landed aristocracy. Having eliminated the feudal lords, the local government system had a better chance to succeed. The continuity in national and provincial political processes also ensured the functioning of local government at the grassroots level. This appears to be an amazing success story. Nonetheless, the local government system started facing difficulties in operational terms. The Ashok Mehta Committee Report of 1978 highlighted these problems and recommended remedial measures (see Ahn 1987). The reservation in 1992 of 33 percent of seats in parliament for women was a major step towards the empowerment of women in rural India. Unlike Pakistan, these bodies are under the control of provincial governments and escaped the intervention and manipulation of the center.

Despite all these positive aspects, the plight of the poor did not receive any significant attention or subsequent improvement. Poverty remained the dominant feature of rural India. Ayesha Jalal (1995) identified this as a structural problem. The District Executive Officer (government functionary) wields enormous financial influence, reducing the importance of elected bodies. Under the veneer of democracy, the authoritarian style of governance has continued to prevail in India. It is clear that the poverty situation needs to be addressed.

Another variable that impacts on the lives of the people is its judicial system. In Pakistan, each time that the army assumed power the Supreme Court endorsed and legitimized the military rule. In 1999, working in complete subordination to the military, the Supreme Court exceeded its powers by even allowing the military ruler to amend the constitution. The latest blow struck by General Musharraf was the imposition of martial law by "Emergency" decree on November 3, 2007, and, as Chief of Army Staff, the Supreme Court and the four High Courts were dismantled and reconstituted with hand-picked judges. The superior judiciary has yet to evolve in Pakistan as an institution. The District and Session Courts continue to suffer from neglect and are the breeding ground for corruption and malpractice. The dispensation of justice is in a precarious condition in Pakistan.

India's experience in the context of a superior judiciary is entirely different. It has the essential elements of an institution and its functional operations have never been curtailed or interrupted. Unlike Pakistan, the judicial activism functioned within the democratic framework without eroding the legitimacy of an elected government. At the highest level, people have an expectation that justice will be dispensed. However, the lower levels have problems of litigation, malpractice, and corruption. The higher judiciary in India plays a positive role, enabling the three organs of the government to function smoothly, which provides the necessary stability to the political system. Its absence in Pakistan keeps alive the issue of the legitimacy of the government and the stability of the political order remains a burning issue in Pakistani politics. Governance problems therefore become acute, causing a deficit of trust in government. The trust level in India is higher, but corruption and the criminalizing of politics mean that it fluctuates.

Rule of law

Good governance requires fair legal frameworks that are enforced impartially. It also requires full protection of human rights, particularly those of minorities. Impartial enforcement of laws requires an independent judiciary and an impartial and incorruptible police force (AusAID 2000). The way the judiciary implements the rule of law is one of the mechanisms by which it builds the trust of the people in government.

On three occasions since independence, military coups have ended democratic rule in Pakistan. The judiciary not only failed to stop extra-constitutional regime change, but also endorsed and abetted the consolidation of illegally gained power. The Musharraf government deepened the judiciary's subservient position among national institutions, ensured that politics tempered the rule of law, and weakened the foundations for democratic rule. Substantial changes in the legislative framework for the appointment, promotion, and removal of judges, as well as the jurisdiction of the ordinary courts, are needed to restore confidence in the judiciary. However, judicial independence from political influence and financial corruption cannot be restored by mere technical, legislated change. Reform depends as much upon a credible commitment by the government to respect the rule of law. There has been a lot of unrest among the people on the issue of missing persons in the country. People at every level are perplexed about the disappearance of their nearest and dearest. The Human Rights Commission of Pakistan filed a constitutional petition with the Supreme Court in February 2007 on the issue and lobbied for the creation of a commission to investigate the seizing of people by the intelligence agencies (*Dawn*, April 8, 2007). The Supreme Court gave the government time to produce those people, but the government was unable or unwilling to cooperate.

Media

In today's world, the mass media, which include television, radio, newspapers, books, and magazines, have become the ears and eyes of society and act as a model of social responsibility. The media also can exert a powerful influence on government by identifying and highlighting the impacts of policies and policy gaps. Three major factors affect the media's selection of material: editorial policy, investigative reporting, and now also community problems. The media can act as a catalyst for positive change between government and society by acting as a watchdog. Chomsky's propaganda model is widely applied in the developing countries. As Chomsky puts it:

> A propaganda model focuses on this inequality of wealth and power and its multilevel effects on mass-media interests and choices. It traces the routes by which money and power are able to filter out the news fit to print, marginalize dissent, and allow the government and dominant private interests to get their messages across to the public. (Herman and Chomsky 1988: 1)

The Indian government has given lot of freedom to its mass media and that has really established their position in the region. Given their stronghold, the propaganda carried by the Indian media attracts a lot of attention. In Pakistan, the media received some minor freedoms under the regime of President Musharraf. With the establishment of a democratically elected government in Pakistan, the media's independence has gained much more ground.

Basic necessities of life

One of the other basic requirements of good governance is to provide all people with proper healthcare, education, protection from natural disasters, and law and order. People pay taxes to the government with an understanding that they will receive certain basic services. As mentioned earlier, according to the 2006 report on *Human Development in South Asia*, "There are over 867 million people without access to basic sanitation, more than 400 million adults are unable to read or write, and 300 million are undernourished" (MHHDC 2007: 2). These deplorable statistics reveal the extent to which the various governments have underperformed. Public services such as healthcare, education, childcare, natal and postnatal services, water, and sanitation and basic infrastructure such as roads, transport, credit, power, irrigation, and employment need to be expanded and provided free or at a manageable cost. The *Human Development in South Asia* report also pointed out that Pakistan's GDP growth rate since 1990 had stayed in the range of 4 percent – the country was lagging in terms of human development in relation to Bangladesh and India. In Bangladesh, which ranks third after China and India in terms of the absolute number of poor people, the government has introduced various programs for improving the lives of its people.

Transparency and anti-corruption

Transparency means that decisions and their enforcement are undertaken in accordance with rules and regulations. It also means that information is freely available and directly accessible to those who will be affected by such decisions and their enforcement. Furthermore, it means that enough information is provided and that it is provided in easily understandable forms.

The government in Pakistan has claimed that all the policies of the government are transparent and people have the right to evaluate that transparency, but these claims are not all fulfilled in these structures. The universally accepted standards of transparency are in deficit in South Asia generally.

The fundamental causes of corruption are economic structures, an institutional incapacity to design and implement reform strategies, and a lack of political will to combat corruption. Corruption is a problem of good governance: it is a symptom of something that has gone wrong in the management of the state. It also indicates that institutions designed to govern relationships between citizens and the state are used instead for personal enrichment and the provision of benefits to the corrupt. The expanding role of government in development has placed the bureaucracy in a monopolistic position and enhanced the opportunities for administrative discretion. Corruption results from excessive regulation, increased bureaucratic discretion, and the lack of adequate accountability and transparency of the system. The state intervenes in the economy to provide a framework for economic and social activities (Cheema 2005).

As Noman (1988) puts it, corruption in Pakistan is pervasive and entrenched. Cross-country surveys commonly rank Pakistan as worse than average in terms of its level of corruption and red tape (Mauro 1995). The Nawaz government tried to reduce corruption by arresting offenders and filing cases against corrupt individuals, but no positive results were achieved. Such was also the case with the Musharraf's regime, which established an independent National Accountability Bureau (NAB) to eradicate corruption, but the measures did not bear fruit. In the 2005 report by the Human Rights Commission of Pakistan, it was observed that corruption had become widespread. According to Section 1.d of the National Accountability Ordinance, those convicted of corruption by the NAB are prohibited from holding political office for 10 years. However, the NAB disproportionately targeted opposition politicians for prosecution and did not prosecute members of the military. These laws created unrest and a breach of trust. The Musharraf government's treatment of the issue was perceived as a false promise by the president to weed out corrupt individuals (Abbas 2007).

The participation context

The issue of participation is of paramount importance, because it establishes the link between the people and the political system. The link is formalized through the political process and is activated by the instrument of the electoral politics of free and fair elections, which confer credibility and legitimacy on the political system. Participation also stimulates hope and a sense of empowerment among the people that they can change the government if its performance is inadequate. This continuous political process operated through democratic electoral activity reinforces belief and faith in the political system. This process is seen as validating the perceived viability of the state and its potential. In more than one way, the democratic political process constructs "certainty" among the populace.

As successor states to the British Raj, India and Pakistan inherited the same federal structures at the time of independence. India, borrowing heavily from the government of India Act 1935 for its constitution, kept the flavor of federal criticism, yet was successful in operating its political system with formal democracy. The mature and seasoned political leaders, supported by a well-knit nationally organized Congress Party, contributed to the political process. Additionally, the secular ideology served as a facilitator in India's diverse society, and, in the absence of a dominant ethnic group, the Indian army dampened its appetite for military intervention. However, the civil bureaucracy continued to play a dominant role, aiding and assisting the elected governments over time. Participatory politics through electoral activity is thus institutionalized in India.

In obvious contrast to the Indian case, Pakistan took a different constitutional and political route, though having the same historical experience as India. In the course of its 60-year history, Pakistan has changed its governance model from, in turn, vice-regal, to parliamentary, to presidential, and to extended periods of martial law. It now is a hybrid system with both a president and a parliament, with the balance of power favoring the president. The jockeying for power is a recurring theme throughout the political system. Pakistan, unlike India, missed out on the contribution that a charismatic leader could have made in stabilizing and consolidating the political power structure. The Islamic ideology was used as a national blanket to cover and suppress ethno-religious, linguistic, sectarian, and regional divisions in the name of national unity and integration. The civil-military dominance continued to be the most entrenched interest group in the politics of Pakistan. The legitimization by the judiciary of every military ruler did not help to create an environment in which the rule of law and the supremacy of the constitution were respected. In the process, Pakistan experienced "guided democracy," "controlled democracy," "indirect democracy," "remote controlled democracy," and "military democracy." In 2008, however, multi-party elections led to the formation of the present civilian government and the suspension of emergency rule. Federalism, though a declared part of each constitution, remains elusive, causing alienation among groups and regions and resulting in a greater demand for autonomy, accompanied by the eruption of violence, insurgency, and a pull towards secession.

Pakistan is still a long way from a stable and mature democracy. Participatory politics in Pakistan are manifested through protests, demonstrations, and agitation. Electoral activity is manipulated and rigged elections keep alive the issue of the legitimacy of successive governments. The constitutional deviation on the role of the military changed the political landscape, often privileging martial interests rather than a strict constitutional interpretation. This distorts the constitution, and the gulf between the original constitution and the actual practice of politics widens. The consensus document of the 1973 constitution awaits implementation. Participatory politics, with reference to the constitution, has yet to be institutionalized.

Sri Lanka presents another case in the South Asia context. As a former British colony, it inherited the colonial structures with a trace of parliamentary democracy. Sri Lanka has the highest literacy rate in the region (96 percent), but ethnicity surfaced as a key issue and locked the country into a spiral of armed confrontation between the rival ethnic groups.

In these seemingly abnormal circumstances, the government was able to function normally and elections were held at regular intervals, providing some sort of continuity to parliamentary politics. In view of the violence in Sri Lanka, it is difficult to argue that participatory politics occurs in an environment that is conducive to institutionalization.

Bangladesh seceded from Pakistan after a bloody civil war in 1971 and the intervention of the Indian army. The British and Pakistani legacy seemed to shape the political landscape in Bangladesh. Declared an international "basket case" by Henry Kissinger, Bangladesh has survived and continues to function with its own set of problems and difficulties. The assassination of Sh. Mujib-ur-Rehman (the father of the nation) disrupted the political process and the Pakistani legacy of military rule became a complicating factor in political affairs. The return of civilian rule and the completion of a full five-year term suggested significant movement towards political development. It seems, however, that the five-year term of government has not been the most robust indicator of political advancement, because for almost two years an interim government ran the affairs of government and the leading national political leaders were facing charges of corruption. This injected political uncertainty into Bangladesh. The dialectics of military and civilian rule have created conditions that inhibit predictions concerning the institutionalization of participatory politics in Bangladesh.

Nepal presents another fascinating case as an heir to a centuries-old monarchy, punctuated by British influence. It remained stable for a few years under monarchial rule, only to be usurped by calls for participation and an end to the monarchial system. The 1990s saw a major upsurge in demands for limiting the power of the monarchy. Insurgency by the Maoists intensified the violence, forcing their co-option in the government. General elections were deferred twice and the Maoists opted out of the government, insisting that the institution of the "monarchy" be terminated before holding the elections. The 2008 national election was a landmark event in Nepal. The Maoists took part and won more seats than any other party and they formed a coalition government. The monarchy was abolished. These and related events have set the stage for a more stable democratic system.

The development context

The development paradigm has occupied center stage among social scientists for many decades. Whereas anthropologists, sociologists, and political scientists explained development and its processes from their particular perspective, it is the economists who have dominated the field and influenced decision-makers around the world. The impact of these development policies emerged during the governance crises of the 1990s in most of the developing countries. The globalization paradigm, in terms of the privatization of the free-market economy and deregulation, is currently seeking to correct the imbalances. The results of these initiatives do not seem encouraging at the present.

It will be interesting to briefly review the South Asian countries and how they negotiated the development paradigm. The inherited colonial structures, the construction of state systems in the region, and economic philosophies more or less defined the parameters. The colonial structures remained unchanged except for minor changes or modifications. The accent remained on state construction through different instruments, and economic policies were directed in favor of centralization.

India persisted with the inherited civil bureaucracy and the central command economy, and further expanded the scope of its operations. The public sector developed to accommodate the rising expectations of the people. The imperatives of state construction aided the expansion of the public sector and also provided limited space for the private sector to grow. The state-building functions remained dominant and led to the imposition of emergency rule in 1975 under Indira Gandhi. The pace of economic growth stayed slow until 1990. With the infrastructure development in place, India was in a much better position to cope with the forces of globalization. The pace of economic growth picked up and is now around 10 percent. However, the "India Shining" slogan of the BJP (Bharatiya Janata Party) government in the 2004 elections did not help it to win because the poor rural population was not touched by the economic growth. The expanded public sector was sluggish and inefficient and the transition to the private sector has yet to benefit the estimated 40 percent of the Indian population who are poor.

Pakistan, in its haste to build a strong center, focused on state construction. The dialectics between state- and nation-building saw an uneasy and conflict-ridden interaction. The extended military rule in Pakistan strengthened the centralizing tendencies. The attempt to build a strong center alienated the federating units and the federation appears to be weak and faces many intractable issues and problems. Pakistan practiced the capitalist model of "functional inequality" in the 1960s and switched to the socialist model in the 1970s. The 1980s saw Pakistan in the grip of "Islamization," and the so-called Islamic economy was introduced. After a turbulent period of political instability in the 1990s, Pakistan made some half-hearted attempts to privatize. Since 9/11, Pakistan has been fully engaged in the war against terrorism and has made some modest attempts to privatize. It is interesting to note that the economy of Pakistan recorded growth above 6 percent when it was closely aligned with the United States. As a nuclear state, Pakistan faces serious internal threats and political instability remains a persistent problem, giving rise to serious governance concerns and law and order issues.

Sri Lanka continued to function with inherited colonial structures but was mired in a bloody civil war for almost 30 years. Although the hostilities ended in May 2009, Sri Lanka is still engaged in the struggle for state construction, and development does not seem to be a priority.

Bangladesh inherited both the British and the Pakistani legacies. This mixture did not facilitate a smooth evolution of development. Though declared to be an international basket case, it has managed to survive without changing its economic policies. It has interacted with the globalizing forces, but this has made no significant impact on its poor, and the governmental apparatus is suffering from exhaustion. The recent political crisis added to the complexities of governance, as an interim government ruled the country for over two years. In this climate of uncertainty, development has been put on the back burner.

Nepal, continued to operate as a monarchy after 1947, without any major change until electoral national politics intervened. The 2008 elections, the formation of an elected government by the Maoists, and the abolition of the monarchy have created a new political landscape in the country. The issue of state construction is paramount and subordinates other concerns and issues. Nepal has a poor economy and it is difficult to speculate about the future prospects for the democratic system.

Development performance in South Asia

Development performance, including economic development and access to services and employment opportunities, is an important determinant of trust in government. The record of South Asian countries in this regard has been mixed.

As successor states to extended British colonial rule, the primacy of the colonial structures remained and this resulted in tendencies towards centralization. Pushes for integration and unity drove the centralizing trends. These initiatives were also driven by a desire to stoke the nascent spirit of nationalism. The building of a strong center alarmed the provinces and uneasy relations emerged between the two. In the case of Pakistan, this led to the successful secessionist movement that resulted in the birth of Bangladesh. India, which takes immense pride in being the largest functioning democracy in the world, had to suffer emergency rule during Indira Gandhi's regime, the imposition of "Governor Raj" (involving the suspension of the provincial government) about eight times, the uprising in Kashmir, and the Naxalite-Maoist insurgency in 29 states. Bangladesh has had its share of military rule, which could be operated under a strong center. Sri Lanka, though having undertaken parliamentary reforms, continues to have insurgency concerns. Nepal, ruled by a monarchial system, faced violence from the anti-monarchial Maoists, who demanded an immediate end to the institution of the monarchy. The opposition between a strong center and the demand for autonomy continues to be a theme in South Asian countries.

Looking at the poverty index and the general performance of these countries reveal a discouraging situation. If we examine Bangladesh, then according to the World Bank (2007) half the population of the country is living below the national poverty line. India, which is recognized as having been a fast-growing economy for the past decade, has 29 percent of its population living below the national poverty line. The World Bank does not report on the Pakistani situation because the statistics are contested.

These figures reveal a dismal picture, which would be even worse if individuals living on less than US$3–4 per day were included. This certainly is reason for pessimism, and raises serious questions about the policies pursued in the context of governance and in particular about pro-poor service delivery.

As asserted previously in the section on decentralization and local governance reform, the development performance in Pakistan and India reflects the relative health of their respective judiciaries. Pakistan's performance lags significantly behind India's, with impacts on levels of trust.

The security context

Since the birth of India and Pakistan as independent states in August 1947, both countries have been locked in a security competition. Indeed, the sources of conflict are rooted in the partition of the Indian subcontinent, which had been ruled formally by the British for a hundred years. The British finalized the partition in haste. It was a momentous event that involved the division of territory, uprooting millions of people, and causing the death of perhaps a quarter of a million persons in the violence that resulted from this massive migration. Moreover, the final outcome of the partition left both states dissatisfied. From India's perspective, the partition was unnecessary, unnatural, and tragic. Pakistan, on the other hand, interpreted the partition as necessary and inevitable but "essentially incomplete," because Kashmir, a Muslim majority state, remained with India. This stands out as a core conflict issue that bedevils relations between the two countries.

Besides the issue of Kashmir, the menu of conflicts has increased overtime. Having fought three major wars, there was limited military action over Sir Creek in the Rann of Kutch in 1964 and a low-intensity war over the Siachen Glacier since 1984. The Wullar Barrage and the construction of other barrages in the area of Indian-held Kashmir raise apprehensions that India is planning to strangulate Pakistan economically. The

Brasstacks Crisis of 1986–1987, the Kashmir Crisis that erupted in the spring of 1990, and the Kargil conflict of 1999 are manifestations of the ongoing conflicts. In the wake of 9/11, India deployed a million troops along the international border and exerted extreme pressure for a year and a half to extract concessions on infiltration into Indian-held Kashmir (Indians called it cross-border terrorism), while Pakistan was engaged in the "war on terrorism" as a coalition partner of the United States. The Mumbai blasts of November 2008 disrupted the peace process that started in 2004 with many orchestrated confidence-building measures. The peace process, however, failed to deliver on any of the conflict issues. The surge in terrorist activities and India's enhanced presence in Afghanistan further complicate the power equation in the region, increasing the level of distrust between the two countries and thereby minimizing the prospects for the peaceful settlement of disputes.

Besides this menu of conflicts, there exist competing political visions and contested identities. Here is a classic case of a distorted "mirror image," with each thinking the worst of the other. India has managed a liberal democracy that espouses secularism but appears to be fighting a battle against revisionist parties and groups. The BJP is viewed as a fundamentalist Hindu-dominated party, thereby diluting Indian claims to secularism. Pakistan, on the other hand, is engaged in establishing an Islamic order to be organized as a liberal democracy. This orientation would facilitate Pakistan's acquisition of a pan-Islamic or transitional identity. Pakistan also challenges India's world-view, which seeks regional dominance in the short run and aspires to become a major power in global politics in the long run. The stability of its political system, consistent annual economic growth of 8 percent, and a strategic partnership with United States stoke India's ambitions to become a regional hegemon. Pakistan fears that India could threaten its sovereignty and independence. The Indian ambitions are threatening because they could reduce Pakistan to a subordinate political entity in the region. Thus have such opposing perceptions locked the two states in an enduring rivalry.

It would be appropriate, therefore, to describe India and Pakistan as "dissatisfied" states, though the nature of their dissatisfaction varies. India aspires to a dominant regional role, which is challenged by Pakistan. Even Bangladesh and Sri Lanka have yet to acknowledge this particular role, despite India's coercive behavior towards them. This posturing, along with the political and strategic circumstances, has led India and Pakistan into often disrupting the status quo, thus increasing tensions periodically.

The intractable nature of this competition has vitiated the security environment of the South Asia region (which now includes Afghanistan as member of the South Asian Association for Regional Cooperation). Now that both India and Pakistan are nuclear states, they have tended towards covert subversive operations, with limited objectives. Recent events have shown that such activities can spin out of control (India's alleged involvement in Sind, Baluchistan, and jihadi activities, and Pakistan's alleged involvement in Kashmir, supporting elements in Assam, and infiltrating the dissatisfied Muslim minority). The redeeming feature of the present situation is that the deterrence value of nuclear weapons has ensured strategic stability between the two countries. Since 1971, India and Pakistan have not seriously entertained the idea of a conventional war to achieve their respective political objectives.

The cold war between India and Pakistan has not abated, though the global Cold War came to an end in 1990. Both countries have demonstrated a remarkable degree of continuity in their behavior patterns. In the security competition, India has so far failed to establish hegemonic status in South Asia. It is locked in an arms race with Pakistan, particularly in the nuclear field. In view of this strategic stability, support for separatist movements has been the principal thrust of their security efforts.

Huge defense expenditures have prevented both countries from addressing their basic socioeconomic problems. Poverty stands out as a serious problem and the continued lack of government attention leads to violence and internal conflicts. The lack of a solution to the socioeconomic problems erodes the creditability of governments in both countries. India seems to be more secure today but it continues to face internal security problems (Maoist movements in 29 states and uprisings in Kashmir) and terrorist threats pose a different kind of challenge. Pakistan's internal security problems are more acute and are coupled with continuing political stability. Pakistan's security paradigm is defined and operated by the military establishment. Though there is an elected set-up in Pakistan, the civil–military power imbalance still persists. The US presence in this region to fight terrorism has injected other dimensions into the region's security issues.

The interplay of issues of participation, development, and security in South Asia has created a significant trust deficit. Given the significant post-colonial challenges, interaction with the pressing forces of globalization, and persistent security issues, it is not surprising that these countries have not been models of good governance.

Conclusion

My survey of South Asian countries suggests that deficits in governance, participation, development, and security are applicable limiting factors in

trust in government. Excluding India, which resolved the issue of participation through electoral politics, the remaining countries are caught in
the struggle to manage these issues. Even though recent political changes
and democratic transitions in Pakistan, Nepal, and Bangladesh have improved the prospects for pluralism and multi-party systems, the political
systems are still struggling for stability. Recurring patterns of instability
aggravate key areas of governance – causing a decline in trust in government and in some cases leading to the alienation of groups and parties,
which challenge the authority of government.

On the issue of development, the performance of this region is clearly
poor. Having embraced a huge agenda of development to bring unity and
integration, these countries failed to address the issue of social justice
and could not distribute economic benefits equitably. After six decades,
the poverty level has increased, and more rapidly in recent years. This is a
disturbing situation, because these countries are also confronting violence and terrorism, which create distortions in the image of the government. Even India, which enjoys political stability, is up against the
problem of poverty. The "India Shining" slogan of the BJP did not find
favor with the poor in rural India. The trust level in India may be higher
compared with other countries, yet trust generally remains in short sup-
ply in this region.

The security issue has complicated the situation, particularly between
India and Pakistan. Both have spent huge sums to bolster their defense
systems and ended up as nuclear states. Pakistan, having established strategic stability, faces serious internal threats that bring the government
into disrepute. As a nuclear state, it faces rising doubts internally about
the capacity of the government to maintain law and order. The issue of
trust in government in Pakistan is at its lowest ebb.

REFERENCES

Abbas, A. (2007) "On the Horns of Dilemma," *Dawn* (Lahore), April 8.
Ahn, Chung-Si (ed.) (1987) *The Local Political System in Asia: A Comparative Perspective*. Seoul: Seoul National University Press.
AusAID [Australian Agency for International Development] (2000) *Good Governance: Guiding Principles for Implementation*. Canberra: Australian Agency for International Development.
Cheema, G. Shabbir (2005) *Building Democratic Institutions*. Westport, CT: Kumarian Press.
DeSouza, Peter Ronald, and Jayadeva Uyangoda (2005) "Political Trust, Institutions and Democracy in India, Sri Lanka and Pakistan," presentation at the World Bank Conference on "New Frontiers of Social Policy: Development in a Globalizing World," Arusha, Tanzania, December 12–15. Available at: <http://

siteresources.worldbank.org/INTRANETSOCIALDEVELOPMENT/Resources/
DeSouza_Formatted.pdf> (accessed 29 January 2010).

Herman, E. S., and N. Chomsky (1988) *Manufacturing Consent: The Political Economy of the Mass Media*. New York: Pantheon.

Human Rights Commission of Pakistan (2005) *State of Human Rights in 2005*. Lahore: Human Rights Commission of Pakistan.

Jalal, Ayesha (1995) *Democracy and Authoritarianism in South Asia*. Lahore: Sange-e-Meel Publications.

Mauro, P. (1995) "Corruption and Growth," *Quarterly Journal of Economics* 110, pp. 681–712.

MHHDC [Mahbub ul Haq Human Development Centre] (2007) *Human Development in South Asia 2006 – Poverty in South Asia: Challenges and Responses*. Karachi, Pakistan: Oxford University Press.

Noman, O. (1988) *The Political Economy of Pakistan 1947–85*. London: KPI.

Paracha, Saad Abdullah (2003) *Devolution Plan in Pakistan: Context, Implementation and Issues*. Budapest: Open Society Institute, International Policy Fellowship Program. Available at: <http://www.policy.hu/document/200808/paracha.pdf&letoltes=1> (accessed 8 February 2010).

Stern, R. W. (2001) "Democracy in India," in R. W. Stern, *Democracy and Dictatorship in South Asia: Dominant Classes and Political Outcomes in India, Pakistan and Bangladesh*. New Delhi: Research Press.

UNESCAP [United Nations Economic and Social Commission for Asia and the Pacific] (n.d.) "What Is Good Governance?", <http://www.unescap.org/pdd/prs/ProjectActivities/Ongoing/gg/governance.asp> (accessed 29 January 2010).

World Bank (2007) *Bangladesh: Strategy for Sustained Growth*. Bangladesh Development Series, Paper No. 18. Dhaka: World Bank Office. Available at: <http://siteresources.worldbank.org/SOUTHASIAEXT/Resources/Publications/448813-1185396961095/4030558-1185396985915/fullreport.pdf> (accessed 8 February 2010).

6

Trust in government in the Pacific Islands

Meredith Rowen and Gerard A. Finin

This chapter explores trust and governance issues that were identified at two Regional Forums on Reinventing Government in the Pacific Islands, convened in October 2004 in Samoa (UNDESA 2004) and February 2006 in Fiji (UNDESA 2006). Participants included ministers, senior government officials, members of parliament, and civil society representatives, and members from academia within Pacific Island universities. Points raised at these two meetings were then further analyzed within the Workshop on Promoting Trust in Government, held in January 2008 in Hawai'i (UNDESA 2008), alongside results from the Northeast Asia, Southeast Asia, and South Asia sub-regions.

Following a contextual look at statehood and national identity, the chapter explores the changing role of leadership within the Pacific Islands, with particular emphasis on traditional governance structures. It then proceeds to examine the relationship between trust and the quality of governance, arguing that they are not always directly equivalent. Finally, the chapter presents cases of successful techniques and innovations that particular Island governments have employed to strengthen trust and improve governance within national and sub-national contexts.

Trust in government is essential, because it facilitates interactions between government, civil society, and the private sector to collaborate as partners in governance. As such, it provides the basis for successful policy decisions, implementation, and assessment. As of 2005, dissatisfaction with government had reached 65 percent in Asia and the Pacific (Cheema 2007). Although this figure is by no means exceptional when

Building trust in government: Innovations in governance reform in Asia, Cheema and Popovski (eds), United Nations University Press, 2010, ISBN 978-92-808-1189-6

placed in the context of similarly high rates in all other regions of the world, including developed and developing countries, it does prompt a further examination of trust levels and their causes within the Pacific Islands.

Although trust is not tangible, it has concrete consequences for governance and governments. The cooperation that trust engenders is a necessary, albeit insufficient, ingredient for effective governance. The more trust there is in government, the less government will have to invest valuable resources to gain public cooperation. Moreover, a lack of trust can engender many forms of defiance, and in extreme cases may make governing all but impossible. While a certain degree of skepticism may be healthy within a well-functioning, democratic society, an utter lack of confidence – or mistrust – may signal a fundamental breach in governance or lack of legitimacy. Trust cannot ordinarily be quickly established or installed mechanistically, but rather is a dynamic value that is cultivated over time.

Background

The Pacific Islands illustrate tremendous cultural, political, and geographic diversity – both within the major sub-regions of Melanesia, Micronesia, and Polynesia and at the country and island levels. Its governance systems have evolved over time to include elements from traditional or customary practices, its colonial past, and more modern introductions. The ways in which these systems have meshed varies widely within the region. Not only did implanted institutions, constitutional arrangements, legal regimes, and electoral systems differ, but forms of traditional governance are also distinct in terms of leadership, custom, processes, and scope.

Despite their differences, Pacific Islands share a few commonalities, with implications for current levels of both social and political trust in a regional context. At independence, many small island states had to contend with political boundaries and institutions that did not adequately reflect local identities or customs, and limited infrastructure that served mainly to support administrative control and enclave economies. Colonialism had also resulted in the formation of new interest groups and allowed the marginalization of sectors of the population who were not useful to the colonial apparatus to varying degrees in different states. Traditional forms of governance acted as an important counterbalance to colonial authority and persisted in areas of life ungoverned by these administrations, particularly in the case of outlying islands and hard to reach localities. They were also frequently incorporated on an ad hoc basis to reinforce or supplement colonial control.

The formal incorporation of traditional practices into implanted structures depended on a number of factors, including: the geographic concentration of the population, its homogeneity, and the degree to which traditional governance styles were directly compatible with colonial structures. Governments were more likely to adopt traditional governance practices in cases where the latter were highly centralized and hierarchical, with clear lines of authority (Wesley-Smith 2004). During the independence movements of the 1960s to 1990s, traditional and colonial structures became progressively intertwined, leading to "blended" systems that incorporated elements of both, with great variations throughout the region. At present, the region has both presidential and parliamentary democracies, combinations of the two systems, a constitutional monarchy, and one interim military government. In countries such as Samoa, traditional governance practices play a large and explicit role in central and local government. In others, traditional governance has a strong informal influence on interactions between state and citizen, but its legal basis is more tenuous.

As social and cultural identities did not always align with national boundaries, most island populations did not have the opportunity to construct national identities and arrive at areas of consensus on the role of government prior to the formation of their countries. Instead, these issues have had to be addressed during and since independence. Terence Wesley-Smith has observed that a strong sense of nationhood has been difficult to achieve in areas of Oceania where there are large numbers of ethnic groups, languages, and traditionally defined societies:

> This is particularly the case in places like Papua New Guinea, Solomon Islands, and Vanuatu where extreme cultural and linguistic fragmentation defies the creation of common identities, and in territories that have attracted significant numbers of permanent settlers from Europe or Asia. It is not easy to foster a sense of solidarity across the profound cultural, economic, and religious divide between indigenous Fijians and the descendants of migrant workers from India, who now represent some 44 percent of the population of Fiji. Nor is it easy to persuade fragmented indigenous Kanak tribal groups that they share a national identity with each other, let alone the settlers of European, Asian, and Polynesian origin who have been numerically and economically dominant in New Caledonia for many decades. (Wesley-Smith 2004: 9)

These dynamics have affected the development and maintenance of social and political trust in the Pacific Islands. When social trust is low, people are more reluctant to engage in mutually beneficial interactions with other members of society. A lack of social trust and reduced interaction may further inhibit the ability of citizens to recognize the legitimacy of other citizens' needs in the context of competition for government services and redress. Moreover, when political trust is lacking and citizens do not feel empowered to effect change through existing governance systems, people are more inclined to challenge these systems (Ghaus-Pasha and Rowen 2007).

In recent decades, several countries have had to grapple with a trust deficit, which has led to both civil strife and military coups in Melanesia. For example, in the Solomon Islands, "the perceived failings of and declining confidence in government was a crucial – and causal – ingredient in the civil unrest of 1998–2003. Poor levels of service delivery, an inability to ameliorate the inequality of distribution of socioeconomic projects and uneven sharing of development benefits, corruption, and a widespread perception that government has not been responsive to the citizenry are the oft cited causes of the crisis of trust" (Lane 2006: 14).

However, the region has accomplished significant progress in achieving new areas of consensus between communities, which is not an easy feat. Papua New Guinea recently held a peace and reconciliation ceremony at Duisei village in January 2010, and the Solomon Islands is in the process of developing a truth and reconciliation commission, using its own innovations to adapt the South African model, in order to strengthen areas of understanding and reduce resentments between citizens. Moreover, even countries that have not experienced conflict to this degree are creating new ways of engaging citizens and encouraging their participation in policy processes.

Where conflict situations have emerged, traditional governance systems have played an important role in filling gaps left by government. Traditional leaders have been particularly useful in supporting mediation efforts and providing essential services at the local level. According to ESCAP (2010), Pacific Islanders tend to question the ability of central governments to successfully resolve provincial differences when these occur. Notably, local governance structures and leaders – which are often more trusted – have stepped in to play a larger role in managing land disputes, which are one of the main causes of conflict in the region. In some cases, these interventions have produced new modes of indigenous governance and have helped to revitalize structures of local governance (White 2004). Particularly relevant in this regard are activities related to the administration of justice, the provision of basic health services, and education activities.

In general, local governments across the Pacific Islands appear to be more highly trusted, in large part because of their increased accessibility for citizens and the greater degree to which traditional governance practices are incorporated. In many parts of Oceania, governance at the community level, outside national capitals, is for the most part considered competent. Importantly, this is where most islanders reside. In contrast, the institutions and processes associated with the nation state and centralized government are still often regarded with a certain degree of suspicion and lower political trust (Wesley-Smith 2004). Whereas traditional institutions and processes tend to prioritize social harmony and consensus-building, using a longer-term perspective many national-level political systems within the Pacific Islands are viewed as more top-down and attenuated. Because citizens are often unfamiliar with how national governance processes and institutions work, they tend to rely heavily on traditional systems of kin and personal connections to elected national leaders in order to achieve services (Mellor and Jabes 2004).

At present, specific issues that may be affecting trust in government in the Pacific Islands include: the need for improved clarification of the interface between traditional and modern governance systems; strengthened legislative and ombudsman oversight of the executive branch; improved policy formulation and decision-making capacity within cabinets; better policy implementation; strengthened human resource development; and greater transparency in communicating the functions, processes, and current activities of layers of government. Regional forums on government have also highlighted the need to better institutionalize political parties, which frequently suffer from limited policy platforms; unclear ideological differentiation; and weak organizational capacity. Where these problems exist, parties may not be active in civic education, consensus-building, interest group mediation, or policy deliberation (Rich 2008).

However, although improvements in trust and governance are generally agreed to be mutually reinforcing, it is important to remember that the quality of governance and the degree of trust in government are both locally determined and culturally defined. Hence, though there may be much room for innovations to improve governance, certain issues may be perceived as higher priority by citizens in any given state. The following sections will take a brief look at modern and traditional governance styles in each of the three sub-regions and will then examine popular expectations for government.

Changing patterns of leadership

A major theme that emerged from the Forums was how government reinvention must take into account older indigenous forms of governance, custom, and leadership. There is broad agreement across the Pacific region that there is no "purely" traditional or customary form of governance. Rather, systems of governance are always evolving and changing to meet circumstances. The frequently discussed dichotomy between so-called indigenous and introduced systems (or modernity vs. tradition, state vs. custom, etc.) of government is in reality better viewed as a continuum. Numerous speakers noted that models suggesting that traditional forms of governance can be entirely displaced by "modern" institutional structures fail to appreciate the extent to which everyday life in Pacific Island societies embraces a practical adaptive approach to organizing the functions of government with elements of both old and new.

Consequently, much discussion addressed the topic of how Pacific Islanders could work toward more effective "hybrid" or blended structures of governance. Rather than being seen as a fixed-sum model, evidence suggested that both traditional and modern structures of Pacific governance could be strengthened to more effectively serve Pacific Island constituencies.

Over time, the idea of chief has changed substantially. Institutions such as "paramount chief" and "council of chiefs" invented during the colonial era have been incorporated into numerous post-independent Pacific nation states. Current roles of chiefs may include mediation, consensus-building, legislation, cultural preservation, the organization of celebrations, basic service provision, and promoting the work of church and government. To a greater extent than is frequently recognized, local communities are governed based on a shared understanding of values and principles. Concepts associated with respect and the maintenance of relationships, as well as notions of dignity and caring, remain prominent in Pacific societies. This is not to romanticize governance in local Pacific communities or to suggest that local government is by any means without imperfection, but rather to underscore that this is where transparency and accountability are frequently most apparent.

However, institutionalizing indigenous modes of governance can be challenging. Geoffrey White (2004) has identified a series of potential incompatibilities between modern modes of public administration and traditional practices in the Pacific Islands. First, many traditional forms of governance emphasize oral practices and trust that eschew written forms of documentation. In contrast, contemporary forms of public administration see accurate and comprehensive documentation as critical to transparency and openness. Second, to the extent that traditional forms of governance emphasize personal qualities rather than structural positions, issues of responsibility and accountability may be problematic. In some instances, the absence of an outstanding person for a traditional leadership position or a dispute about who should assume a position may require that a position will remain vacant for some time. It is also clear that throughout Melanesia the majority of traditional leadership roles favor men, although this may be changing over time. Third, it is important to note the lack of specificity associated with the scope of responsibility for traditional leaders or chiefs. This differs from the level of specificity of responsibilities and authority for leadership positions in government, business, or churches. Not withstanding these considerations, traditional leaders have offered an important source of stability and continuity, particularly in the face of crisis and conflict situations.

Throughout much of Oceania, there is no one national custom and tradition per se. Rather, individual islands or groups of islands within nation states, especially in Melanesia and Micronesia, tend to have customs and traditions particular to a specific geographical area. Noteworthy is the fact that traditional forms of governance, which cannot be completely divorced from traditional leadership, may not in all cases be the most democratic. Moreover, traditional leaders appear to be most effective in societies where custom and tradition have not been radically transformed.

Polynesia

In Polynesia, strong traditional governance structures at the time of colonization led to the early emergence of locally controlled states (e.g. Samoa), which meant that older systems and values became well incorporated into evolving governance processes. A larger sense of nationhood within the nations of Polynesia, as well as a greater degree of effective integration of political and customary structures, has enabled both a greater degree of political stability, in general, and local leadership, in particular (Tuimaleali'ifano 2001; Kling 2008). Traditional governance within Polynesia tended to be centralized and hierarchical. This characteristic often helped to ensure its continuity and incorporation into colonial structures. Even so, only a few of the current states within Polynesia had populations that were wholly united under a single leader at the time of colonization.

In contemporary Polynesia, many traditional leaders play a dominant role in the governance of their societies. In both Samoa and Tonga, traditional leaders and values were enshrined in the principles of the new state at an early date. In Samoa, the constitution included specific reference to "the way of the chiefs"; protection for the use of Matai titles; incorporated specific positions in local governance into the legal framework; and ensured that the Matai played a central role in land disputes through the creation of a Land and Titles Court. Moreover:

> Two of the highest holders of titles were made joint heads of state with tenure for the whole term of their lives. Though provision was made for their successors, the latter had to be members of Parliament, who were only the matai as

the "representatives of forty-five territorial constituencies created in the constitution were to be matai." Hence, the prime minister, eight cabinet ministers, the council of deputies, the speaker and his or her deputy and all backbenchers were to be holders of titles, thus "effective power was placed in the hands of matai, who were elected in turn by other matai ... furthermore, no change could be made to the matai laws as it could be done only through the laws relating to Samoan custom and usage." (University of the South Pacific 2000)

Similarly, the earliest constitution of the Kingdom of Tonga from 1875 provided special land rights to Tongan nobility, which comprised select persons from among several hundred thousand chiefs. Because traditional values and norms were well incorporated into actual governance practices, there is a stronger sense of national identity and social trust. Trust was traditionally tied not only to interpersonal relations but also to *mana*,[1] which was acquired by birth lineage and associated with belief systems.

Micronesia

Experience from Micronesia sheds further light on the current and potential roles of traditional institutions of governance.[2] During colonial times, traditional leaders were rarely directly involved in governance but they were consulted, because of their influence at the local level. After independence, traditional chiefs in Micronesia were able to influence politics and governance primarily because their blessing was normally needed to win elective office. In a few cases, traditional leaders became elected leaders at national level. However, some evidence from different areas of the Pacific supports the view that traditional leaders are most effective at the local or district level, because this is where they are known and trusted.

The current degree of integration between traditional and modern governance systems varies widely in Micronesia in terms of legal protection for traditional governance, as well as political authority and unofficial influence at levels of central and local government. The constitution of Yap State of the Federated States of Micronesia provides official recognition and legal roles for traditional leaders, who are active in both central and local government. In other states, traditions may have a legal basis, but leaders themselves do not. Differences are also evident in terms of the degree to which citizens want the roles and power of traditional leaders to expand or be incorporated into contemporary government. This is frequently distinguished from a more broad-based desire to protect custom and tradition.

A common concern is that efforts to formalize the status of chiefs might lead to abuse of power or to diminished respect for leaders seen as bureaucratic appointees rather than as leaders recognized for their traditional knowledge, skill, and involvement with local communities:

> [M]any leaders in Pohnpei as well as in the other states believe that it would be disrespectful for the traditional leaders to serve in public offices alongside the commoners. They would be opened to criticism and ridicule by other leaders who are not their social equals, customarily speaking. It is customarily inappropriate for ordinary people, even in official capacity, to debate with and criticize a traditional leader. (Haglelgam 2006: 11)

Even elected non-traditional leaders who control public financial resources are sometimes uncomfortable with traditional leaders, who still command much respect and deference. However, rising expectations for service provision at the village level may encourage people to increasingly turn to municipal officials if these expectations are unmet.

Melanesia

These experiences contrast with Melanesia, where the tenuous reach of colonial administrations extended infrequently into local affairs, and the legal basis for the role of chiefs in various aspects of government is sometimes unclear. However, examination of experience from the Solomon Islands noted that, despite variation in their local status, chiefs are now increasingly evident in the political discourse of both local communities and the nation:

> They have not been replaced by newer leaders of church and state so much as transformed or *dis*placed, sometimes forming a kind of parallel universe, intersecting at strategic points with structures of the state (and church). Just as chiefs once played an important part in colonial systems of indirect rule, so today they often mediate between localized rural communities and the state, usually in informal ways not well represented in the rational codifications of government bureaucracy. (White 2004: 4)

Melanesia is also noteworthy for the relatively egalitarian nature of traditional leadership, as chiefly status can be obtained through personal accomplishment. Today, not all chiefs are well versed in traditional knowledge, and neither are they entirely immune to manipulation or charges of corruption. Still, a leader knowledgeable in custom, history, and local practices for resolving conflicts will likely be more effective. Discussants noted how it was only in the 1970s that many remote communities in the larger nations of Melanesia were slowly provided with access to the veneers of modern political practices and administrative organizations. Even today, some islanders in more rural areas live in largely traditional communities with their own systems of governance and justice.

Governance surveys on the Pacific

To better examine the current state of trust in government, it is useful to look at how governance within the Pacific Islands is perceived. In *Governance Matters VII* (Kaufmann et al. 2008), the World Bank examined all countries to determine their quality of governance over multiple years, providing both their percentile rank (relative performance versus all other countries) and their governance score. According to the report, these indicators aggregate the views on the quality of governance provided by a large number of enterprise, citizen, and expert survey respondents.[3] The data are gathered from a number of survey institutes, think-tanks, non-governmental organizations, and international organizations. Among the governance indicators that were selected for this project were: voice and accountability; rule of law; control of corruption; government effectiveness; and regulatory quality.

Table 6.1 displays the percentile rank for a number of Pacific Island countries in 2007.[4] The data represent how well they fared in comparison with both developed and developing countries at the international level. To place the data in some context, both Australia and New Zealand scored above the 90th percentile in each category, whereas the Caribbean as a region tended to score in the mid to high 60th percentile. Hence, Palau's rating in the first column means that, in the area of voice and accountability, it nearly reached the highest (90th) percentile worldwide.

According to this measure, the Pacific Islands generally scored most highly in perceptions of voice/accountability and rule of law, although some countries that have recently emerged from conflict situations received lower scores in the latter category. On average, the region tended to receive its lowest scores in the areas of regulatory quality, government effectiveness, and control of corruption, in that order.

In each category, there is considerable variation between the results for different countries because of the heterogeneity of the region. Nonetheless, the data suggest that a lingering perception exists of the need for improvement in several governance areas. The following sections will proceed with a brief look at the relationship between trust, expectations, and select governance dimensions, with a view toward providing an explanation for some of these data.

Table 6.1 World percentile rank of selected Pacific Island countries on various governance indicators, 2007

	Governance indicator				
	Voice and accountability	Rule of law	Control of corruption	Government effectiveness	Regulatory quality
Palau	89.4	80.5	n.a.	36.5	n.a.
Marshall Islands	88.0	53.8	36.2	18.5	18.4
FS Micronesia	80.8	71.9	42.5	38.4	38.3
Nauru	81.3	62.4	49.8	35.1	23.3
American Samoa	78.4	85.7	67.6	70.1	62.6
Tuvalu	72.1	84.3	54.1	40.8	19.9
Kiribati	69.2	75.7	60.9	34.1	13.6
Samoa	67.3	81.9	64.3	49.3	52.4
Vanuatu	60.1	68.1	63.3	45.5	32.5
Solomon Islands	53.8	24.3	32.9	20.4	12.6
Papua New Guinea	51.9	21.0	9.2	25.1	30.1
Tonga	45.7	64.3	12.6	32.2	22.8
Fiji	32.2	46.2	42.0	35.5	34.0

Source: Data from Kaufmann et al. (2008).
Note: n.a. = not available.

Transparency

In the Pacific Islands, the relationship between transparency and trust is not always a direct one. Contemporary forms of public administration see accurate and comprehensive documentation as critical to transparency and openness. However, many traditional forms of governance within the Pacific Islands place emphasis on oral practices that eschew written forms of documentation. Because local governance often relies more heavily on oral systems, there is often less transparency at this level. Nonetheless, it is at the local level in Oceania where trust is often the highest.

In 2005, the Pacific Media and Communication Facility reported that, with a few exceptions, access to government information within the Pacific Islands ranged from ad hoc to difficult, and the quality and timeliness of the information varied significantly (CHRI 2006). Causes included a frequent lack of coordination between central government information departments; unclear guidelines for disclosure; and the sense that media coverage of government information was intrusive and low priority. To date, most of the Pacific Islands have not passed a freedom of information law – the exception being Cook Islands' Official Information Act 2008.[5] A relevant issue for trust, therefore, when looking at individual countries, is the degree to which the population has expectations of this access.

Given relatively low levels of transparency, depending on the country and level of government, trust may not always accurately correspond to the quality of governance. This is a key point, because civil society can play an important role in pressuring government to focus on issues that may be inadequately addressed. It can also have a say in how policy objectives are implemented and later assessed. If citizens are not receiving complete, useful, or timely information, they may not know where their efforts are most needed or best applied. For example, the Asian Development Bank has noted that most Pacific Islanders are effectively shut out from participating in the legislative process, because information on the legislative agenda is rarely available in advance, nor are draft bills published prior to parliamentary consideration (Mellor and Jabes 2004: 19). Hence, the quality of citizen contributions to the governance process depends upon improvements in transparency.

E-government has provided one recent option to improve access to government information. However, Pacific Island governments and their populations still face many barriers to its widespread use because of high infrastructure, connection, and equipment costs; a lack of digitized government information; the monopoly of telecommunication services; and the need for training programs. In the early part of the twenty-first century, less than 25 percent of the population of most Pacific Islands were found to have Internet access, although there was widespread interest in seeking to enhance Internet infrastructure within and between the Pacific Islands countries (UNESCO 2002). Currently, most governments have some degree of online representation (see Table 6.2). However, in some cases it is still difficult to find a comprehensive entry portal. Ministries, parliament, and local governments may host their own sites, but may not be connected via one joint site. Where entry portals do exist, continued and reliable access to them can vary over time.

Corruption

High perceptions of corruption are a particular area where trust in government could be improved. A 2007 discussion paper by the Pacific Institute of Advanced Studies in Development and Governance identified ministerial favoritism, misappropriation, embezzlement, abuse of discretionary power in regulation, and limited use of reports generated by government auditors as present to differing degrees within the region (PIAS-DG n.d.). Confused lines of accountability present another issue,

Table 6.2 Pacific Island governments on the web

Country	URL (accessed 1 February 2010)
Cook Islands	http://www.cook-islands.gov.ck
FS Micronesia	http://www.fsmgov.org/
Fiji	http://www.fiji.gov.fj/
Kiribati	http://www.mfep.gov.ki
	http://www.parliament.gov.ki/
Marshall Islands	http://www.rmiembassyus.org/Government.htm
Nauru	http://www.naurugov.nr/
New Caledonia	http://www.gouv.nc/portal/page/portal/gouv
Palau	http://www.palaugov.net/
Papua New Guinea	http://www.pngonline.gov.pg/
	http://www.pm.gov.pg/
Niue	http://www.gov.nu/
Samoa	http://www.govt.ws/
Solomon Islands	http://www.commerce.gov.sb/
	http://www.parliament.gov.sb/
Tokelau	http://www.tokelau.org.nz/
Tonga	http://www.pmo.gov.to/
Tuvalu	http://www.tuvaluislands.com/gov_info.htm
Vanuatu	http://www.vanuatugovernment.gov.vu/

Note: This list is not all inclusive and provides only a small sample of web presence.

since members of parliament frequently participate in the planning and delivery of services by the central government. However, Transparency International (TI) considers particular sectors within the Pacific Islands to be at highest risk: police, customs, land and titles administration, forestry, fisheries, ports, health, education, retirement funds, tendering processes, trade in passports and Internet domain names, and offshore banking (Larmour and Barcham 2005).[6]

A recent analysis highlighted the complexity of this topic and called into question perceptions of widespread corruption in the Pacific Islands. Peter Larmour (2008: 1) notes "a striking difference between reports of public perception of corruption and reported personal experience with corruption," whereby "public perception of corruption is not tantamount to legally actionable evidence of corruption." In reference to one Pacific Island country, he concludes that there may be less corruption than the military and the populace thought.

The Tebbutt research for TI Fiji suggests that there is a gap between perceptions of corruption (widespread) and experiences of bribery (minor, but worrying). The National Integrity Systems surveys show deep suspicion throughout the region of "grand" corruption by ministers. Definitions of corruption matter in several ways. Audits, reviews, and inquiries will become arbitrary and interminable without some specification of what exactly they are looking for (and whether, exactly, it is an offense). Differences between popular and official or legal understandings also affect the legitimacy of the campaign. Popular expectations have been cranked up, queues have formed outside the government buildings. And, if nothing is found or can be done, people will get disappointed and angry – and no doubt suspect more corruption. (Larmour 2008: 31)

In some cases, a lack of consensus exists about the definition of corruption within the Pacific Islands. Local traditions tend to place high value on social harmony and obligations, with less differentiation between individual and community resources. These values often conflict with the implicit values of institutional structures that strictly define the separation between what is public and private. Moreover, respect to chiefs and elders may be accompanied by a higher degree of tolerance for discretionary practices (Larmour and Barcham 2005). The merging of these two approaches can therefore lead to an extreme result: all actions that are not perceived as "fair" or where one party appears to take advantage of another may then be erroneously perceived as corruption. This implies that Pacific Island governments could potentially increase the trust that they receive from citizens by proactively initiating public dialogues on the subject of corruption.

Trends toward increased participation

Participation by civil society and the private sector in policy identification, formation, and assessment can play a key role in pressuring the government and establishing satisfactory conditions for improved government effectiveness (Heppell 2008). Many recent initiatives within the Pacific Islands have emphasized the importance of community participation in improving trust, through: parliamentary select committees; consultations with traditional leaders, churches, and civil society groups; and national leadership conventions. All of these address the need for ongoing dialogue and emphasize the importance of promoting peace and harmony within society. Some Pacific Island governments have created specific mechanisms to incorporate civil society input as a formal step of the policy process. However, these initiatives have in numerous cases experienced initial challenges in terms of how to achieve "buy-in" or acceptance of the consultation process and its goals.

In terms of improved participation in governance processes within the Pacific Islands, a first barrier can be public perceptions that the government should be entirely responsible for policy development and implementation. Citizens may believe, at least initially, that the government is not fulfilling its mandate if it too frequently turns to the public for input (Baaro 2006). When governments do use open forums for policy debate, "meeting fatigue" can then provide a second barrier to participation, as even legislators themselves can grow weary of conducting more dialogue, even when that offers the opportunity to present their views. Finally, as a third barrier, governance partners such as civil society organizations may be resistant to changing the ways in which they contribute to the governance process, because their members may believe that they are already doing what needs to be done. Each of these barriers must be overcome through ongoing dialogue in order to establish a strong collaboration culture, which is particularly essential where there are income discrepancy issues between different areas or districts. The following section examines these issues through specific cases.

Mobilizing community and traditional leadership

Recognition of the importance of trust has played an important role in the success of many recent innovations to improve governance within the Pacific Islands. In the cases of Kiribati and Palau, a focus on mobilizing community and traditional leadership has helped to ensure that development initiatives were people centered. The Kiribati National Leadership Convention and the Palau Leadership Symposium provide excellent examples of the importance of national consultations to enhance the parliamentary process.

In Kiribati, the government discovered the value of holding an inclusive conference, open to the public, every three years in order to strengthen transparency and encourage participation in the governance process. The initial rationale for the conference was to promote consensus for a code of conduct for public officials under the first government of Anote Tong, who had prioritized transparent and accountable governance in his election platform. However, the government quickly learned that civil society organizations wanted to provide their input on a wider range of issues.

The first Kiribati National Leadership Convention was held in May 2005 in Tarawa. Government officials, elected representatives, leadership from all registered churches, traditional *unimwane*[7] associations of older men, heads of island councils and their clerks, private sector leaders, and women and youth groups were invited to discuss the major challenges that faced the country and identify strategies to address them. The preparatory committee spent some time deliberating on how to conduct the meeting and decided not to have a traditional meeting in the *maneaba*[8] setting, which would place constraints on who could speak. Moreover, a minimum of three conference table seats were set aside for each of Kiribati's participating islands (Baaro 2006). Topics covered at the convention included population growth, overcrowding, land issues, social peace and harmony, and community participation and ownership.

The strength of the innovation was that it blended traditional and other systems of consultation and dialogue, providing a clear framework for follow-up and implementation (Baaro 2006). As such, the convention took a broader approach to nation-building to foster an environment of shared collective responsibility at the national level, while forging stronger partnerships and collaboration between national institutions and civil society. Other island states had also held leadership conventions, but Kiribati made an effort to ensure considerable collaboration with key non-state actors to jointly organize and manage the convention. This process later helped to foster a positive environment for constructive dialogue and partnerships at the highest level. It further enabled citizens to discuss public policy within the larger context of issues with which they identified. The convention received financial support from New Zealand, Australia, the Pacific Islands Forum, the Republic of China, and the United Nations Development Programme.

In response to the initiative, the convention received high levels of representation and a largely positive response from the public. There was a very strong sense of appreciation by civil society leaders of this first significant move by the government to include the community on discussions on major socioeconomic challenges. To date, some of the positive outcomes of the convention have included more coherence between legislative initiatives and the concerns of the populace, as well as better collaboration between civil society organizations, which now organize programs to address social issues identified by the convention, and the government, which funds these programs. Moreover, the convention outcomes have included specific actions to be taken by the family, the community, the churches, community organizations, and the government. It highlighted the support from the general public for a dialogue process that strengthened partnerships and the mobilization of collective action and shared responsibility in nation-building. Under the Kiribati Development Plan of 2008–2011, the convention is now being used as a means of addressing inequality and identifying areas of need and strategies for poverty reduction (KDP 2008).

In contrast to Kiribati, Palau used a national and state Leadership Symposium to address specific economic development issues and manage its relationship with the United States of America under the Compact of Free Association (COFA). Its specific objective was to pre-empt the possibility of facing conditionality in coming years by taking a proactive approach to Palau's major needs and priorities (Mikel 2006). Within this context, the symposium was designed to: (i) prepare for the upcoming review with the United States on the financial provisions of the compact; (ii) undertake an inventory of Palau's performance to date within the context of the current agreement; and (iii) identify what needed to be done as a nation to enhance opportunities for sustainable economic development, either within the COFA framework or separately. The government hoped that the symposium would help to develop a consensus on national priorities and policy direction for a development strategy framework by mobilizing public and private sector support, ensuring leadership buy-in, and identifying parties responsible for implementing recommendations and initiatives.[9]

The President of the Republic of Palau called the first symposium to be held between 7 to 9 February 2006. Participants included leaders from the executive and legislative branches at the national level, governors and speakers from state government, non-governmental organizations, and members of the Chamber of Commerce. These participants then examined and formed recommendations on six focus areas: (i) priorities to guide Palau's discussions with the United States regarding the renewal of COFA financial and other provisions; (ii) the identification of laws and regulations that should be passed to meet national goals and objectives; (iii) infrastructure requirements to meet development goals; (iv) means of enhancing private sector development; (v) improving the sustainability of public financial management, including anti-corruption efforts; and (vi) strengthening human resource development.

The Palau Leadership Symposium led to several outcomes. First, it enabled the creation of a communiqué, later converted into an action plan, that outlined strategic objectives and actions to be undertaken within each of the six focus areas. These actions were incorporated into the planning and budgeting process, and resulted in new banking, foreign investment, and tax laws. Consequently, national debt fell from US$35 million in 2006 to US$28 million in the following year (Remengesau 2007). Second, Palau has continued to use the symposium as an important tool for the promotion of a broad-based understanding of different development options. Since the time of the Leadership Symposium, education and health symposiums have since been held, as well as a separate Economic Symposium, held in February 2007 to further address private sector development issues, as well as COFA and economic development in general. The latter event provided the opportunity for local business leaders and government and non-governmental representatives to discuss the economy, environment, society, and security. Following panel discussions and presentations by guest speakers, students spoke of their visions of the future.

Budgetary and fiscal innovation

A key issue for trust in government within the Pacific Islands concerns how resources are deployed, given the islands' relative scarcity, limited private sectors, and frequent dependence on foreign aid. Some donors believe that small island nations have poorly managed budgetary and fiscal policy, little basis for a self-sustaining diversified economy, and limited prospects. The inability of some Pacific Island governments to constrain spending to conform to revenues suggests to some policymakers that the best and perhaps only long-term option is to rely on activities centering on migration, remittances, aid, and bureaucracy.

Two small island states, discussed during the Regional Forums, offer a dramatically different view of public finance within the Pacific Islands. Tuvalu in Polynesia and Yap State in the Federated States of Micronesia (FSM) offer examples of jurisdictions that have achieved impressive fiscal records as a result of good financial and public sector management over the last two decades. The different approaches employed by these states have helped to promote sustainable public finance and strengthen national autonomy. They have also served to improve the confidence of the international donor community and to demonstrate the potential of other island states to pursue their own innovations in line with national priorities.

Tuvalu

Tuvalu offers a fascinating example of how the forces of globalization may at once strengthen and weaken vulnerable small island states. In its early years of nationhood, Tuvalu had to make annual requests to bilateral donors for contributions to sustain basic government services, such as health and education. Over time, donors grew weary of providing these seemingly interminable annual budget subventions. For its part, Tuvalu had grown equally disillusioned with what its citizens saw as interference in the budgetary matters of a sovereign state (Finin 2002). However, as one of the world's most resource-poor island chains, Tuvalu had limited options.[10]

Well before independence, Tuvalu officials had attempted to discuss the idea of establishing a major public trust fund with UK negotiators, as there had been a tradition of successful overseas investments facilitated by colonial and church leaders earlier in the century. This proposed fund would help Tuvalu to finance chronic budget deficits, underpin economic development, and achieve greater financial autonomy.[11] The idea gained momentum in 1979 when Kiribati gained independence and inherited US$68 million from the Revenue Equalization Reserve Fund (RERF), originally capitalized from colonial taxes on the Ocean Island phosphate mining operation, but Tuvalu received no share.

Over the next few years, Tuvalu and its Ministry of Finance patiently continued to advocate the establishment of the trust fund. In 1982, Tuvalu proposed to the United Kingdom a "once and for all" contribution, in lieu of ongoing annual budget support. However, it continued to receive negative responses (Finin 2008). The United Kingdom responded that Her Majesty's Government did not provide aid in advance of demonstrated need, as a matter of policy. Similar overtures were made to Australia and New Zealand, but both nations declined. New Zealand's initial disinclination to rely on world markets to fund public activities in some of the Pacific's remotest atolls received further thought and discussion over several years, as this novel idea for "development assistance" was refined. Following the submission of a formal prospectus outlining the specific purposes and structure of the proposed fund's management, with multiple structural checks and balances, New Zealand, by far the smallest of the three major donors, stepped forward with a pledge of A$8 million, contingent upon the participation of Australia and the United Kingdom.

On June 16, 1987, the Tuvalu Trust Fund (TTF) was established at a signing ceremony in the New Zealand High Commissioner's Office based in Suva, Fiji. Australia, New Zealand, and the United Kingdom together contributed just under US$25 million, with Tuvalu investing US$1.6 million. Japan and the Republic of Korea also made modest contributions. By international agreement, the parties established an international board chaired by Tuvalu and an independent international advisory committee that meets in Tuvalu twice each year (one month prior to the board meetings) to review economic and financial developments.[12] To ensure that the trust fund would be self-perpetuating, the parties agreed that the real capital value would always be maintained. Professional fund managers in Australia were hired to ensure that the fund's value would grow. Draw-down distributions (returns) received by the Tuvalu government were calculated annually by adjusting for inflation and subtracting administrative costs.

The first three years saw considerable disappointment, as market conditions declined. The first year, the fund yielded virtually no draw-down revenues for the government.[13] This experience led Tuvalu to create a second account that the government alone would control. This "B Account" acted as a buffer and allowed the Ministry of Finance to weather years when returns did not maintain the fund's real balance and there was no distribution. To date, Tuvalu has experienced four years when the maintained value of the fund has been insufficient to allow any distribution to government.

However, the pace of world markets in the 1990s brought windfalls that not only bridged revenue shortfalls but even allowed Tuvalu to make substantial additional contributions to the fund's corpus. In most years, Tuvalu's annual recurrent costs have exceeded normal revenues, despite adhering to some of the most frugal fiscal policies in the entire region.[14] An emergent private sector with very limited scope for rapid expansion left little realistic hope that revenues from Tuvalu's internal tax base would grow substantially in the short term. Therefore, government policymakers made determined efforts to reinvest trust fund returns, in view of the long-term need for greater economic sustainability and less reliance on aid. As a result of its consistent and significant new infusions into the fund's corpus, Tuvalu became the major shareholder of the fund by 1998.

Today, Tuvalu is more secure economically than many neighboring states with far superior resource endowments and many more comparative advantages. The success of the Tuvalu Trust Fund was a major step forward in advancing the sovereignty of the country and its long-term future. The fund has become a model for financial sustainability that other Pacific Island nations and multilateral lending institutions now attempt to emulate. Still, the fund has not proven to be the panacea some had anticipated. Even with major injections of new capital into the fund and a number of years yielding windfall growth, the fund has served almost exclusively as a means to support the annual recurrent budget, given perennial shortfalls from other revenue sources. It has not supported major development projects.

On balance, however, the fund allows Tuvalu to manage its economy in a manner that has avoided major budgetary shortfalls and the debt trap that envelops some other small island states. Perhaps the strongest testimony to its overall success was the establishment in 1999 of an entirely new international trust fund called the Falekaupule Trust Fund. Capitalized with assistance from the Asian Development Bank at US$12 million, it is designed to underwrite the costs and projects of island local governments. Ironically, the tremendous achievements of the fund in securing greater self-reliance and financial sustainability have yielded another unanticipated benefit – additional bilateral aid from donors who are anxious to see their funds put to good use in a well-managed economy. As such, Tuvalu offers intriguing lessons for Western nations in their efforts to be innovative in assisting small developing states that are striving to achieve greater self-reliance.

Yap State

The case of Yap provides an alternative example of measures that may be taken within the Pacific Islands to achieve fiscal innovation in ways that are compatible with local culture and priorities. One of four states within the Federated States of Micronesia, Yap demonstrates that small Pacific Island governments can achieve consensus to maintain fiscal conservatism. Its approach to public sector management has enabled it to limit expenditures, prioritize saving, and achieve regular budget surpluses.

Like Tuvalu, Yap cannot rely on its limited natural resources or private sector to generate substantial revenues for public coffers. Nonetheless, Yap is unusual in that only a quarter of its funds comes from locally generated revenue. The majority comes from its Compact of Free Association with the United States (COFA), while the remainder comes from national revenue-sharing. Yap also has its own investment portfolio or "trust fund" and uses investment advisors and techniques that are not dissimilar to those employed by its Pacific neighbors. However, its expenditure decisions have enabled Yap to become more financially secure than almost any other Island government in the North Pacific.

In 1991, Yap secured a medium-term note for US$71 million, based on anticipated COFA funds. Over the next 10 years, it paid off the note as funds were received. Because earnings exceeded the loan interest, the proceeds from this venture provide the primary basis for the growth of the investment portfolio. This growth required considerable discipline, as well as long-term planning and implementation, which is quite unusual. Currently, the investment portfolio is worth an estimated US$50 million, which is roughly equivalent to four times the government's annual budget. These funds are then managed by the Federated Development Authority in a pooled investment fund, which includes investments from the national government and its other three states (Underwood 2006).

Yap has amassed these surpluses by avoiding expenditures on items that typically receive tremendous political pressure in other states. It employs a long period of discussion and consensus-building prior to financial commitments, keeps a low minimum wage for civil servants, avoids large capital investment projects, and refrains from investing in projects that benefit special interests. Furthermore, successive governments have demonstrated this fiscal conservatism even during natural disasters and changes in foreign aid:

> In its first confrontation with dramatic political turmoil due to budgetary shortfalls, Yap's political leadership bit the bullet and no one paid a political price. The Yap State Legislature was very cooperative in devising and implementing

the plan to shed government employees and participated in forcing the retirement of workers. The philosophy of the Yap State Legislature according to Senator Clement Mulalap, Chair of the Finance Committee for the past eight years, is "We don't spend what we don't have." In fact, he remarks, good politics in Yap is not to spend money. (Underwood 2006: 5)

A primary reason why Yap has been able to maintain its fiscal conservatism relates to cultural values and expectations. Its traditions have led to an emphasis on practicality, prudency, and the need to use resources sparingly with the utmost care. For the general public, these values have translated into low demand for consumer items and high savings rates by individuals. Yap's value systems have also meant that government is expected to spend within its means and plan for the future. Since resources must be used frugally, adequate discussion and consideration must be given to their use. Furthermore, traditional leaders in Yap play a significant role in ensuring that government policies accord with these values:

It should not surprise anyone that the Yap constitution offers the most extensive recognition of customs and traditions [in the Federated States of Micronesia] and provides for active and functional role of the traditional chiefs in the state government. The constitution creates two councils of traditional leaders: the Council of Pilung for traditional chiefs of Yap Islands Proper and the Council of Tamol for the traditional chiefs of the outlying islands and atolls.... The two Councils have sparingly exercised their constitutionally bestowed power to veto legislation. But in the few cases in which the two councils have exercised their veto power, they have adopted a broad interpretation of their power to veto even appropriation measures. (Haglelgam 2006: 11, 12)

Some have argued that Yap's good financial performance could not be easily replicated, since the majority of government operating revenues come from external sources. Moreover, participants at the Regional Forums also pointed out that there is a need to balance frugality and savings with attention to the basic needs of citizens in areas such as health and education. The equitable distribution of resources to the outer islands was also raised as an issue that has sometimes been overlooked. Nonetheless, the experience of Yap provides a viable alternative approach for Pacific Islands that look to forge their own development paths while maintaining consensus and working with existing institutions and ideologies of governance. Yap is still in a strong fiscal position, contrary to conventional wisdom, which argues that small island economies are inherently prone to expenditure patterns that exceed real revenues.

Enhancing trust through transparent governance and dialogue

In post-conflict situations within the Pacific Islands, trust has also played a critical role in rebuilding societies as part of peace and reconciliation processes. During reconstruction, there may be a tendency to exclude certain groups from the peace process, because of security issues or worry that varied interests will delay agreement and action. Often, too, there are conflicting concerns – wanting to include everyone in the process, yet not wanting full participation in the early stages.

Experiences in Papua New Guinea have shown that it is essential to strive for consultation processes that are as inclusive as possible. This means that agreement can be more difficult and takes longer to achieve. However, once achieved, agreements tend to be more enduring and accepted by the populace as a whole because of the ownership generated by participation in the process. Transparent processes are also essential when developing new constitutions or legal documents during post-conflict periods. Since the process of rebuilding trust is a slow one by definition, concerted efforts must also be made to ensure that all contributors are aware of even the most minor changes to agreements and documentation.

Papua New Guinea

The Bougainville peace process that took place within Papua New Guinea in Melanesia offers interesting lessons for the role of trust in reconciliation processes, because both social and political trust were largely lacking between the parties to the extended resource-based conflict. A sustained and inclusive process of political negotiations began in 1997, encompassing four phases of talks, which eventually led to the Bougainville Peace Agreement of 2001 (Regan 2002).[15] These four phases focused on: (i) establishment of the process, lines of communication, and a lasting ceasefire; (ii) consolidation of the process and coalescence of political groups; (iii) substantial political negotiations between the Bougainville parties and the Papua New Guinea government; and (iv) agreement implementation and drafting of constitutional laws on autonomy.

Success in negotiating between the parties to the Bougainville conflict required flexibility, openness, inclusiveness, transparency, accountability, and consistency of process. These principles were "intuited" by the parties to the conflict, rather than agreed to in accordance with theoretical models (Hassall 2006). At the onset of this process, one of the primary challenges was how to establish lines of communication and a dialogue between the parties to the conflict, which had been caused by widespread mistrust and perceptions of insecurity.

One of the reasons that flexibility, openness, and inclusiveness were required was that the parties to the dispute were loose alliances rather than military formations. According to Dr Edward Wolfers (2006b), Senior Advisor in the Bougainville Peace and Restoration Office, it was not always possible to determine where power and responsibility were located. Some groups in the dispute had unclear hierarchies and organizational structures, and still experienced internal differences. Consequently, it was not possible to simply arrange meetings with select leaders to discuss and resolve differences.

To address this situation, many negotiations were open to the public, which meant that it was difficult to anticipate who would attend. This approach had both problematic and helpful characteristics. On the one hand, the approach led to short-term difficulties in holding meetings, because gatherings were often rowdier and had greater numbers of participants, many of whom claimed to hold the same position or authority. Furthermore, the open nature of negotiations tempted the occasional participation of individuals who had limited political interest in the proceedings. On the other hand, however, the approach was inclusive. It ensured that internal differences – which are often present within one or more sides to a conflict – would not be pre-emptively ignored or decided in haste by others who did not have the authority or legitimacy to do so. It thus enabled differing views and actors on both sides of the conflict to gradually sort out internal differences, so that they could then reach a broader agreement. This inclusive approach enabled a stronger foundation for agreement among citizens when it later occurred (Wolfers 2006a). The case of Bougainville shows that the short-term difficulties of holding open meetings were more than outweighed by the longer-term results of a broader-based consensus for peace.

Transparency and accountability also played a key role in the slow process of strengthening trust, since parties to the dispute needed to be able to assure themselves at all times that nothing devious was taking place behind the scenes. Transparency entailed keeping the cabinet informed of the peace process, radio broadcasts, joint awareness teams, an agreed mechanism for implementation, and a bipartisan national committee. It further meant not having military secrets or plans. Once the parties to the dispute began working on an agreement, it also meant that no changes to agreement documentation could take place behind closed doors – even if it was a question of fixing a typographical error. Furthermore, transparency was required at all levels: within government, among the parties to the dispute, and throughout the area as a whole. Accountability entailed increased sensitivity to the years of mistrust that had developed among the parties to the conflict and an extra effort on both sides to ensure that even minor oral agreements were kept and transparency maintained. Eventually, it included the absorption of hundreds of people into the bureaucracy, so that rebel groups would have a stake in government and the constitutional process.

Cooperation continues on the development of a process to determine a permanent status for Bougainville, which is currently an autonomous province within Papua New Guinea. There is now a peace agreement viewed as a "joint creation" by the parties to the conflict, an agreement to reinvent government, a constant process of coalition-building between factions, growing trust and a sense of mutual security on Bougainville, and the discontinuation of the diversion of resources into conflict rather than development (Wolfers 2002). As of February 2009, negotiations were again under way for the central government to hand Bougainville additional powers, following a meeting of the joint supervisory body with the national government (Radio New Zealand International 2009).

Conclusion

The degree of trust that citizens have in government and in each other within the Pacific Islands context is intimately related to concepts of local, regional, and national identity, as well as concepts related to legitimacy. In many areas of the Pacific, the concept of nation state is still being constructed. In partial consequence of the colonial legacy and the subsequent policies of independent governments, the institutions and processes associated with centralized government are still often regarded with a certain degree of suspicion and lower political trust. By the same token, a deficit of social trust is also in evidence in some Pacific Islands, as social and cultural identity does not always correspond to national boundaries.

However, the proposition of low political and social trust must be qualified, in view of the great variation across the Pacific Islands with respect to how the governed view governance. For example, smaller communities within society often benefit from high levels of trust. Within the Pacific Islands, kinship represents an important institution unto itself, because it structures the everyday lives of many islanders, influences residence groups, and determines the membership of many economic enterprises, as well as political and religious associations (Rapaport 1999). Kin and other social groups have a long history of interaction and a mutually evolved understanding on socially acceptable practices, which over time have led to the development of a greater degree of mutual confidence. At the village level, there is normally consensus on shared values and principles, and the expectation that political processes will adhere to them.

As a result of these expectations, local governments have incorporated traditional governance practices to a much greater extent than central governments. Owing to this blending between modern and traditional systems, local governments tend to be more accessible to citizens and also more highly trusted. Still, the Regional Forums underscored that local or community governance is by no means perfect in the Pacific and, although values and principles are usually shared and understood, they have also had to withstand multiple influences brought by the different waves of globalization.

Specific country factors have played an important role in trust formation and maintenance. For example, Tuvalu experiences a close overlap between social and political trust because of the extremely small size of its population. Not only is Tuvalu the fourth-smallest country in the world in terms of land mass, but it also is the third-least-populated country in the world, with fewer than 12,000 people. As a result, the average citizen has greater access to the institutions and officials of government through social connections. In contrast, Papua New Guinea is a much larger country, with approximately 6 million people, the large majority of whom live in rural areas, over 850 indigenous languages, many traditional societies, and limited infrastructure. In conjunction, these factors can mean that the average citizen may have little knowledge of government above the provincial level.

Ongoing demographic trends are also affecting trust in government. In many countries such as Vanuatu, younger age groups now represent a sizeable portion of the population. When faced with a lack of employment or with other governance shortfalls, these younger populations can lose faith in the ability of government to meet their needs. They may also be more skeptical of traditional leaders and question their authority. As people move increasingly from small outer islands and rural towns to larger islands and national capitals, this will continue to place additional stress on government. Relocating citizens may find that they are unfamiliar with these governance structures and do not know how to interact with them, other than by reverting to the use of interpersonal connections. In combination, urban population growth, out-migration, and younger populations may further broaden the gap between state and citizen.

Numerous successful innovations in governance and trust-building are currently being implemented throughout the Pacific Islands with diverse applications for their adaptation by neighboring countries. These innovations cover a wide range of focus areas, which include strengthening institutions, processes, and human resource capacities; creating new platforms for dialogue and consensus-building; and encouraging civic participation and engagement. In reference to these innovations, the Regional Forums highlighted the importance of improving the interface between modern and traditional governance systems. By drawing on the strengths of local cultures, more can be accomplished than by relying exclusively or predominately on imported governance systems. Traditional norms and values are critical and must be actively incorporated into the innovation process. This will help to enhance state capacity, as well as the ability of public officials and citizens to improve services, and overall conditions for small island states.

Importantly, trust in government and the quality of governance are not always directly equivalent in the Pacific Islands. On the one hand, governance processes that have more legitimacy and trust are not always the most transparent. This lack of transparency is currently inhibiting the ability of many citizens to understand how government functions, how to achieve services, and how to interact with policy processes. Expectations for greater transparency, however, may be comparatively low. On the other hand, there is some evidence that areas of significant trust deficits, namely in perceptions of corruption, may be considered worse than they are in reality.

Therefore, trust in government should be viewed perhaps as a perceptual indicator that sheds additional light on citizen interpretation of the quality of governance in the Pacific Islands. Changing government in ways that produce greater trust requires time and, perhaps, initially modest expectations. To the degree that governments within the region wish to earn more trust through cooperative efforts that include expertise from the outside, it is important to recognize that, in the final analysis, trust is dependent on the implicit calculus and assessments made by islanders themselves; the quality of governance and the degree of trust in government are both locally determined and culturally defined.

Notes

1. In Polynesian culture, *mana* is a spiritual quality considered to have supernatural origins. To have *mana* is to have influence and authority, and efficacy, i.e the power to perform in a given situation. The essential quality of *mana* is not limited to persons – peoples, governments, places and inanimate objects can possess *mana*. *Mana* can be obtained in two ways: through birth and through warfare.
2. Micronesian societies normally recruit traditional leaders from chiefly clans, passed on to an individual based on customary rules and practices (Finin 2008). Most leadership positions are held by males, but in some cases a female may appoint a male relative to act on her behalf as a surrogate.

3. Hence, the data could be interpreted as encompassing perceptions from people outside of the region.
4. Governance score was measured on a scale of –2.5 to +2.5. Because very few countries in any region reached the upper levels of this measure, we chose to focus on the percentile ranking of Pacific Islands as a potentially more useful reflection of the quality of governance within the region.
5. Most countries within the region have a comparatively good record of media activism and freedom of expression when viewed in the context of other developing regions. Moreover, the report qualifies that, at the national level, there is already some constitutional protection for freedom of information, via freedom of the press (Federated States of Micronesia, Fiji, Palau, Papua New Guinea, Marshall Islands, and Tonga), and the right to seek and receive information as part of the broader right to freedom of expression (Federated States of Micronesia, Fiji, Kiribati, Solomon Islands, and Tuvalu). As of 2006, the constitutions of four countries (Cook Islands, Nauru, Samoa, and Vanuatu) did not guarantee freedom of the media or freedom to communicate ideas and information. However, the local chapter of Transparency International was finalizing a model Freedom of Information Bill within Vanuatu (CHRI 2006).
6. On a positive note, a consistent finding from multiple sources was a lack of corruption in national judicial systems, which were generally found to have higher levels of accountability, and auditors also played an important role. According to Larmour and Barcham (2005), the oversight role of auditors was limited, however, by the weakness of parliamentary accounts committees, which failed to read, debate, or act on their reports. Within the region, ombudsmen were rarer than auditors.
7. *Unimwane* are an important local governing body holding several meetings throughout the year. On the outer islands, their opinion can outweigh governmental decree. *Unimwane* are highly respected and are honorable guests at any *botaki* (party).
8. A *maneaba* is a pavilion-style structure with low hanging thatch or a tin roof and cement floor. It acts as a community center as well as a general meeting area.
9. Palau is one of the largest per capita aid recipients within the Pacific Islands region. The COFA agreement with the United States covered a 15-year period from 1994 to 2009.
10. Prior to independence, the United Kingdom encouraged residents of the Ellice Islands (now Tuvalu) to remain part of the larger and wealthier Gilbert Islands (now Kiribati) as a means of avoiding greater unemployment, a reduced standard of living, and further isolation (Finin 2002).
11. Tuvalu Trust Fund Board (2007: 3). It is notable that Ellice Islanders' impressive history of mobilizing cash resources included the establishment in 1950 of a £10,000 endowment to finance the appointment of a resident missionary. See Kofe (1976: 74).
12. The Falekaupule Trust Fund Board consists of representatives from Tuvalu's eight inhabited islands. It oversees the fund's investment strategy and makes decisions on the annual distribution from the Fund for use by the individual islands for development purposes. See Paeniu (2006).
13. Most funds are invested in Australian markets.
14. Tuvalu mints its own coins but relies on the Australian dollar as its currency, leaving little scope for monetary policy.
15. According to Edward Wolfers (2002, 2006b), different parties to the conflict and observers view the peace process as having begun in either 1990, 1994, or 1997, depending on one's perspective. He adds that Papua New Guinea is also unusual in having hosted a number of different peace missions, some simultaneously, and for having invited them, not having them imposed.

REFERENCES

Baaro, Makurita (2006) "Innovative Strategies for Resource Mobilization," paper prepared for the Regional Forum on Reinventing Government in the Pacific Islands, Nadi, Republic of the Fiji Islands, February 20–22. Available at: <http://unpan1.un.org/intradoc/groups/public/documents/un/unpan022602.pdf> (accessed 1 February 2010).

Cheema, Shabbir G. (2007) "Building Trust in Government: Findings from Major Surveys," United Nations Department of Economic and Social Affairs, New York. Available at: http://unpan1.un.org/intradoc/groups/public/documents/UN/UNPAN025132.pdf> (accessed 23 February 2010)

CHRI [Commonwealth Human Rights Initiative] (2006) "Information Disclosure Policy: A Toolkit for Pacific Governments." Commissioned by the Pacific Media and Communications Facility, an initiative of the Australian Agency for International Development, July. Available at: <http://www.undppc.org.fj/userfiles/file/Pacific%20-%20Info%20Disclosure%20Toolkit%20-%20Jul-06.pdf> (accessed 1 February 2010).

ESCAP [United Nations Economic and Social Commission for Asia and the Pacific] Pacific Operations Centre (2010) *Draft Pacific Regional Report. Five-Year Review of the Mauritius Strategy for Further Implementation of the Barbados Programme of Action for Sustainable Development of SIDS (MSI+5)*. ESCAP/EPOC/PHLD/MSI.1/2010/01, January 25. Available at: <http://www.unescap.org/EPOC/pdf/Draft%20Pacific%20MSI+5%20Regional%20Report_25Jan2010.pdf> (accessed 23 February 2010).

Finin, Gerard A. (2002) "Small Is Viable: The Global Ebbs and Flows of a Pacific Atoll Nation," East-West Center Working Papers, Pacific Islands Development Series No. 15, April. Available at: <http://www.eastwestcenter.org/fileadmin/stored/pdfs/PIDPwp015.pdf> (accessed 23 February 2010).

Finin, Gerard A. (2008) "The Pacific Islands Region: Toward Understanding the Context of Trust in Government," presentation at the Workshop on Promoting Trust in Government through Innovations in Governance in Asia and the Pacific, East-West Center, Honolulu, January 29. Available at: <http://unpan1.un.org/intradoc/groups/public/documents/UNGC/UNPAN029111.pdf> (accessed 1 February 2010).

Ghaus-Pasha, Aisha and Meredith Rowen (2007) *Towards Participatory and Transparent Governance: Reinventing Government*. New York: United Nations Department of Economic and Social Affairs. Available at: <http://unpan1.un.org/intradoc/groups/public/documents/un/unpan026997.pdf> (accessed 1 February 2010).

Haglelgam, John R. (2006) "Governance in Micronesia: Roles and Influence of Traditional Chiefs," paper prepared for the Regional Forum on Reinventing Government in the Pacific Islands, Nadi, Republic of the Fiji Islands, February 20–22. Available at: <http://unpan1.un.org/intradoc/groups/public/documents/un/unpan022608.pdf> (accessed 1 February 2010).

Hassall, Graham (2006) "Establishing Social Trust through Transparent Governance and Dialogue in the Pacific Islands," paper prepared for the Regional

Forum on Reinventing Government in the Pacific Islands, Nadi, Republic of the Fiji Islands, February 20–22.

Heppell, Michael (2008) "Pacific Choice: Improving Government," ADB Capacity Development Series. Mandaluyong City, Philippines: Asian Development Bank. Available at: <http://www.adb.org/Documents/Studies/Capacity-Development-in-the-Pacific/Improving-Government.pdf> (accessed 1 February 2010).

Kaufmann, Daniel, Aart Kraay, and Massimo Mastruzzi (2008) *Governance Matters VII: Aggregate and Individual Governance Indicators 1996–2007*. World Bank Policy Research Working Paper 4654, June. Available at: <http://ssrn.com/abstract=1148386> (accessed 11 January 2010).

KDP [Kiribati Development Plan] (2008) *Kiribati Development Plan: 2008–2011*. Ministry of Finance and Economic Development, Government of Kiribati. Available at: <http://www.sprep.org/att/IRC/eCOPIES/Countries/Kiribati/87.pdf> (accessed 1 February 2010).

Kling, Zainal (2008) "Orang Besar – Orang Kaya: The Big Man – Rich Man in Malay Society," Perak, Malaysia. Available at: <http://ipm.upsi.edu.my/web/images/Gallery/5._zainal_kling_big_man_rich_man.pdf> (accessed 19 January 2010).

Kofe, Laumua (1976) "The Tuvalu Church: A Socio-historical Survey of Its Development towards an Indigenous Church," Suva, Fiji. Thesis submitted to the Pacific Theological College.

Lane, Marcus B. (2006) *Coastal Governance in Solomon Islands: An Evaluation of the Strategic Governance Issues Relating to Coastal Management*. IWP-Pacific Technical Report (International Waters Project) No. 29, Secretariat of the Pacific Regional Environment Programme.

Larmour, Peter (2008) "Guarding the Guardians: Accountability and Anticorruption in Fiji's Cleanup Campaign," Pacific Islands Policy 4, East-West Center, Honolulu, Hawaii. Available at: <http://www.eastwestcenter.org/fileadmin/stored/pdfs/pip004.pdf> (accessed 1 February 2010).

Larmour, Peter and Manuhuia Barcham (2005) "National Integrity Systems in Small Pacific Island States," Asia Pacific School of Economics and Government discussion paper, Australian National University. Available at: <http://unpan1.un.org/intradoc/groups/public/documents/APCITY/UNPAN024517.pdf> and <http://pandora.nla.gov.au/pan/71814/20070521-0000/www.crawford.anu.edu.au/degrees/pogo/discussion_papers/PDP05-9.pdf> (accessed 1 February 2010).

Mellor, Thuy and Jak Jabes (2004) *Governance in the Pacific: Focus for Action 2005–2009*. Manila, Philippines: Asian Development Bank.

Mikel, Antonio (2006) "Republic of Palau National/State Leadership Symposium," presentation prepared for the Regional Forum on Reinventing Government in the Pacific Islands, Nadi, Republic of the Fiji Islands, February 20–22. Available at <http://unpan1.un.org/intradoc/groups/public/documents/un/unpan022593.pdf> (accessed 1 February 2010).

Paeniu, Bikenibeu (2006) "Lessons from the Tuvalu Trust Fund," presentation prepared for the Regional Forum on Reinventing Government in the Pacific Islands, Nadi, Republic of the Fiji Islands, February 20–22.

PIAS-DG [Pacific Institute of Advanced Studies in Development and Governance] (n.d.) "Governance Thematic Areas," Pacific Islands Governance

Portal: Supporting the Pacific Islands Governance Network. University of the South Pacific, Suva, Fiji. Available at: <http://www.governance.usp.ac.fj/top-menu-29/thematic-areas-236> (accessed 19 January 2010).

Radio New Zealand International (2009) "PNG to Hand Back Power to Bougainville – Says President," Wellington, New Zealand. Posted online on February 17 at: <http://www.rnzi.com/pages/news.php?op=read&id=44868> (accessed 1 February 2010).

Rapaport, Moshe (1999) *The Pacific Islands: Environment & Society*. Honolulu, Hawaii: Bess Press.

Regan, Anthony J. (2002) "Phases of the Negotiation Process," in Andy Carl and Sr Lorraine Garasu (eds) *Weaving Consensus: The Papua New Guinea-Bougainville Peace Process*. Accord issue 12. London: Conciliation Resources.

Remengesau, Tommy E., Jr (2007) "State of the Republic Address," Senate Chamber, Palau, 10 April. Available at: <http://www.palauoek.net/senate/News/RemengesauSORA2007.pdf> (accessed 1 February 2010).

Rich, Roland, with Luke Hambly and Michael G. Morgan (2008) *Political Parties in the Pacific Islands*. Canberra, Australia: ANU E Press.

Tuimaleali'ifano, M. (2001) "'Aia Tatau and Afioga Tutasi: 'Aiga versus Tama a 'Aiga. Manipulation of Old and New Practices: An MP for Faletatai and Samatau in Samoa's 2001 Elections," *Journal of Pacific History* 36:3, pp. 317–325.

Tuvalu Trust Fund Board (2007) *Tuvalu Trust Fund: 20th Anniversary Profile 1987–2007*. Vaiaku, Funafuti, Tuvalu. Available at: <http://www.undppc.org.fj/_resources/article/files/TuvaluTrustFundProfile.pdf> (accessed 23 February 2010).

Underwood, Robert A. (2006) "Yap State Finances: Rock Solid in the Land of Stone Money," paper prepared for the Regional Forum on Reinventing Government in the Pacific Islands, Nadi, Republic of the Fiji Islands, February 20–22. Available at: <http://unpan1.un.org/intradoc/groups/public/documents/un/unpan022607.pdf> (accessed 1 February 2010).

UNDESA [United Nations Department of Economic and Social Affairs] (2004) *Report on the Findings of the Regional Forum on Reinventing Government in the Pacific Islands. Apia, Samoa, 4–6 October*. New York: United Nations.

UNDESA [United Nations Department of Economic and Social Affairs] (2006) *Report on the Findings of the Regional Forum on Reinventing Government in the Pacific Islands. Nadi, Republic of the Fiji Islands, 20–22 February*. New York: United Nations.

UNDESA [United Nations Department of Economic and Social Affairs] (2008) *Report on the Workshop on Promoting Trust in Government Through Innovations in Governance in Asia and the Pacific. Honolulu, Hawai'i 28–30 January 2008*. New York: United Nations.

UNESCO [United Nations Educational, Scientific and Cultural Organisation] (2002) *Internet Infrastructure and e-Governance in Pacific Islands Countries: A Survey on the Development and Use of the Internet*. Wellington, New Zealand: Zwimpfer Communications Limited for UNESCO, May. Available at: <http://www.unesco.org/webworld/publications/2002_internet_survey_ report.rtf> (accessed 1 February 2010).

University of the South Pacific (2000) "The Pacific-Peace.Net Portal: Samoa," Project of the United Nations Development Programme – Pacific Centre, Pacific Institute of Advanced Studies in Development and Governance (PIAS-DG), University of the South Pacific, Suva, Fiji. Available at: <www.pacific-peace.net>; temporarily cached at <http://74.125.93. 132/search?q=cache:8d_2KuhihMIJ:www.pacific-peace.net/countries/samoa/ +%22territorial+constituencies%22+matai&cd=4&hl=en&ct=clnk&gl=us>.

Wesley-Smith, Terence (2004) "Reinventing Government: The Politics of State Failure and Regional Intervention in the Pacific," Concept paper prepared for the Regional Forum on Reinventing Government in the Pacific Islands, Apia, Samoa, October 4–6. Available at: <http://www.hawaii.edu/cpis/files/UN3.pdf> (accessed 1 February 2010).

White, Geoffrey (2004) "Indigenizing Local Governance: Chiefs, Church, and State in a Solomon Islands Society," draft paper prepared for the Regional Forum on Reinventing Government in the Pacific Islands, Apia, Samoa, October 4–6. Available at: <http://unpan1.un.org/intradoc/groups/public/documents/ un/unpan022609.pdf> (accessed 1 February 2010).

Wolfers, Edward P. (2002) "Joint Creation: The Bougainville Peace Agreement – and Beyond," in Andy Carl and Sr. Lorraine Garasu (eds) *Weaving Consensus: The Papua New Guinea-Bougainville Peace Process*. Accord issue 12. London: Conciliation Resources.

Wolfers, Edward P. (2006a) "Establishing Social Trust Through Transparent Governance & Dialogue," Speaking-notes for presentation on international peace missions in Bougainville, delivered at the Regional Forum on Reinventing Government in the Pacific Islands, Nadi, Republic of the Fiji Islands, February 20–22. Available at: <http://unpan1.un.org/intradoc/groups/public/documents/ un/unpan022619.pdf> (accessed 1 February 2010).

Wolfers, Edward P. (2006b) "International Peace Missions in Bougainville, Papua New Guinea, 1990–2005: Host State Perspectives," paper prepared for the Regional Forum on Reinventing Government in the Pacific Islands, Nadi, Republic of the Fiji Islands, February 20–22. Available at: <http://unpan1.un.org/ intradoc/groups/public/documents/un/unpan022601.pdf> (accessed 1 February 2010).

7

Trust in government: Evidence from China

Teresa Wright

The high level of government trust shown by citizens of still-authoritarian China is one of the most perplexing political phenomena of the late twentieth and early twenty-first centuries. Contrary to predictions that the violent crackdown by the Communist Party of China (CPC) on the protests in the spring of 1989 would de-legitimize the government to such an extent that democratic revolution would be imminent, since the early 1990s the Chinese citizenry has displayed remarkably strong confidence in the central government. Even more surprisingly, popular trust in national political leaders and institutions has been apparent even among the hundreds of thousands of Chinese citizens who have participated in tens of thousands of yearly protests since the early 1990s.[1] To be sure, these widespread "mass disturbances" indicate some degree of unhappiness with the political system. Yet almost none of the protestors have challenged CPC rule. Instead, demonstrators typically have directed their anger at local employers and/or officials, and expressed support for central authorities. Simultaneously, they generally have not criticized the political system from a Western, liberal perspective. Rather, most have voiced their criticisms from the left, calling on ruling elites to live up to their socialist claims to legitimacy. Thus, even China's most aggrieved citizens have displayed little desire to end CPC rule. Simultaneously, many citizens – especially those who have prospered in recent years – have shown strong interest in joining the CPC and working with, rather than against, the existing political establishment. Through an analysis of public opinion polls, interviews, and data on the political behavior of China's

Building trust in government: Innovations in governance reform in Asia, Cheema and Popovski (eds), United Nations University Press, 2010, ISBN 978-92-808-1189-6

major socioeconomic sectors, this chapter provides evidence of these political attitudes within the Chinese citizenry.

Popular political attitudes and behavior in contemporary China

In a variety of nationwide surveys, Chinese respondents display a remarkably high level of confidence in the national political system. In two well-respected polls conducted in China in 2001 and 2002 – the World Values Survey (WVS) and East Asian Barometer (EAB) – 97 percent and 98 percent of respondents (respectively) expressed "quite a lot" or "a great deal" of confidence in the national government (World Values Survey 2001; East Asian Barometer 2002). Relatedly, 98 percent (WVS) and 92 percent (EAB) expressed "quite a lot" or "a great deal" of confidence in the CPC. Further, 72.9 percent of WVS respondents reported being "fairly satisfied" (67.1 percent) or "very satisfied" (5.8 percent) with "the people in national office," whereas only 1.5 percent reported being "very dissatisfied." In addition, 94.8 percent expressed "a great deal" (33.5 percent) or "quite a lot" (61.3 percent) of confidence in China's national legislative body, the National People's Congress (World Values Survey 2001).[2] Similarly, a 2008 survey by WorldPublicOpinion.org found that 83 percent of Chinese believed that they can trust the national government to do the right thing "most of the time" (60 percent) or "just about always" (23 percent). Meanwhile, 65 percent expressed the view that "the country is run for the benefit of the people." Among the 19 nations (both democratic and not) surveyed in the World Public Opinion poll, Chinese citizens displayed the greatest trust in and support for the political system (WorldPublicOpinion.org 2008). Further, the Chinese public seems to believe that the existing system is not static or frozen, but rather open and changing in a positive direction. In the 2001 WVS, 67 percent stated that they were "satisfied" or "very satisfied" with the "way democracy is working" in China, and, in the 2002 EAB, 88.5 percent reported being "quite satisfied" or "very satisfied" with the "way democracy is developing" in China (East Asian Barometer 2002; World Values Survey 2001).

Related to these popular views, social trust appears to be much higher in China than in most countries around the world (Tang 2005: 104, citing World Values Surveys). In the 2001 WVS, 54.5 percent of Chinese respondents agreed that "most people can be trusted." By way of comparison, in the United States, 35.8 percent of WVS respondents (in 2000) agreed with this statement. Indeed, if one correlates levels of interpersonal trust and political freedom, China is the "biggest outlier" in the world, evidencing an almost unheard-of combination of exceptionally high levels of social trust and very low levels of political rights and civil liberties (World Values Surveys 1990–1996 and Freedom House 1990–1995, cited in Tang 2005: 104). Interpersonal trust is important because it has a demonstrated connection to political trust. As reported by Chen and Lu (2007: 431), "the empirical evidence from the 2000 World Values Surveys show[s] that generalized trust increases people's faith in political and public institutions in all countries surveyed" (see also Tang 2005: 114). This finding also is supported by a wide array of studies of "social capital" in Western democracies (e.g. Brehm and Rahn 1997; Putnam 2000). Similarly, in China, a six-city survey by Tang Wenfang (2005: Ch. 5) found that social trust helps to promote individual confidence in various national and local governmental institutions. Tang (2005: 114) concluded that "[interpersonal] trust can therefore increase support for the system in democratic as well as non-democratic countries."

Looking at another indicator of popular political views, surveys show that an overwhelming majority of Chinese citizens prioritize social stability and economic prosperity over liberal political freedoms and rights. For example, in 1995–1999 Beijing surveys, Chen Jie (2004: 32) found that "over 90 percent of respondents preferred a stable and orderly society to a freer society that could be prone to disruption." Similarly, in a 1999 multi-city survey conducted by Tang (2005: 72), nearly 60 percent of respondents agreed that "the most important condition for our country's progress is political stability. Democratization under the current conditions would only lead to chaos." Further, when asked to identify their criteria for good government, 48 percent of Tang's respondents chose "economic growth," whereas only 11 percent selected "democratic elections" and 7 percent "individual freedom" (Tang 2005: 70). In a 1995 Beijing survey undertaken by political scientists Daniel Dowd, Allen Carlson, and Shen Mingming, 56 percent of respondents named "national peace and prosperity" as their most important value, whereas only 5.8 percent chose "political democracy" and 6.3 percent "individual freedom" (Dowd et al. 1999: 371). In the 2001 WVS, when respondents were presented with four options, 40 percent chose economic development as the top national priority, and only 5 percent chose "seeing people have more say" in their work or community. In another set of four options, 57 percent chose "maintaining order" as their top priority, 26 percent chose "fighting rising prices," 12 percent chose "seeing people have more say in government," and about 5 percent chose "protecting freedom of speech" (Z. Wang 2006: 234, citing World Values Survey 2001). Additionally, in Tang's 1999 six-city survey, 67 percent of respondents reported being satisfied with their "freedom of speech" (Tang 2005: 60–61).

Concurrently, many Chinese citizens have demonstrated a preference for socialist economic benefits and guarantees. For example, in the 2001

WVS, 52.8 percent responded that "government ownership of business should be increased," as compared with 20.2 percent who believed that "private ownership of business should be increased" (18.3 percent fell in between). When asked in the same survey whether society should pursue the more socialist goal of "extensive welfare" or the more neo-liberal aim of "lower taxes," 47 percent chose "extensive welfare" and 14 percent "lower taxes"; virtually all of the remainder either leaned toward "extensive welfare" (18 percent) or were undecided (14.8 percent) (World Values Survey 2001).[3] Similarly, a late 2004 nationwide survey undertaken by Chunping Han and Martin King Whyte found that "very large majorities ... would like the government to take measures to alleviate poverty and reduce inequality" (Han and King 2008: 13). Preferences for socialist values are especially apparent among those who feel that their socioeconomic status has declined in the reform era. As Tang found in his 1999 six-city survey, "the lower social classes were more anti-Western than others and still adhered to revolutionary ideologies [i.e. Marxism-Leninism and Maoism]" (Tang 2005: 75).[4] Such sentiments have been particularly apparent in the rhetoric of former state-owned enterprise workers who have taken to the streets in protest.

Thus, as of the late 2000s, the overall conclusion of available survey data is clear: despite nearly three decades of dramatic economic reform and growth in China, popular support for the CPC-led political regime is strong and public interest in liberal democratic change appears weak. Further, those at the lower end of China's socioeconomic spectrum display a substantial commitment to socialist economic values.

Political attitudes and behavior by sector

A closer look at the political attitudes and behavior evinced by each of China's major socioeconomic sectors further illustrates these points. These sectors include: private entrepreneurs, professionals, rank-and-file public sector workers, rank-and-file private sector workers, and farmers. Although the political attitudes and behavior found within each group differ in some important respects, all display generally high support for the central authorities.

Private entrepreneurs

Turning first to private entrepreneurs (defined officially as the owners of businesses with eight or more employees), there is little apparent interest in pursuing alternatives to the current political system. To the contrary, a substantial portion of private entrepreneurs has eagerly pursued greater integration in existing party and state entities. Even though private entre-preneurs were officially banned from CPC membership through 2002, since the early 1990s there has been a substantial rise in the percentage of private entrepreneurs who are party members. In a 1991 survey of private entrepreneurs, 7 percent reported being CPC members (Tsai 2007: 77). By 1993, this proportion had nearly doubled, rising to 13 percent. In the latter half of the 1990s, it continued to grow, reaching 18.1 percent in 1997 and 19.9 percent in 2000 (Zhang et al. 2003: 31; Zhang and Liu 1995: 408). After the turn of the millennium, the numbers continued to climb. In 2002, an estimated 29.9 percent were party members, and another 11.1 percent indicated interest in joining (*Lianhe Zhaobao*, cited in Hong 2004: 33). By 2003, the percentage of private entrepreneurs who were party members had risen to nearly 34 percent. Since then, this percentage has remained at roughly the same level (Alpermann and Gang 2008: 6; Tsai 2005: 1140). By way of comparison, as of 2007, only 5.5 percent of the entire population was a CPC member (Xinhua 2007). Indeed, private entrepreneurs have a higher percentage of CPC members per capita than any other social sector (Hong 2004: 33).

Among private entrepreneurs who are party members, from the early 1990s through the present the vast majority joined the CPC prior to en-tering into private business. In surveys conducted in the late 1990s, 25 percent of all private entrepreneurs fit into this category. By 2005, this percentage had risen to just over 34 percent (Dickson 2003: 107; 2007: 838; see also Alpermann and Gang 2008; Zhang et al. 2003). Simultane-ously, the portion of private entrepreneurs joining the party after going into business also has increased, rising from just over 13 percent of pri-vate business owners in 1999 to slightly less than 16 percent in 2005 (Dickson 2007: 838).

Even private entrepreneurs who are not party members have not shown interest in challenging the ruling regime. To the contrary, many have indicated a desire to join it. In Dickson's 2005 survey, for example, nearly 31 percent of private businesspeople without a CPC affiliation had applied to join the party, and over 50 percent expressed interest in be-coming a member (Dickson 2007: 838).

Moreover, it has been suggested that private entrepreneurs who have not sought CPC membership have not been motivated by a desire to dis-tance themselves from the party. Rather, they simply have not felt that it has been worth the effort to join, because CPC membership requires much more than simply signing up. In order to join the party, one must submit a formal application (supported by two sponsors) and undergo a probationary period of assessment. The applicant then must be approved by various levels of the party hierarchy. Further, upon admission, one is required to take part regularly in party meetings and activities and to pay party dues. Given these requirements, many private entrepreneurs who *already* have a close relationship with one or more party members or party-state officials have declined to join the party. With pre-existing political connections, they have viewed party membership as more of a bother than a necessity. As David Goodman reports, when asked in the early 2000s about their lack of membership in the CPC, many private business owners responded: "Why should I join the CPC? I have grown up locally and my (father, mother, or some other relative) was the (village head, county party secretary, or some other local position of leadership)" (Goodman 2004: 159–160). Thus, among private businesspeople who have not attempted to become CPC members, there has been little evidence of antagonism toward the party, and clear indications of a desire to have close connections with it.

In addition, even business owners who have become successful through high-tech and creative efforts that do not rely on political connections have demonstrated little inclination to challenge the political status quo. In one indication of this group's political acquiescence, in 1998, its "dutiful tax payments" "amounted to 2.25 times more than those rendered by all the other private enterprises combined" (Goodman 2004: 159–160, citing *Liaowang Xinwen Zhoukan*, 21 December 2002). Although researchers find that these private entrepreneurs "have deliberately kept their distance from [the] power establishment," high-tech and creative business owners have appeared quite willing to cooperate with it (Goodman 2004: 159–160, citing *Liaowang Xinwen Zhoukan*, 21 December 2002).

Along with joining the party, in the second half of the reform era private entrepreneurs have embedded themselves in the party-state by joining government-sponsored business associations, such as the Self-Employed Laborers' Association, the Private Enterprises' Association, and the Industrial and Commercial Federation (Dickson 2003: 74). These quasi-corporatist organizations are designed both to "maintain state control" over private entrepreneurs and to represent their interests (Dickson 2003: 25). In Dickson's surveys in the late 1990s, nearly 70 percent of private enterprise owners were members of at least one CPC-created business association (Dickson 2003: 74). Similarly, Alpermann's 2002–2004 study of rural private entrepreneurs found that more than 70 percent were members in at least one government-sponsored association. Of those, 63 percent described themselves as "active" participants (Alpermann 2006: 46). Moreover, Dickson's late-1990s surveys showed that private enterprise owners did not perceive any incompatibility between the associations' dual functions of state control and member representation. The reason was that these businesspeople "[saw] themselves as partners, not adversaries of the state" (Dickson 2003: 57).

In addition, in the later portion of the reform era, private entrepreneurs have displayed the belief that local village elections provide private business owners with an attractive opportunity for political participation, thus undercutting their potential desire to seek an alternative political system. Research conducted by political scientist Jianjun Zhang in the early 2000s found that, in some wealthy areas, virtually all candidates for village elections were wealthy private entrepreneurs (Zhang 2007: 427–429). Similarly, Dickson's surveys in 1999 and 2005 reported that roughly 14–16 percent of private enterprise owners had been candidates in village elections (Dickson 2007: 845).[5] In Dickson's 1999 poll, over 40 percent of the private enterprise owners who had been successfully recruited by the party had run in village elections (Dickson 2003: p. 123). Importantly, private entrepreneurs do not appear to see candidacy in village elections as a way to challenge the ruling regime. In Dickson's 1999 survey, nearly 68 percent of private business owners agreed that, if a non-CPC member was elected to a village committee, then he or she should join the CPC (Dickson 2003: 125).

Private entrepreneurs also have displayed substantial interest in joining other state entities. Most importantly, these include: (a) the Chinese People's Political Consultative Conference (CPPCC) and the lower-level Political Consultative Conferences, which represent members of the CPC, members of China's other legal political parties (all of which were allied with the CPC during the party's civil war with the Kuomintang), and individuals without a party affiliation; and (b) the National People's Congress (NPC) and the lower-level People's Committees, which technically serve as the legislative and administrative arms of the state. As of the late 1990s, an estimated 8,500 private entrepreneurs belonged to Political Consultative Conferences at the county level or higher, and 5,400 private entrepreneurs belonged to People's Committees at the county level or higher (He 2003: 90). In addition, Dickson's 1999 and 2005 surveys of private entrepreneurs show that approximately 5 percent had served or were serving on local Political Consultative Conferences (nearly 61 percent of whom also were CPC members), and 10–11 percent had served or were serving on local People's Committees (close to 78 percent of whom also were CPC members) (Dickson 2003: 122; 2007: 844). Citing Chinese media sources, Zhaohui Hong reports that, as of 2002, more than 17 percent of private entrepreneurs were members of the NPC, and just over 35 percent were members of the CPPCC at various levels (*Lianhe Zaobao*, 31 March 2003, cited in Hong 2004: 34). By way of example, the Zhejiang delegation to the 15th NPC in 2003 comprised 78 representatives, of whom 14 (18 percent) were private entrepreneurs (Peng and Liu 2003, cited in Hong 2004: 34). Given that private entrepreneurs comprise less than 1 percent of China's population, their level of participation in these state entities is quite high. Indeed, a 2005 study concluded that, "in some parts of the country, private entrepreneurs already make up a very substantial proportion of the local policy elite" (Lang and Guo 2005, cited in Yang 2006: 157). As these statistics suggest, rather than seeking to change the existing political system, beginning in the early 1990s private businesspeople increasingly have chosen to become part of it. In sum, as the reform era has progressed, China's private entrepreneurs generally have become more supportive of, and embedded in, the existing political system.

Professionals

Professionals form a second major socioeconomic sector in Chinese society. Broadly construed, professionals have "specialized secondary or postsecondary educations" and "perform non-routine white-collar jobs" (Wang et al. 2006: 326). As such, this stratum includes teachers, intellectuals, medical doctors, lawyers, accountants, engineers, and other technical personnel. Because these individuals often are viewed as the kernel of an emergent "middle class" in reform-era China, many believe that they will become champions of democratic political change. Yet, since the early 1990s, educated professionals have displayed a remarkable desire to be part the political establishment and little interest in opposing it.

Unfortunately, little research has been done on the political attitudes and behavior of professionals in contemporary China. Fortunately, however, substantial research has been undertaken on college-educated individuals. Because virtually all professionals have a university or vocational-technical college degree, an examination of the attitudes of China's college-educated population provides a window into the minds of current and future professionals.

Since 1989, China's college-educated population has displayed a reduced desire to challenge the political establishment and a heightened interest in joining it. Whereas there has been a slight decrease in the overall number of young people recruited into the CPC since the early 1990s, the number of *college-educated* youths has climbed substantially (Rosen 2004: p. 169). As political scientist Stanley Rosen notes (2004: 169 and fn 56), the overall percentage of party members under the age of 35 declined slightly in the late reform era, from 23.1 in 1998 to 22.3 in 2000. Meanwhile, the portion of university students who are CPC members rose exponentially – from 0.8 percent in 1990 to nearly 8 percent in 2001 (Rosen 2004: 168 and fn 52). Further, in 2001, an estimated 33 percent of those attending college had applied to join the party (Rosen 2004: 168 and fn 52). Other surveys in the early 2000s have found that "40 percent of students expressed interest in joining the Party, with the number increasing to 50 percent for new students" (Rosen 2004: 169 and fn 56). Among graduate students, 28.2 percent were party members by 2000 (Rosen 2004: 168). In 2007, the official Xinhua news agency proudly proclaimed that, between 2002 and 2007, 32.5 percent of new CPC members were college graduates (Xinhua 2007). Moreover, rather than seeking jobs that are distant from the party-state, many young people have reported "a strong desire" to be employed as a government or party official (Rosen 2004: 170).

Moreover, since the early 1990s, college students have voiced virtually no public political dissent. Although awareness of the brutal crackdown on the demonstrations of 1989 surely has helped to motivate their quiescent behavior, even when opportunities for political dissent have arisen in the post-1989 period, virtually none have indicated any interest. Perhaps mostly notably, when the opposition China Democracy Party formed in 1998, 41 of its top 151 leaders had a college education, but only two of these individuals had entered college in 1990 or later (Wright 2002).

Even so, post-1989 college students are not committed communists. Numerous surveys show that there is no identifiable difference in the ideological orientation of student CPC members and non-members (Guo 2005: 388). For example, "in one survey of over 800 graduating Party and CYL [Communist Youth League] members at 16 universities in Beijing ... only 38 students expressed a belief in communism" (Rosen 2004: 170). Similarly, a "political education instructor at Beijing University ... said that he had never met a student who really believed in communism" (Rosen 2004: 170). To the contrary, many studies indicate that student CPC members are "even more receptive to privatization and capitalism than ordinary students" (Guo 2005: 389).

In sum, from the early 1990s through the present, college-educated individuals have displayed increased interest in joining the existing political establishment and diminished interest in pressing for liberal democratic transformation. To the extent that these individuals also hold jobs as "white-collar" professionals, these political attitudes and behaviors may more generally characterize China's professional sector.

Still, these political attitudes and behaviors are not universal within this group. Since the early 1990s, a small segment of defense lawyers, intellectuals, and journalists have criticized the CPC's repression and called for political, economic, legal, and human rights. The most organized and publicized example was the establishment of the China Democracy Party in the late 1990s. Since then, overt domestic political dissent on the part of professionals has been almost non-existent, yet a small number not only has remained active but also has joined with ordinary citizens in protests (see Goldman 2005).

In addition, among professionals more generally, there have been some cases of disruptive collective actions to contest actions that threaten the quality of the areas around their homes. As local officials have sought to promote development and economic growth (both to increase the government's – and their own – coffers through taxes and kickbacks, and to improve their chances of promotion), they often have approved development projects that impinge upon the quality of life and property values of existing homeowners. Notable examples of homeowner-related protests on the part of professionals include collective actions in 2007–2008 against the extension of Shanghai's high-speed "mag-lev" train, and demonstrations in 2007 in Gulei (Fujian province) and 2008 in Chengdu (Sichuan province) to oppose the construction of petrochemical factories and oil refineries. In addition to these cases, there have been myriad smaller acts of contention regarding the building of roads and the loss of open space in areas in or adjacent to "middle-class" housing developments.

Yet, rather than indicating growing *political* restiveness on the part of China's new "middle class," political scientist Yongshun Cai found that professionals who engage in homeowner-related protests have been overwhelmingly "moderate" and – even while criticizing and opposing local officials – have displayed faith in and support for the central regime. In one example of this mentality, demonstrators raised a banner accusing local authorities of "cheating the premier at the top, and cheating the people at the bottom" (Cai 2005: 792). In addition, they consciously chose strategies and slogans that were legal according to central policy. Although participants stressed that this tactical choice was necessary in order to reduce the likelihood of repression, they also expressed no antagonism toward the ruling regime and no desire for systemic political transformation. Overall, Cai (2005: 798) concludes that, even when China's "middle-class" professionals engage in collective resistance, they "wish to advance their interests without threatening the political order."

Rank-and-file state sector workers

A third major socioeconomic sector comprises rank-and-file workers in the state sector, such as manual laborers in state-owned enterprises (SOEs). Many in this category have suffered greatly since the mid-1990s, when approximately one-third of SOE employees were laid off as a result of large-scale SOE reform (Solinger 2004: 50; Weston 2004: 69). Among them, a substantial number have sunk into poverty, with little hope of financial improvement (Solinger 2004: 50–52). Meanwhile, still-employed state sector workers have experienced cuts in pay and benefits, as well as more exacting and undesirable working conditions.

This reality has bred great dissatisfaction, and in some very notable cases has led state sector workers to rise up in protest. Yet, even at the height of state sector worker unrest in the early 2000s, protestors did not advocate for democratic transformation. To the contrary, disgruntled laid-off SOE workers have aimed their protests at local party-state representatives, and have looked to central elites for protection. As Lee states, former SOE workers have exhibited a "bifurcation of regime legitimacy," such that they have accepted and supported the central authorities, yet have disparaged and risen up in protest against local officials (Lee 2007: 21).

Even the most extensive, lengthy, and conflict-ridden protests by former SOE employees have not featured calls for an end to CPC rule. Rather, most have appealed to central party elites to make good on their socialist promises to the working class. For example, leaders of large-scale protests in the northwestern city of Liaoyang in 2002 "used highly respectful language that in no way challenged the dominance of the Communist Party. Instead, they represented themselves as allies of Party central and as guardians of socialism" (Weston 2004: 75). As the protest leaders wrote in a letter to then CPC General Secretary Jiang Zemin: "Respected and beloved Secretary General Jiang, we do not oppose the leadership of the Party or the socialist system ... [O]ur efforts [are] aimed to help the country ... eliminate all the corrupt worms boring away at and ruining our socialist economic system" (Weston 2004: 75).

It may be that the respectful language of these protestors has been simply a self-protective tactic designed to obscure their true political desires. Yet extensive interviews with disgruntled SOE workers clearly show that, even if these individuals are deeply cynical about CPC rule, their desired outcome has been not the demise of the party but rather its recommitment to the social guarantees, equality, and values of the past. As Lee (2007: 28) reports, the central party-state has been viewed by laid-off SOE workers as "the source of omnipotent power and paternal authority from which flows protection for workers." When these laborers have risen up in protest, they have done so because market reform has "assaulted [their] prevailing sense of justice, worthiness and humanity" (Lee 2007: 24). Further, Lee (2007: 28) explains that, because the "the central government affirms its moral responsibility for protecting [the weak and disadvantaged]," workers have criticized local officials and managers who have failed to do so, and they have seen national leaders as workers' only possible saviors. Overall, Lee (2007: 112) finds that protestors consistently "pledge[ ] their support for socialism and the central leadership ... [C]onspicuously absent in the vast majority of labor protests is any hint of demands for independent unionism or for democratic rights of political participation, or challenges to regime legitimacy. The most politicized demand to date is removal of specific officials, without questioning the system of communist rule."

Rank-and-file private sector workers

A fourth major socioeconomic sector comprises rank-and-file private sector workers. As a stratum that is both large and critical to China's continued economic growth, its political proclivities are likely to shape China's future trajectory. As of the mid-2000s, domestic private businesses accounted for one-third to one-half of China's gross domestic product, employed more than 100 million people, and, together with foreign-invested private firms, provided an estimated 75 percent of employment and 71 percent of Chinese tax revenues (Liu 2007; Xiao 2003; Zhuang 2007). Given this, much credit for China's economic success must be given to the manual laborers who have comprised the vast majority of private sector employees. Among these workers, an extremely high proportion has included migrants from the countryside who hold a rural residential registration card but have moved to China's towns and cities (both legally and illegally) in search of wage employment. In the mid-2000s, China's estimated 131 million rural migrants made up 70–80 percent of China's textile, garment, and construction workers and 37 percent of service sector employees (Boyd 2005: 29; Lee 2007: 6; Lei 2005: 482). Thus, any study of China's rank-and-file private sector employees is simultaneously a study of China's rural migrants.

Since the early 1990s, this sector has displayed a general political quiescence and only limited dissent. To be sure, labor-related grievances have been widespread. They have centered on wage arrears, unwarranted pay reductions, hazardous working and living conditions, and inhumane management practices. Yet, most aggrieved private sector workers have not seen the central regime as their antagonist. Rather, the focus of their ire has been the employer. In a 1996 survey of migrant workers in Shenzhen, 39 percent had expressed their problem directly with their employer, 23 percent had begun a mediation process within the enterprise, 5 percent had quit the enterprise, and 26 percent had given up on resolving the problem (Anon 1996, cited in Thireau and Hua 2003: 84). Further, those who had expressed their complaints in the workplace and had been dissatisfied with the employer's response have not challenged the national government. Rather, most have worked through centrally sponsored legal channels to seek redress, seeing the national government as their protector. In the 1996 Shenzhen study referred to above, 4 percent had gone to arbitration committees, Letters and Visits Offices, or the courts; another 1.5 percent had contacted the local media (Thireau and Hua 2003: 84).[6] By all accounts, the number of workers seeking adjudication through official channels grew dramatically from the mid-1990s onward, as laborers became aware of the more favorable and protective central policies that had been promulgated in the late reform era (Chan 2001: 26). In most cases, both the employee and the employer have been placated, such that, even when aggrieved workers have remained somewhat dissatisfied, their grievances have been ameliorated (Lee 2007: 177).

Although collective action outside of official channels has been relatively rare among unskilled private sector workers, public protests have occurred. Beginning in the mid-1980s, work stoppages and strikes by rank-and-file private sector workers appeared in coastal Special Economic Zones, rising to more than a hundred per year by the early 1990s (Solinger 1999: 284). In 2005–2006, when a shortage of unskilled labor occurred in Guangdong province, the proportion and number of private sector (mainly migrant) worker protests grew further (China Labour Bulletin 2007: 25). Almost universally, however, collective protests have focused on economic and not political matters. Most often, they have raised demands related to pay arrears and deductions – problems that have been especially prevalent among migrant laborers (China Labour Bulletin 2007: 20; Solinger 1999: 284). To give just one notable example, in the spring of 2004, approximately 4,000 workers at two shoe factories owned by the Taiwanese firm Stella International publicly protested. Along with delays in wage payments and forced and uncompensated overtime, employees claimed that deductions for rent and food left them with virtually no income.[7]

Like disgruntled former employees of state-owned enterprises, when aggrieved private enterprise workers such as those at Stella have voiced their complaints, they have indicated a notable belief in the legitimacy and good intentions of the CPC-led regime. Private sector employees submitting complaints to Letters and Visits Offices have referred to central party-state representatives as "comrades," "servants of the people," "uncles," "fair judge," "protective god," and "father and mother of the people." Although such language clearly has reflected a tactical strategy to enhance the chances of a favorable response, most disgruntled private sector workers have viewed the central government as an ally in their cause. As sociologist Isabelle Thireau and historian Linshan Hua (2003: 97) state, complainants generally have assumed that "the government and members of society share similar perspectives on what is just and unjust." For example, most unskilled private sector workers have expressed the belief that the regime's minimum wage standards and rates of compensation for injury and loss are reasonable (Lee 2007: 174). And, although few have displayed a detailed understanding of specific legal provisions, most have referred to national laws to buttress their case, stressing "the distance between what is legal and supposed to be fair and the lived reality" of the aggrieved (Thireau and Hua 2003: 98). Indeed, complaints to Letters and Visits Offices "often depict two types of . . . legal violations: both the workers and the state whose decisions are not obeyed . . . letters contain expressions stating that 'workers' legal rights and interests should be protected as well as the state's dignity." Like aggrieved state sector workers, many also have charged that local officials have not been properly implementing national laws (Thireau and Hua 2003: 99). These views have been widely shared among the migrant workers who have comprised the majority of unskilled private sector workers. In extensive interviews, Lee found that, as with SOE workers, migrant laborers have had a "bifurcated view of the state," wherein a "righteous and legalistic center" is "far removed from corrupt and predatory local agents"(Lee 2007: 201).

Further, rather than rejecting the legitimacy of the party-state, in many cases protesting private sector workers have called for greater integration within it – supporting Dickson's assertion that citizens generally want to be more embedded within the system, rather than autonomous from it. For example, in many public demonstrations, private enterprise employees have voiced the desire to form a factory-level branch of the CPC-affiliated All-China Federation of Trade Unions (China Labour Bulletin 2005; 2007: 27). Similarly, protesting private enterprise workers often have demanded the same protections that the regime affords to workers in the state sector.

Nonetheless, unskilled private sector workers have shown more indifference toward the CPC-led regime than has been the case for private enterprise owners, professionals, and state sector workers. This has been seen perhaps most prominently in their attitudes toward membership in the CPC. Although the party has shown little interest in recruiting unskilled rural migrants, a number of these individuals were party members before they moved to the city. Dickson notes that, as of the late 1990s, 2–3 percent of the migrant population were CPC members and, in more economically developed areas, this percentage reached nearly 10 percent (Dickson 2003: 44). Yet it appears that, once a formerly rural party member goes mobile, his or her political relationship with the party becomes quite attenuated. As Dickson relates, most of these individuals decline to register with the party branch in their new urban neighborhood or workplace, because doing so requires attendance at meetings and study sessions, as well as the payment of dues (Dickson 2003: 44). Consequently, rural migrants who are CPC members generally are so in name only, and they lack any meaningful political relationship – positive or negative – with the party.

Farmers

As the largest socioeconomic sector in China, farmers have great potential political influence. Despite extensive urbanization and migration, as of the end of 2006, 737 million (56 percent) of China's 1.3 billion residents resided in the countryside (Xinhua 2006). Although this marks a dramatic decline in comparison with the early 1990s, China's farming population is expected to drop to no lower than 40 percent by 2030 (*Renmin Ribao* 2006).[8]

Farmer protests have comprised a major portion of the tens of thousands of yearly "mass disturbances" that have occurred in China since the early 1990s. Peasants also have submitted hundreds of thousands of collective petitions to government authorities. Yet, despite their activism, China's farmers have shown little proclivity toward challenging the existing CPC-led political system. As with former SOE employees and rank-and-file private sector workers, farmers have sometimes shown great disdain for local officials yet remarkable trust in the central government. When they have engaged in protest, they have appealed to national leaders to enforce what in the peasants' view are benevolent and well-intentioned laws. Even so, there have been signs that peasant support for the central regime may be declining. Further, relative to other socioeconomic sectors, farmers have appeared more open to fundamental political change.

In 1993, the central authorities reported well over 6,000 cases of "turmoil" in the countryside. In nearly 1,000 of these instances, 500 or more protestors were involved. In all, more than 8,000 deaths occurred, and 200 million *yuan* worth of property was destroyed. In 1995 and 1996, similar waves of peasant uprisings occurred (Bernstein and Lu 2000: 753–754; Bernstein 2004: 3–4). In 1997, nearly 900,000 peasants in nine provinces participated in collective petition efforts and public demonstrations that in many cases involved violent confrontations with the authorities. In 1999 roughly 5 million farmers participated in such political activities, and in 2003 nearly 2 million did so (Bernstein 2004: 3–4). Since 2005, government statistics on the frequency of popular unrest have not been forthcoming, but both official media reports and independent observations suggest that peasant uprisings have remained frequent and widespread.

In addition to street protests, millions have participated in collective petition efforts. Although data since 2006 are not available, the total number of petitions skyrocketed in the first half of the 2000s (*China Daily* 2004). In 2003, the government petition office received over 10 million petitions. In 2005, this number rose to 13 million. Official and scholarly reports estimate that approximately 60 to 80 percent of these petitions were initiated by peasants, and related to land disputes (Yu interview in Zhao 2004).

The content and geographic distribution of peasant grievances shifted over the course of the 1990s and 2000s. Between the early 1990s and the early 2000s, the major peasant concern was excessive taxes. As political scientists Thomas Bernstein and Xiaobo Lu (2000: 753–754) report, dis-content with tax and fee burdens during this period was "widespread and chronic." Because local government exactions were much steeper in central and western provinces than in coastal zones, peasants in the former reported much higher levels of dissatisfaction; they also displayed a much greater proclivity to engage in collective protest actions.[9] Since the tax reforms of the early 2000s, protests and petition efforts revolving around excessive taxation have virtually disappeared, and China's western and central villages have been relatively quiet. Meanwhile, peasant discontent and unrest seem to have increased in China's coastal provinces, where most cases of land requisitions have occurred. In 2004, 87 percent of known cases of rural disturbances reportedly arose from land disputes.[10]

Despite these shifts in grievances and geography, peasants' basic political attitudes were remarkably consistent between the mid-1990s and the late 2000s. In a 2002 survey in five provinces and the municipality of Chongqing by sociologist Ethan Michelson, farmers reported general satisfaction with the ability of local leaders to resolve most basic villager problems (Michelson 2008). Yet when it comes to tax disputes and land requisitions, peasants often have expressed grave discontent with local authorities. In these cases, farmers have insisted that their outrage is not simply caused by the material hardship that local government actions have caused. Rather, their dissatisfaction has derived from their view that tax and land revenues have gone almost entirely into the pockets of local political leaders and their cronies.

Meanwhile, peasants have displayed faith in the central government. In surveys conducted by political scientist Lianjiang Li between 1999 and 2001, a substantial majority of villagers expressed the belief that the national government was well intentioned but that, when it came to tax disputes, the local authorities thwarted the capacity of the center to implement its benevolent policies. As a farmer engaged in tax protests in the late 1990s stated: "Damn those sons of bitches [township and village cadres]! The Center lets us ordinary people have good lives; all central policies are very good. But these policies are all changed when they reach lower levels. It's entirely their fault. They do nothing good, spending their whole day wining and dining. The only thing they don't forget is to collect money" (Zhu 1999, cited in O'Brien and Li 2006: 43). Myriad studies and interviews have uncovered an identical frame of mind among rural protestors. Indeed, research on rural tax and land conflicts universally has concluded that what has encouraged peasants to undertake collective action in the first place has been their belief that local authorities have not been implementing central policies designed to protect peasants' interests (Guo 2005; O'Brien and Li 2006; Xiao 2003). Relatedly, O'Brien and Li's 2003–2004 survey found that 78 percent of respondents agreed or strongly agreed that "the Center is willing to listen to peasants who tell the truth and welcomes our complaints," and 87 percent agreed or strongly agreed that "the Center supports peasants in defending their lawful rights and interests" (O'Brien and Li 2006: 45).

Still, compared with other socioeconomic groups, peasant support for the CPC-led political system has appeared weak. First, farmers have shown relatively little interest in joining the CPC or participating in its affiliated organizations. As of 2006, only 3.07 percent of those living in the countryside were party members, as opposed to 8.9 percent of urban residents.[11] Further, farmers have appeared more likely than other socioeconomic sectors to believe that "the well-being of the country should depend on the masses instead of state leaders" (Yang 2006: 203). When they feel wronged, peasants have reported less reluctance than urban residents to argue with the political authorities. In addition, farmers have shown more support for free-market capitalism and a greater belief in core democratic values such as free and fair elections and freedom of speech and expression (Yang 2006: 194, 200, 203, 207; Bernstein and Lu 2000: 759).

The future trajectory of peasants' political attitudes and behavior may depend on the extent to which the central regime succeeds in promoting mechanisms within the existing political system that satisfactorily address peasant grievances. Important in this regard is the degree to which village elections are meaningful. As political scientist Melanie Manion finds, high-quality local elections seem to promote both public trust in government and government trustworthiness (Manion 2006: 319). Although Kevin O'Brien and Rongbin Han note that procedural improvements have been more impressive than have been changes in the actual exercise of power, free and fair village elections do seem to have become more prevalent over time (O'Brien and Han 2009). To the extent that this trend continues, one might expect that peasant support for the existing political system will only rise in the future. Of course, to the degree that meaningful local elections become the norm in China, the political system will in reality be more democratic than is currently the case.

Similarly, the perceived responsiveness of the petition and hearing systems is important. Christopher Heurlin and Susan Whiting's 2005 survey of 17 provinces found that, in 68 percent of petition cases (virtually all of which concerned land compensation), the government either refused to increase the peasants' compensation (36 percent) or took no action at all (32 percent) (Heurlin and Whiting 2007: 20; Li 2008). Li's 2003–2005 survey of villagers in two provinces uncovered even more disturbing results: over 60 percent of petitioners had been subjected to one or more forms of local repression, including being subjected to fines (28.2 percent); having their homes demolished or destroyed (21.8 percent); having their homes ransacked, properties confiscated, and valuables taken away (31.4 percent); being beaten, or having their family members beaten (46.8 percent); and being detained, arrested, and sent to labor camps (41.1 percent). Still, in Li's survey roughly 40 percent reported satisfaction with the result of their petitioning effort (Li 2008). In Heurlin and Whiting's research, among the 32 percent of cases where petitions resulted in increased compensation, 12 percent of respondents were satisfied with the amount (2007: 20).

Not surprisingly, Li found that peasants who have had good experiences with petitioning have expressed increased trust in the central government, whereas those with bad experiences have displayed diminished faith in and lowered support for the ruling regime.[12] Interestingly, regardless of a person's assessment of the outcome, those who had petitioned the central authorities in Beijing reduced diminished trust in the national regime. As a whole, these petitioners were roughly 31 percent less likely than other peasants to agree that the center truly cared about farmers, nearly 41 percent were less likely to agree that the center welcomed farmers to petition, and approximately 47 percent were less likely to agree that petitioning Beijing was very useful (Li 2008). Thus, even though beneficent national laws and pronouncements have encouraged peasants to take action within existing political structures, when their efforts have come to naught they have become disillusioned with the political system as a whole. As one petitioner relates: "when we returned [home], seven of us were detained for a few weeks. It's useless to seek justice. Opposing graft and corruption means time in prison. There is no place to look for justice" (Li 2004: 247).

For some, the response has been despair. Among Li's respondents, more than 13 percent of unsuccessful petitioners said that they would give up. But for most others, the reaction has been rage and determination (O'Brien and Li 2006: Ch. 4). In Li's survey, roughly 82 percent of failed petitioners said that they would continue petitioning until their goals were achieved; approximately 74 percent asserted that they would publicize policies and mobilize the masses to defend their lawful rights; slightly more than 45 percent said that they would "do something that cadres would be afraid of"; and nearly 56 percent said that they would establish an organization to defend farmers' lawful rights (Li 2008). Some even expressed the desire to bring down the regime (although this was not common). In the words of one peasant whose repeated collective petition efforts had failed: "If we do not get the expected response in a given period of time, then we will go all out to mobilize the masses to struggle for peasant's right to life and democratic rights by starting a democratic revolutionary movement" (Li 2004: 247; see also Cao 2000: 253).

It must be emphasized that the vast majority of peasants in the late reform era have not petitioned the government or engaged in protests. As of the mid-2000s, only about 1.4 percent of China's rural residents undertook petition efforts, and only 0.25 percent participated in public "disturbances."[13] Yet to the extent that these actions continue to rise and the government's response is not seen as satisfactory, peasant discontent may be expected to become more widespread and deeper. Given that most unsuccessful petitioners have not given up but rather have continued their activism – often in a more confrontational way – peasant-based challenges to the ruling regime are likely to increase.

Into the future

Looking at Chinese society as a whole, it seems clear that China's economic liberalization and growth since the early 1990s have not led to public dissatisfaction with the central government. To the contrary, public trust in the national political system is strong, especially when compared with other, even democratic, countries. Even so, popular political attitudes are never static and, in China as elsewhere, are likely to change.

One factor that is most certain to change is the public's memory of China's socialist economy prior to the reform era. As of 2008, individuals who are under 30 years of age have had no direct experience of the Maoist economic system. They comprise slightly more than 43 percent of the total population, but less than 20 percent of the adult population.[14] By 2050, they will make up virtually the entire population. As this demographic shift takes place, the effect of China's socialist legacies on the political attitudes and behavior of the public will fade and eventually disappear. When the quasi-capitalist system of the reform era becomes the only lived experience of China's citizenry, the populace will no longer judge the performance of the current economic system against that of China's Maoist past. The public also will be less likely to expect the socioeconomic security and benefits that the ruling regime offered in the pre-reform period.

The precise impact of this generational change on the political attitudes and behavior of the Chinese populace is difficult to predict. Surveys conducted in the late 1990s by Chen (2004) and Tang (2005) found, that as the age of the respondent declined, support for the ruling regime was lower, and openness to liberalization and democratization was higher. Yet researchers also find a significantly higher level of nationalism among young people. Importantly, as seen in Chinese students' emotional opposition to criticism of China's Tibet policy in conjunction with the 2008 Beijing Olympics, this nationalism often coincides with a distrust of the West and a belief that powerful countries such as the United States press China to liberalize its political system in order to weaken China's international reputation and strength. Thus, even while there appear to be signs of greater interest in democracy and somewhat diminished faith in the national government, there is little to indicate that China's citizens are moving toward a greater embrace of the political systems that are dominant in the West.

Notes

1. Official sources counted 87,000 "disturbances to public order" in 2005, up from 74,000 in 2004, 58,000 in 2003, and 10,000 in 1996 (I. Wang 2006). Figures from 2006 to the present have not been made available.
2. In the United States, 37.8 percent of 2000 WVS respondents expressed confidence in the government, and 38.1 percent expressed confidence in Congress.
3. At the same time, it should be noted that, on questions asking respondents to value "egalitarianism" v. "competition" and "people should take more responsibility" v. "the government should take more responsibility," the responses were almost evenly mixed.
4. It is important to emphasize that this adherence to socialist economic values does not mean that workers and other citizens wish to return to the state-planned economy of the past.
5. It should be noted that this percentage declined slightly between 1999 and 2005 in Dickson's surveys.
6. Thireau and Hua (2003: 89–90) note that the vast majority of unskilled private enterprise workers who lodged complaints with government offices went to Letters and Visits Offices. Meanwhile, workers who were educated and skilled, or were affiliated with the state sector, were more likely to approach arbitration committees. In large part, this difference resulted from manual private sector workers' lack of resources, as arbitration costs nearly four times their mean monthly wage, whereas submitting a complaint with a Letters and Visits Office is free.
7. When some machinery and other items belonging to the factory were damaged in the course of the protest, several dozen employees were arrested – including two 16-year-old workers who had been under-aged when hired. As a result of the help of a lawyer hired by China Labour Bulletin (a labor activist group based in Hong Kong), as well as domestic media coverage that was sympathetic to the workers, Stella expressed its "sadness" at the detention of the workers, who were ultimately released (China Labour Bulletin 2004; 2007: 20–24; see also Albert Shanker Institute 2008: 46–54).
8. In 1990, 74 percent of China's citizens were rural residents; in 2001, 64 percent lived in rural areas (Xinhua 2006). Rural residents earn income from a variety of sources, but virtually all are engaged in agriculture. As of 2000, 70 percent did not earn a regular income from non-farm wage labor, and only 2.5 percent had registered individual family enterprises (China Agricultural Bureau 2001: 95; China Statistical Bureau 2000: 369).
9. In a 2002 survey of rural households in six provinces, Michelson (2007: 475) found that 85–90 percent of villagers in the central provinces of Hunan and Henan reported at least one grievance, as opposed to only 22–26 percent of villagers in coastal Shandong

and Jiangsu provinces. On the geographic distribution of collective disputes in the 1990s and early 2000s, see Bernstein and Lu (2003).

10. Peasants' major complaints are that land is illegally or forcibly confiscated, or that compensation is too low (Yu interview, in Zhao 2004).

11. In 2006, of a total of 73 million CCP members, an estimated 50.37 million (69 percent) were urban residents and 22.6 million (31 percent) were rural residents. The total urban population in 2006 was roughly 563 million, and the total rural population was roughly 727 million.

12. In Li's survey, successful petitioners became 45.7 percent more likely to agree that the central government truly cared about farmers and 63.7 percent were more likely to agree that petitioning Beijing was very useful. Conversely, "local repression had a negative correlation with trust in the Center" (Li 2008).

13. If one assumes that 80 percent of the petitions submitted in 2005 related to land disputes (and therefore were initiated by peasants), then some 10.4 million of China's 737 million peasants submitted a petition. In 2003, about 2 million of China's approximately 800 million population participated in public protests.

14. As of 2007, 22.8 percent of the population were between the ages of 15 and 29.

REFERENCES

Albert Shanker Institute (2008) *A Cry for Justice: The Voices of Chinese Workers*. Washington DC: Albert Shanker Institute. Available at: <http://www.shankerinstitute.org/acryforjusticefinal.pdf> (accessed 3 February 2010).

Alpermann, Bjorn (2006) "Wrapped up in Cotton Wool: Political Integration of Private Entrepreneurs in Rural China," *China Journal* 56, pp. 33–61.

Alpermann, Bjorn, and Shuge Gang (2008) "Social Origins and Political Participation of Private Entrepreneurs in Beijing," unpublished paper.

Bernstein, Thomas (2004) "Unrest in Rural China: A 2003 Assessment," Center for the Study of Democracy Paper 13, University of California, Irvine.

Bernstein, Thomas, and Xiaobo Lu (2000) "Taxation without Representation: Peasants, the Central and the Local States in Reform China," *China Quarterly* 163, pp. 742–763.

Bernstein, Thomas, and Xiaobo Lu (2003) *Taxation without Representation in Contemporary Rural China*. Cambridge: Cambridge University Press.

Boyd, Mary (2005) "Migrant Labour Mechanisms: The Down and Dirty," *China Economic Quarterly* Q3.

Brehm, John, and Wendy Rahn (1997) "Individual-level Evidence for the Causes and Consequences of Social Capital," *American Journal of Political Science* 41, pp. 999–1023.

Cai, Yongshun (2005) "China's Moderate Middle Class: The Case of Homeowners' Resistance," *Asian Survey* 45:5, pp. 777–799.

Cao, Jinqing (2000) *Huanghe biande Zhongguo* [China along the Yellow River]. Shanghai: Shanghai wenyi chubanshe.

Chan, Anita (2001) *China's Workers under Assault: The Exploitation of Labor in a Globalizing Economy*. Armonk, NY: M. E. Sharpe.

Chen Jie (2004) *Popular Political Support in Urban China*. Palo Alto, CA: Stanford University Press.

Chen Jie and Lu Chunlong (2007) "Social Capital in Urban China: Attitudinal and Behavioral Effects on Grassroots Self-Government," *Social Science Quarterly* 88:2, pp. 422–442.

China Agricultural Bureau (2001) *Zhongguo xiangzhen qiye nianjian 2001* [China Rural Enterprise Yearbook 2001]. Beijing: Zhongguo nongye chubanshe [China Agricultural Bureau Press].

China Daily (2004) "The Land Beneath Their Feet," March 16.

China Labour Bulletin (2004) "Release and Sentence Reductions for Stella Shoe Factory Workers," January 10, <http://www.china-labour.org.hk/en/node/4072> (accessed 3 February 2010).

China Labour Bulletin (2005) "Xianyang Textile Workers Detained for Leading Historic Seven-week Strike Are Released," April 20, <http://www.china-labour.org.hk/en/node/8357> (accessed 3 February 2010).

China Labour Bulletin (2007) "Speaking Out: The Workers Movement in China (2005–2006)," CLB Research Report No. 5, December. Available at <http://www.clb.org.hk/en/files/File/research_reports/Worker_Movement_Report_final.pdf> (accessed 3 February 2010).

China Statistical Bureau (2000) *Zhongguo tongji nianjian 2000* [China Statistical Yearbook 2000]. Beijing: Zhongguo tongji chubanshe [China Statistical Bureau Press].

Dickson, Bruce (2003) *Red Capitalists in China*. Cambridge: Cambridge University Press.

Dickson, Bruce (2007) "Integrating Wealth and Power," *China Quarterly* 192, pp. 827–854.

Dowd, Daniel, Allen Carlson and Shen Mingming (1999) "The Prospects for Democratization in China: Evidence from the 1995 Beijing Area Study," *Journal of Contemporary China* 8:22, pp. 365–381.

East Asian Barometer (2002) Available at: <http://www.jdsurvey.net/bdasepjds/easiabarometer/eab.jsp> (accessed 3 February 2010).

Goldman, Merle (2005) *From Comrade to Citizen*. Cambridge, MA: Harvard University Press.

Goodman, S. G. David (2004) "Localism and Entrepreneurship: History, Identity and Solidarity as Factors of Production," in Barbara Krug (ed.) *China's Rational Entrepreneurs: The Development of the New Private Business Sector*. New York: Routledge.

Guo, Gang (2005) "Party Recruitment of College Students in China," *Journal of Contemporary China*, 14:43, pp. 371–393.

Han, Chunping, and Martin King Whyte (2008) "The Social Contours of Distributive Injustice Feelings in Contemporary China," in D. Davis and F. Wang (eds) *Creating Wealth and Poverty in Contemporary China*. Palo Alto, CA: Stanford University Press.

He, Li (2003) "Middle Class: Friends or Foes to Beijing's New Leadership," *Journal of Chinese Political Science* 8, pp. 87–100.

Hong, Zhaohui (2004) "Mapping the Evolution and Transformation of the New Capital Holders in China," *Journal of Chinese Political Science* 9:1.

Heurlin, Christopher, and Susan Whiting (2007) "Villagers against the State: The Politics of Land Disputes," paper presented at the annual meeting of the American Political Science Association, Chicago, IL, August 30.

Lee, Ching Kwan (2007) *Against the Law.* Berkeley: University of California Press.

Li, Lianjiang (2004) "Political Trust in Rural China," *Modern China* 30:2, pp. 228–258.

Li, Lianjiang (2008) "Political Trust and Petitioning in the Chinese Countryside," *Comparative Politics* 40:2, pp. 209–226.

Liu Haoting (2007) "Private Firms Propel Innovation," *China Daily,* September 6.

Manion, Melanie (2006) "Democracy, Community, Trust: The Impact of Elections in Rural China," *Comparative Political Studies* 39:3, pp. 301–324.

Michelson, Ethan (2007) "Climbing the Dispute Pagoda: Grievances and Appeals to the Official Justice System in Rural China," *American Sociological Review* 72, pp. 461–485.

Michelson, Ethan (2008) "Justice from Above or Below? Popular Strategies for Resolving Grievances in Rural China," *China Quarterly* 193, pp. 43–64.

O'Brien, Kevin, and Rongbin Han (2009) "Path to Democracy? Assessing Village Elections in China," *Journal of Contemporary China* 18:60, pp. 359–378.

O'Brien, Kevin, and Lianjiang Li (2006) *Rightful Resistance in Rural China.* Cambridge: Cambridge University Press.

Peng Cong and Liu Lantao (2003) "Zhongguo fuhao zai renda" [Wealthy Chinese in the People's Congress], *Mingxin Caixun,* June 27.

Putnam, Robert (2000) *Bowling Alone.* New York: Simon & Schuster.

Renmin Ribao [People's Daily] (2006) "Urbanization is Reducing China's Rural Population," February 23.

Rosen, Stanley (2004) "The State of Youth/Youth and the State in Early 21st-century China: The Triumph of the Urban Rich?" in P. Gries and S. Rosen (eds) *State and Society in 21st Century China.* New York: Routledge, pp. 159–179.

Solinger, Dorothy (1999) *Contesting Citizenship in Urban China.* Berkeley: University of California Press.

Solinger, Dorothy (2004) "The New Crowd of the Dispossessed," in P. Gries and S. Rosen (eds) *State and Society in 21st Century China.* New York: Routledge, pp. 50–66.

Tang Wenfang (2005) *Public Opinion and Political Change in China.* Stanford, CA: Stanford University Press.

Thireau, Isabelle, and Linshan Hua (2003) "The Moral Universe of Aggrieved Chinese workers," *China Journal* 50, pp. 83–103.

Tsai, Kellee (2005) "Capitalists without a Class," *Comparative Political Studies* 38:9, pp. 1130–1158.

Tsai, Kellee (2007) *Capitalism without Democracy: The Private Sector in Contemporary China.* Ithaca, NY: Cornell University Press.

Wang, I. (2006) "Incidents of Social Unrest Hit 87,000," *South China Morning Post,* 20 January.

Wang, Shaoguang, Deborah Davis, and Yanjie Bian (2006) "The Uneven Distribution of Cultural Capital: Book Reading in Urban China," *Modern China* 32, pp. 315–348.

Wang, Zhengxu (2006) "Explaining Regime Strength in China," *China: An International Journal* 4:2, pp. 217–237.

Weston, Timothy B. (2004) "The Iron Man Weeps: Joblessness and Political Legitimacy in the Chinese Rust Belt," in P. Gries and S. Rosen (eds) *State and Society in 21st Century China*. New York: Routledge, pp. 67–86.

WorldPublicOpinion.org (2008) *World Public Opinion on Governance and Democracy*, Program on International Policy Attitudes, University of Maryland, May 13. Available at: <http://www.worldpublicopinion.org/pipa/pdf/may08/WPO_Governance_May08_packet.pdf (accessed 3 February 2010).

World Values Survey (2001) Available at: <http://www.worldvaluessurvey.org/> (accessed 3 February 2010).

Wright, Teresa (2002) "The China Democracy Party and the Politics of Protest in the 1980's–1990's," *China Quarterly* 172, pp. 906–926.

Xiao Tangbiao (2003) Ershinian lai dalu nongcun de zhengzhi wending zhangkuang [The Stable Conditions of Mainland Peasants During the Last 20 Years], *Ershiyi Shiji* [The 21st Century] 4.

Xinhua (2006) "NBS: China's Rural Population Shrinks to 56% of Total," 22 October.

Xinhua (2007) "Number of CPC Members Increases by 6.4 Million over 2002," *China Daily*, 8 October.

Yang, Dali (2006) "Economic Transformation and Its Political Discontents in China," *Annual Review of Political Science* 9, pp. 143–164.

Zhang, Houyi and Wenpu Liu (1995) *Zhongguo de siying jingji yu siying qiye zhu* [Chinese Private Economy and Private Entrepreneurs]. Beijing: Zhishi Chubanshe.

Zhang, Houyi, Ming Zhili, and Liang Zhuanyun (eds) (2003) *Zhongguo siying qiye fazhan baogao* [Blue Book of Private Enterprises] 4 (2002). Beijing: Shehui Kexue Wensian Chubanshe.

Zhang, Jianjun (2007) "Marketization, Class Structure, and Democracy in China: Contrasting Regional Experiences," *Democratization* 14:3, pp. 425–445.

Zhao, Ling (2004) "Significant Shift in Focus of Peasants' Rights Activism: An Interview with Rural Development Researcher Yu Jianrong of the Chinese Academy of Social Sciences." Available at: <http://www.chinaelections.net/newsinfo.asp?newsid=3123> (accessed 3 February 2010).

Zhuang, Congsheng (2007) "New Social Strata Has a Vital Role to Play," *China Daily*, October 16.

8

Building trust in government in the Republic of Korea: The case of the National Tax Service reforms

Byong Seob Kim

The purpose of this chapter is to explain how government innovation has improved trust in South Korean governments. For this purpose, I first describe why the Roh Moo-hyun administration (2003–2008) emphasized "principle and trust" as a vision for government innovation. I then present a case study of the National Tax Service reform. Finally, I suggest policy implications in terms of improving trust in government.

Why emphasize trust in government?

It has been shown that trust affects the accomplishment of organizational goals, job satisfaction, and motivation (Dwivedi 1983: 375–376, 381–384). Because trust is sometimes viewed as having a close relationship with national growth or economic prosperity, it is social capital that is considered to enable members of society to confide in each other and form new groups and gatherings (Fukuyama 1995). In addition, more and more researchers have proven that trust in government improves the level of public policy acceptance and reduces administrative costs, while encouraging compliance with laws and regulations (Ayres and Braithwaite 1992; Levi 1997, 1998; Tyler 1990, 1998). Thus, increasing trust in government is becoming an important goal in order for central and local governments

Building trust in government: Innovations in governance reform in Asia, Cheema and Popovski (eds), United Nations University Press, 2010, ISBN 978-92-808-1189-6

to implement their policy measures effectively and so to realize good governance.

However, recent surveys have shown that trust in government has been declining worldwide. In the United States, for example, almost 75 percent of respondents in a survey in 1958 said they trusted the federal government "to do what is right" most of the time or just about always. In 2002, confidence in the government was professed by only 40 percent of respondents (Donovan and Bowler 2004: 17–18). In Europe, the results of the 2004 Eurobarometer survey of 25 European Union member countries showed that two-thirds of respondents did not trust government. Among 15 institutions, government ranked thirteenth, followed by conglomerates and political parties. The survey also revealed a big gap, with confidence in the military, the press, the police, and charity and volunteer organizations all positioned in the top four (Eurobarometer 2004: 10). The decline seems to be a general trend and, regarding it as a government failure, each country is pursuing administrative reform in numerous ways to reverse the trend.

Because South Korea is making a big effort to progress to being a leading nation in the twenty-first century, public confidence in government is becoming more and more important as the major social capital on which national competitiveness and high-morale cosmopolitanism are based. South has had a long history of showing exclusive trust in an "in-group," which is based on personal connections or various personal ties such as kinship and regionalism, while an "out-group" or "between-group" has been relatively belittled, leading to a very low level of social trust. The exclusiveness is perceived to be a legacy of Confucian culture, which emphasizes vertical relationships such as the ones between father and son, ruler and ruled, elder and younger. This legacy, combined with a highly authoritarian political system in which centralized and regulated power is held by a few policymakers, naturally encouraged corruption as the Korean economy experienced explosive growth, steered by the state in conjunction with big business groups for the past 40 years. The coalition between the state and the conglomerates (called *chaebols*) revealed its corrupt nature even in relation to presidents. In particular, powerful state organizations such as the National Tax Service and the Prosecutor's Office were more inclined towards corruption, leading to various scandals. This type of scandal, or "gates" as they are known, was pervasive during the previous Kim Dae-jung administration (1998–2003), and damaged public confidence in government.

Against this background, the Roh Moo-hyun administration, also known as the "Participatory Government," set "principle and trust" as a top priority in its governing philosophy.

Case study: National Tax Service reform

Why the National Tax Service case?

During the twentieth century, the modernization of South Korea was carried out through a top-down approach. The reforms, which were based on the country's underlying legacy of Confucian governance, created an unbalanced institutionalization of governance systems by expanding bureaucracy and restraining democracy. The so-called "developmental state," which is an Asiatic form of the administrative state, paved the way for state-led rapid industrialization up to the 1980s (Jung 2006). In the process, corruption was prevalent owing to excessive regulation governing administrative authority such as the issuance of permits and licenses. Presidential candidates solicited election campaign funds from big businesses with promises of privileged business opportunities. Police officers received bribes for giving traffic violators breaks. The major examples of political corruption were the Slush Fund scandal during the Roh Tae-woo administration (1988–1993) and "Hanbo-gate" during the Kim Young-sam administration (1993–1998). In both cases, tycoons bribed major bureaucrats or the head of the state in exchange for favors. Furthermore, in preparation for the upcoming presidential campaign, the ruling party mobilized the National Tax Service and collected a campaign fund of 16.93 billion won from 23 *chaebols* in a scandal called the Sepoong Affair. As a result of these scandals, South Korea was caught up in the 1997 foreign currency crisis, leading to supervision by the International Monetary Fund (IMF).

Even at a time of major restructuring and government reform implemented to overcome the crisis, "Fur-gate" was revealed in 1999 after the Kim Dae-jung administration took office. The scandal involved the wife of the former chief prosecutor, who had accepted a fur coat and other expensive items from the wife of a tycoon. Even worse, the number of "gates" increased between 2000 and 2002: Lee Yongho Gate, the Jin Seung-hyun Affair, the Chung Hyun-joon Scandal, the Kim Hong-gul and Kim Hong-up Scandal. The last one involved the two sons of the incumbent president, who were found guilty of accepting bribes for influence-peddling. Many more scandals were uncovered in the Kim Dae-jung administration.

As these scandals came to light, civic groups and citizens voiced their displeasure. For example, there was a move to impeach the incumbent chief prosecutor after a scandal involving his younger brother was disclosed in December 2001; a movement for the establishment of a law against corruption was promulgated later in 2001; and an anti-corruption government body was established in 2002. At the same time, civil society demanded a fair and transparent tax administration. It is notable that the increase in the number of scandals and active citizen participation in political matters is closely linked with the degree of democracy, as shown in Freedom House measures of the degree of democracy in the Republic of Korea, which declined over this period (Freedom House n.d.).

During the military regime between 1963 and 1993, civil status and political rights were suppressed by the authoritarian government. The mass media were monitored and the National Intelligence Service wielded significant power over people. Thus, scandals involving power-holders could not be disclosed at that time. In fact, the political environment was incapable of nurturing any growth in civil society. From this perspective, the fact that many scandals were exposed during the Kim administration does not necessarily mean that it was any more corrupt than previous administrations. Rather, the active participation of civil society in politics indicated that Korean society was being increasingly democratized.

In response to demands by civic groups and civilian experts, the presidential candidate at that time, Roh Moo-hyun, pledged reform of both the National Tax Service and the Prosecutor's Office. Roh was elected with their full support.

The following section presents a brief history of the tax administration and the current drive to increase taxpayers' participation and transparency in the tax administration. Finally, the effect of the reform is evaluated by focusing on the Cash Receipt system.

Analysis of the process of reform

During the Japanese colonial period, tax evasion was regarded as a virtue, and people who evaded taxes by escaping scrutiny and investigation by the tax authorities were considered to be patriotic. The national tax administration at that time involved the tax authorities directly contacting taxpayers in order to identify sources of tax revenue and continuously probing to uncover cases of tax evasion.

This public view of taxes continued long after South Korea achieved independence in 1945. When private capital proved to be far from sufficient to finance the state-led economic development that began in the 1960s, the government turned to public capital to fund the project, which required huge financial resources. However, the absence of a culture of voluntary tax compliance only reinforced the practice of tax officials coming into constant contact with taxpayers and tightly monitoring and scrutinizing tax evasions.

If anything, such methods of direct taxpayer contact exposed many problems with the way taxes were administered. In particular, trying to detect and monitor potential sources of tax revenue using a limited number of resources and through direct engagement with taxpayers not only proved inefficient, but made tax evasion a commonplace occurrence. Because taxes were assessed more or less at the discretion of the tax inspector, corruption was to some extent inevitable. It was widely believed by the public that tax officials were "corrupt." The inequitable and unfair system under which some were subject to taxation while others were not only deepened taxpayer mistrust of the national tax administration.

In these circumstances, as social democratization progressed and taxpayers became increasingly aware of their rights, people began to demand transparency in the administration of taxes, fair taxation, and integrity of tax officials. Many reform measures were implemented after the National Tax Service (NTS) of the Republic of Korea was established in 1966, but the most notable are the two measures that will be discussed here.

First of all, in 1999, the NTS underwent a sweeping reform of its organization and function. It was deeply engrained in people's minds at the time that taxes were one of the greatest areas of corruption, so that replacing an institutional instrument in order to root corruption out became a top priority. Although the previous system, based tax types, did have the merit of providing efficient enforcement of the tax laws (a single officer was assigned to a specific "zone" to oversee all tax-related functions, from business registration, to tax returns, to tax audits, to tax collection, to appeals), its structure was inherently vulnerable to corruption and collusive links, which affected the credibility of the tax administration. The specific reform steps were as follows:

1. The organization and function of the national tax administration was completely restructured. District tax offices previously organized around tax types were restructured around functions, such as collection, compliance management, and auditing. The zone management system was abolished in the process, and direct contact with taxpayers was greatly restricted.
2. All areas of the administrative procedure were routinized with manuals, and a computer system was set up to manage compliance.
3. An infrastructure for tax-related social data was set up. In particular, the year 2000 saw the introduction of a system that grants partial income deductions for sums paid with a credit card, and of a credit card lottery system, which gave out lottery prizes. This helped improve the disclosure of income earned in consumer-focused industries. As a result, the rate of credit card payments, which remained flat at around 10 percent of private spending in 1999, increased to 45.7 percent in 2002, contributing greatly to revealing the income earned by the self-employed.

The next significant reform came during the Roh Moo-hyun administration. Although the NTS had since 1999 undergone a sweeping reform in the administration of taxes, with a focus on service improvement and the elimination of corruption, public mistrust persisted.

Although the tax administration environment was experiencing rapid changes brought about by advances in information technologies (IT) and increased taxpayer demands for service diversification, the tax administration system relating to tax returns, tax collection, and tax audits was designed around direct contact with taxpayers. Taxpayers for their part felt secure only through the practice of meeting face to face with the competent tax authority to resolve tax issues. Accordingly, the Participatory Government focused the reform on establishing a system that fundamentally precludes opportunities for tax officials to come into direct contact with taxpayers.

First, the Home Tax Service (first implemented in 2002) underwent a structured upgrade to become a cutting-edge provider of e-tax administration, which meant that taxpayers no longer had to go to the tax office or meet with a tax official to file tax returns.

Second, on the assumption that mistrust of the tax administration arises during the course of a tax audit, a series of measures were implemented to rebuild trust in tax audits and to enhance audit transparency and objectivity. The measures include: abolishing intensive tax audits; disclosing audit selection criteria; dividing the audit function into "selection" and "execution"; and reducing the number and duration of tax audits.

Such reform measures notwithstanding, by far the most remarkable accomplishment was the introduction of the world's first Cash Receipt system in 2005. As already mentioned, substantially more income was brought to light through the increased use of credit cards, but, in a situation where cash transactions still accounted for over half of all private consumption, it was only "half a success." Koreans are well known for traditionally preferring to pay in cash and not asking for a receipt. This penchant for not leaving traces of transactions significantly undermined social transparency and security. Financial resources accumulated through under-the-table cash transactions do not come out in the open to be incorporated into the normal economic system, but tend to flow back again into activities that destabilize society and stunt sound economic growth, such as illegal transactions, bribery, wastefulness, pleasure-seeking, gambling, and real estate speculation.

Cash transactions also make it difficult to identify income earned by the self-employed. This creates a tax burden inequity, with wage-earners dubbed the "glass wallet." The issue of tax burden inequality, coupled with social polarization that worsened in the aftermath of the 1997 economic crisis, created tension between the different social classes. In a situation where the cash transactions of the self-employed fail to be captured as taxable income, public distrust of the national tax administration remained, because it meant that there was always room for a tax official to abuse his or her discretion or to engage in corrupt dealings with the taxpayer. On top of that, an increase in household debt and the credit crisis that followed the 1997 financial meltdown made it impossible to depend solely on the credit card policy.

In the end, in order to enhance social transparency, economic soundness, taxation fairness, and trust in the tax administration, it became imperative that cash transactions be detected. The question was how to keep tabs on the millions of cash transactions that occur on a daily basis among the almost 2 million businesses and over 20 million consumers. With the launch of the Participatory Government, it was determined that the "Cash Receipt system" would be pursued as the government's reform task. On January 1, 2005, after almost a year of preparations, the NTS launched the Cash Receipt system (the first of its kind in the world) – full of hopes that it would not only resolve inequities in the tax burden but also help in achieving social transparency and constructing the future of an advanced and harmonious South Korea.

Overview of the Cash Receipt system

1. When making a purchase in cash at a "registered store" (a store that has installed a device for issuing cash receipts), a consumer presents his or her means of identification (Cash Receipt Card issued by the NTS, credit card, cell phone number, or resident ID number).
2. The (registered) store enters the consumer ID into the receipt-issuing device (which is installed by embedding a cash receipt chip in a credit card reader) and a cash receipt is issued. The transaction is recorded and sent to a Cash Receipt operator, who then passes it on to the NTS.
3. The information gathered is sorted either by consumer or by registered store (business) and is used for the Cash Receipt lottery and the granting of tax credits to registered stores and of income deductions to consumers.

Once the Cash Receipt system was in place, complaints surfaced among business owners. Businesses began resisting the system out of fear it would increase their tax burden. Across the country, some took advantage of the fact that registration and receipt-issuing were not legally enforced and refused to register as a cash receipt issuing store. Others may have reluctantly registered, but used broken devices as an excuse not to issue cash receipts.

Consumer interest in cash receipts was unexpectedly low, owing to Koreans' age-old habit of not asking for receipts, a tradition passed on down the generations and established in Korean society as a "culture" of its own. Tension mounted within the NTS because of anxiety that the system might fail if this situation continued – the Cash Receipt system could not work without business and consumer participation. The system needed something to encourage participation and arouse the interest of businesses and consumers in cash receipts.

First, various tax support programs were implemented. Businesses receive a tax credit on their VAT tax (at 1.0–1.5 percent of the total amount for which a Cash Receipt is issued, up to US$5,000 a year) so that the added tax burden from the extra disclosure of income may be mitigated to some extent. If the issuing of cash receipts results in an increase in revenue (by 130 percent over the previous year), the business owner is granted a reduction in income tax, corporate tax, and VAT, and will also be exempt from tax audits. In addition, cash receipt devices (or "chips" embedded in credit card readers) were installed free of charge for store owners so that they could register as a cash receipt issuer without any extra financial burden.

These tax support programs and various promotions helped to get more businesses involved. However, participation was still low among small businesses such as private training facilities and real estate agencies, which usually do not have enough cash transactions to see any merit in bearing the cost of buying US$300–400 credit card readers.

The NTS hit on the idea that, if cash receipts could also be issued using the Internet, then people would not necessarily have to buy credit card readers! The NTS immediately began implementing a system that now enables small businesses to issue cash receipts over the Internet. For businesses that were registered but refused to issue cash receipts for no apparent reason, a civilian watchdog system was needed to strengthen the scheme and for equity with other businesses. A range of channels including the Cash Receipt website, the Cash Receipt call center, and the NTS website were available to consumers for reporting stores that refused to give cash receipts. Businesses reported to have refused were immediately placed under administrative supervision. The result was quite successful, with negligibly few repeat offenses by those who received supervision. Such channels laid the firm groundwork for the Cash Receipt system to take root rapidly.

Another task remained to be accomplished in order for the Cash Receipt system to be successfully implemented. That was to help consumers cultivate the habit of asking for receipts. This was no easy feat, for it meant changing the very purchasing behavior of Korean consumers unfamiliar with the practice of keeping receipts. Clearly recognizing that raising consumer interest was a top priority, the NTS staked everything on promoting the system to citizens. Promotional targets were separated into groups of wage-earners, housewives, youths, and the self-employed. Annual cash receipt usage rates were analyzed for the purpose of establishing promotional strategies customized to each group's characteristics. An all-out advertising blitz was launched using a variety of media, including television, radio, the Internet, newspapers, and subway walls.

The NTS also encouraged wage-earners to acquire the habit of asking for cash receipts by granting income deductions to those with receipts. Accordingly, for the purchases a wage-earner and his/her non-income-earning family member make, that wage-earner may combine the amounts for which a cash receipt was issued and the amounts paid by credit card; and, where that combined amount exceeds 15 percent of his/her annual earnings, 15 percent of that excess is income deductible when filing year-end tax returns.

However, unlike wage-earners, non-wage-earners have no particular incentives for asking for cash receipts. Indifference from non-wage-earners, who make up most of the consumer base, had been to some extent expected but, without their participation, the Cash Receipt system's success was at risk. To address this, a lottery system was introduced that awards lottery prizes to selected consumers who have asked for cash receipts. It was already proven through experience with the credit card lottery system that lotteries are an effective means of eliciting public participation because they provide incentives equivalent to income deductions. The prize money has gone up substantially (from US$2.7 million to US$5.86 million per year) and, through monthly draws, a total of US$489,000 is awarded to 8,608 winners. This plays a central role in motivating non-wage-earners to use the system.

The most noticeable achievement of the Cash Receipt system is that tax revenue management has become fair, efficient, and transparent owing in large part to national participation, enthusiastic support, and an advanced IT infrastructure. This resulted in enhanced public trust in the NTS and greater integrity of tax officials. Formerly, the NTS monitored cash-intensive industries by way of face-to-face encounters with taxpayers – usually in the form of providing filing instructions – and tax audits. Such methods entail conflict with taxpayers and leave room for corruption. However, by shifting the management of tax revenue streams from a system of direct contact to a system based on IT systems, the Cash Receipt scheme was able to detect cash transactions without coming into conflict with the taxpayer and with greater efficiency. By eliminating the potential for corruption at the very roots, tax revenue management was made more transparent and clearer.

As Tables 8.1 and 8.2 indicate, public satisfaction with the tax administration and the integrity index of tax officials have consistently been on the rise. Although this may be attributed to many different factors, the

Table 8.1 Taxpayer satisfaction with the national tax administration, 1998–2006

Year	1998	1999	2000	2001	2002	2003	2004	2005	2006
Taxpayer satisfaction index	57.3	64.4	73.1	75.8	75.9	76.1	76.5	76.8	80.2

Source: National Tax Service (2007).

Table 8.2 Public Official Integrity Index: Korean National Tax Service, 2002–2006

Year	2002	2003	2004	2005	2006
Average of the index for all state organizations	6.43	7.71	8.38	8.68	8.77
Integrity index for the NTS	5.82	6.80	8.18	8.42	8.77

Source: KICAC (2007).

Cash Receipt system played a defining role because it made revenue management more transparent.

Taxpayer satisfaction with the services provided by the NTS, measured for the first time in 1998 by an independent research institute, increased sharply in 1999 and 2000, then stabilized at around 76 points beginning in 2001. With the launch of the Participatory Government program, taxpayer satisfaction rose further to 80.2 percent in 2006. This followed a string of measures implemented to improve the service to taxpayers, such as offering more tax items that could be filed online and providing better-quality tax consultations, and the improved transparency achieved by the Cash Receipt system.

The Public Official Integrity Index is evaluated every year for the NTS by the Korea Independent Commission Against Corruption (KICAC). In 2002, before the Participatory Government, the index was a mere 5.82 (on a scale of 1 to 10). It significantly improved to 8.77 in 2006.

Next, the Cash Receipt system enabled a more equitable and efficient operation of the tax administration by exposing the cash parts of transactions, which were kept largely hidden, thus greatly improving the transparency of tax sources. Total Cash Receipt values reached US$18.6 billion in the first year (2005), and rose further to US$30.6 billion during 2006. This is remarkable, particularly when compared with the 16 years it took for annual credit card payments to reach US$18 billion.

Estimates of the proportion of taxable resources automatically brought to light as a result of the use of credit cards and cash receipts stood at a mere 12.1 percent of total private consumption spending in 1995 and 15.5 percent in 1999 (see Table 8.3). The figures started to grow with the various credit card incentives introduced in 2000, before reaching a pla-

Table 8.3 Cash receipt and credit card usage as a share of private consumption spending, 1995–2006 (billion won)

Year	Private consumption spending	Total [(1) + (2) + (3)]	Credit card (1)	Debit card (2)	Cash receipt (3)	Proportion (%)
1995	208,461	25,151	25,151	N/A	–	12.1
1999	274,934	42,634	42,634	N/A	–	15.5
2000	312,300	79,592	79,592	N/A	–	25.5
2001	343,416	134,233	134,233	N/A	–	39.1
2002	381,063	174,024	174,024	N/A	–	45.7
2003	389,177	170,530	170,530	N/A	–	43.9
2004	401,469	169,796	167,096	2,700	–	42.3
2005	426,690	216,800	190,463	7,777	18,560	50.8
2006	453,870	258,165	214,820	12,708	30,637	56.9

Source: National Tax Service (2007).

Table 8.4 Estimate of automatic disclosure from use of credit cards and cash receipts, 2004–2006 (trillion won)

Year	2006	2005	2004
Total private consumption spending	**453.8**	**426.7**	**401.4**
Excluded items[a]	226.4	210.5	198.2
Applicable amount from private consumption spending (1)	**227.4**	**216.2**	**203.2**
Applicable credit card amount (2)	155.3	140.7	122.6
Cash receipts for income deduction purposes (3)	28.3	17.8	–
Total amount disclosed [(2) + (3)]	183.6	158.5	122.6
Disclosure as a percentage of applicable private spending [(2) + (3)]/(1)	**80.7%**	**73.3%**	**60.3%**

Source: National Tax Service (2007).
[a] Excluded items: utilities bills, transportation fees, telecommunications costs, public education fees, insurance premiums, overseas spending, etc.

teau in the lower 40 percent range. The numbers picked up with the introduction of the Cash Receipt system – to 50.8 percent in 2005 and to as high as 56.9 percent in 2006, an indication that transparency is improving.

However, measuring the extent to which self-employed incomes have been disclosed as a result of the Cash Receipt system can be much trickier. Because the tax base is influenced by a broad range of factors, including the economic growth rate, economic trends, and the cost of living, it is not easy to estimate the system's direct impact on disclosure. Table 8.4 shows that disclosure obtained through cash receipts and credit cards is estimated to be approximately 80 percent of applicable private spending. The effect of disclosure is clearly visible in the dramatic

Table 8.5 Growth in voluntary individual global income tax payments, 2002–2006 (billion won)

	Attributable year				
	2002	2003	2004	2005	2006[a]
Voluntary payment	1,992.2	2,132.4	2,239.8	2,285.3	2,978.9

Source: National Tax Service (2007).
[a]The increase of 693.6 billion won in the amount of individual global income taxes paid on 2006 income represents 30.35% growth over 2005.

increase in taxes paid voluntarily on income earned for the year ending December 31, 2006 (Table 8.5).

At the end of 2006, with the number of registered stores at 1.4 million and registered Cash Receipt website users reaching 9.35 million and still growing, the Cash Receipt system was fast becoming established as a result of active public participation. The Cash Receipt system, a product of passion and persistence, has now stirred up a strong wind of change in South Korea's transaction culture and is generating the prospect that soon Korea will have as high a standard of transparency and integrity as any other advanced country.

What then are the success factors behind the system introduced to address the long-standing challenge of exposing cash transactions? What was so successful about the system that it attracted the attention of China, the United States, Japan, and the IMF, to name just a few?

The key was coming up with innovative thinking and action, along the lines of: innovative ideas based on advanced IT technology; leadership commitment and passion for success; dedicated staff; incentives in the form of tax breaks and a lottery; and differentiated promotional strategies to suit diverse consumer groups, such as wage-earners, housewives, and students. What cannot be left out is the fact that these innovations were grounded on people's hopes for taxation fairness and were established with the nation's enthusiastic participation and support.

The results cannot be evaluated simply from a tax administrative perspective – for example, secured revenue through the disclosure of self-employed earnings; fairness in the tax burden; public trust in the NTS; and enhanced integrity of tax officials. The reform will have a more far-reaching effect; secured tax revenue will contribute to resolving social polarization issues, and a reduction in the illegal flow of funds will be instrumental in enhancing the transparency of society as a whole and the equitable allocation of resources.

In this example, the leadership of the president and senior officials in the National Tax Service played a major role in devising and implementing the innovative measures, which have resulted in successfully increasing transparency as well as participation by taxpayers.

Conclusion and policy implications

The findings from the analysis of the National Tax Service reform, are as follows:

- Participation and transparency have a positive impact on the level of trust in government.
- Determination and courage from a head of the state or an organization are important in making it possible to maintain the rule of law. This was especially the case in the reform of the Prosecutor's Office, with the unprecedented action of President Rho, who had an open discussion with prosecutors to devise the right direction of the reform and to have them initiate the reform.
- To restore trust in government takes longer once a government has lost the public's faith. As implied in the case study, the National Tax Service reform seems to have gained more in terms of public confidence than the reform of the Prosecutor's Office, which was implemented over a shorter period.

From this study and its findings, several policy implications can be drawn for restoring trust in government:

- It is necessary to understand that trust in government is multifaceted and has many composite factors. Trust can be built by fair and open processes and efficient and effective outcomes.
- Even though a president's leadership is significant in increasing the level of trust in government as a whole, the leadership of state organizations is particularly important. In the new environment of globalization and informatization, the leadership of a head of state and his/her influence on confidence in the public sector are reduced. Therefore, each state organization needs to pursue trust-building. For this purpose, autonomy and a decentralization of power become necessary.
- To find out whether the level of trust has increased, appropriate measurement tools and methods need to be devised. In this chapter, an approximation was used, which limited the analysis. Further study on the scientific measurement of the level of trust in government needs to be carried out.

Acknowledgements

The material on the National Tax Service reform was provided by the National Tax Service of the Republic of Korea. This chapter is a shortened version of a paper published in the *International Review of Public Administration*, 2008, 13(2): 33–47.

REFERENCES

Ayres, Ian, and Braithwaite, John (1992) *Responsive Regulation*. Oxford: Oxford University Press.

Donovan, Todd, and Bowler, Shaun (2004) *Reforming the Republic: Democratic Institutions for the New America*. Upper Saddle River, NJ: Pearson/Prentice Hall.

Dwivedi, R. S. (1983) "Management by Trust: A Conceptual Model," *Group & Organization Studies* 8:4, pp. 375–405.

Eurobarometer (2004) *Eurobarometer Spring 2004: Public Opinion in the European Union*. Brussels: Commission of the European Communities.

Freedom House (n.d.) "Freedom in the World: Country Reports," <http://www.freedomhouse.org/template.cfm?page=21&year=2003> (accessed 2 March 2010).

Fukuyama, F. (1995) *Trust: The Social Virtues and the Criterion of Prosperity*. New York: The Free Press.

Jung, Yong-duck (2006) "The Past, the Present, and the Future of Government Reform: The Case of Korea," *Proceedings of the International Conference for the 50th Anniversary of KAPA on Oct. 13–14, Seoul, South Korea*. Korean Association for Public Administration and Presidential Committee on Government Innovation and Decentralization, pp. 179–211.

KICAC (2007) *Annual Report 2007*. Korea Independent Commission Against Corruption. Seoul.

Levi, Magarete (1998) *Of Rule and Revenue*. Berkeley: University of California Press.

Levi, Magarete (1997) *Consent, Dissent, and Patriotism*. New York: Cambridge University Press.

National Tax Service (2007) *Annual Report 2007*. Seoul: National Tax Service.

Tyler, Tom R. (1998) "Trust and Democratic Government," in Braithwaite, Valerie and Levi, Margaret. *Trust and Governance* edited by. New York: Russell Sage Foundation, 269–294.

Tyler, Tom R. (1990) *Why People Obey the Law*. New Haven, CT: Yale University Press.

9

Promoting trust in government: The case of Indonesia

Prijono Tjiptoherijanto and Meredith Rowen

The financial crisis of the late 1990s had a profound impact on Indonesia and instigated a concurrent multidimensional crisis on the political and socioeconomic levels. As a result, the issue of "good governance" moved to the forefront of popular debate, thus enabling the implementation of a series of reform measures over the next few years. Beginning when the late President Suharto left office in May 1998, the Reformation Era had the objectives of democratization, decentralization, and good governance as its main pillars. Its measures have included, to varying degrees: constitutional reform, political reform, administrative reform, improved regional autonomy, and anti-corruption initiatives. Together, the impact of these measures has been wide-reaching. Although their impact on trust in government has been generally positive, by aiming to improve governance with a particular focus on strengthening transparency, they have also generated complex results in other instances. This chapter contains a general overview of the context in which these reforms were implemented, the impact of the reforms on governance and trust, and recommendations for remaining areas of reform to be addressed in upcoming years.

Governance before the Reformation

As an introduction to the current state of trust in government, it is useful to look at the perceived quality of governance within Indonesia as an

Building trust in government: Innovations in governance reform in Asia, Cheema and Popovski (eds), United Nations University Press, 2010, ISBN 978-92-808-1189-6

important indicator. Good governance is much more than the routine operations of the government. It requires a redefinition of government–citizen relationships in which civil society, business, and other interest groups have a stake. It also represents the most important state guarantee to ensure that political and economic activities benefit the whole society and not just a select group of influential individuals or institutions. In the absence of good governance practices, corruption and discretion flourish.

A number of studies conducted prior to the Reformation Era examined the quality of governance within Indonesia in a regional context and indicated the need for improvement. Huther and Shah (1998) developed a good governance quality index, which rated 12 countries within Northeast, Southeast, and South Asia on the basis of four sub-indexes, namely:

1. *Citizen Participation Index:* An aggregate measure using indexes of political freedom and political stability.
2. *Government-Orientation Index:* An aggregate measure using indexes of judicial efficiency, bureaucratic efficiency, and lack of corruption.
3. *Social Development Index:* An aggregate measure using indexes of human development and egalitarian income distribution.
4. *Economic Management Index:* An aggregate measure using indexes of outward orientation, central bank independence, and an inverted ratio of debt to gross domestic product.

This governance quality index is three-tiered: good, fair, or poor. The results for selected countries in Asia are summarized in Table 9.1. The comparatively lower ranking of Indonesia represents lower scores in the four

Table 9.1 The quality of governance in selected Asian countries

No	Country	Quality index	Governance quality
01	Singapore	65	Good
02	Japan	63	
03	Malaysia	58	
04	Republic of Korea	57	
05	Sri Lanka	45	Fair
06	Philippines	44	
07	India	43	
08	Thailand	43	
09	China	39	Poor
10	Indonesia	38	
11	Nepal	36	
12	Pakistan	34	

Source: Adapted from Huther and Shah (1998: Table 2.1).
Note: This is a modification of the approach used by Hood and Jackson in their study of administration doctrines. See Hood and Jackson (1991: 178–179).

sub-index areas. This governance deficit had many practical implications for Indonesia, in which trust in government was waning and means of rapidly improving service delivery and access were required in order to meet the needs of its growing population. Poor performance at the local level was frequently represented in low human development indicators. Moreover, in 2003, the World Bank constructed an index for government effectiveness, comparing the quality of public bureaucracy, policy-making, and service delivery as components of six elements to provide a measure of governance (Kaufmann 2003). When government effectiveness was tested against data from 175 countries, the analysis confirmed that government effectiveness contributed to higher national income. In practice, this implied that improvements in governance could help to generate improvements in living standards for the general population, while helping to restore trust in government. Transparency and accountability were identified as specific areas that could benefit under the Reformation Era.

Democratization and constitutional reform

As the basis for reform measures to improve transparent and accountable governance, Indonesia began by amending the state constitution to reform various aspects of the state and nation in a way that was both democratic and decentralized. These amendments have altered the status and powers of the president (First Amendment, 1998); provided that each individual has the right to recognition and protection before the law, as well as the right to equality of treatment, and protected the individual against retroactive application of laws (Second Amendment); expanded the powers of the Supreme Court and provided for the establishment of a Constitutional Court and Judicial Commission (Third Amendment, 2001); and provided for the direct election of the president and vice president (Fourth Amendment, 2002) (United Nations Commission on Human Rights 2003). This process entailed government reinvention, including the reform of laws and regulations. The resulting goals included the strengthened authority of legislative institutions, improved regional autonomy, the establishment of laws and regulations on "clean, anti-corruption, collusion, and nepotism-free governance," as well as a series of important changes in the norms and managerial dimensions of state administration that have produced various innovations in government management in Indonesia.

As a result, Indonesia has made important strides toward introducing democratic governance. Previously, under the New Order Government of 1966 to 1998, the House of Representatives elected the president, who in turn selected the vice president. Therefore, the direct election of both the president and vice president by the people of Indonesia represented a major change in governance during the Reformation Era. Furthermore, several laws and regulations have been passed to limit the power of the executive at the central government level to modify governmental structures, while fixing the number of ministries and departments within the bureaucracy. In the past, the president had complete discretion over the formation of ministries and institutions within each government. Even the vice president did not have a voice on this matter. Other significant changes included the ability to form more political parties, the establishment of an independent General Elections Commission (KPU) to supervise elections, and direct elections for the heads of local government. The Constitutional Court, which makes decisions on electoral law, has further shifted power away from the party system and enabled more competition between candidates within political parties.

Additional reform measures have enabled the population and civil society organizations to benefit from freedom of the press, freedom of expression, and freedom of association, which they previously did not enjoy.[1] These freedoms have enabled a vibrant and active media to contribute to the democratic process. They have further provided the opportunity for increased transparency and accountability of governmental processes and decision-making, while opening room for participatory government. As such, they have provided an important basis for building trust in government. Nonetheless, the case of Indonesia illustrates the importance of responsible reporting and journalistic accountability, as a correlate to the increased freedom of the press. A current concern involves ensuring that news items are accurate and well researched, and accurately identifying rumours as distinct from fact. Similarly, increased freedom of expression now enables street demonstrations, which have the potential to become violent. Hence, one of the challenges for Indonesia in the area of democratization has been how to temper and balance the introduction of increased democratic rights with an improved understanding of civic responsibility, without lessening the former freedoms.

Decentralization

Decentralization measures introduced during the Reformation Era complemented efforts to improve democratic governance. In the case of Indonesia, trust in government tends to be higher at the provincial level, where governments are fairly powerful, in contrast to trust in the central government, which lost confidence in the late 1990s. In some cases, provinces even have foreign relations, prompting discussions in recent years within the country over whether there would be value in changing to a federal system. Within this general context, the recent decentralization process has focused on the devolution of power to sub-regional rather than provincial governments. The decentralization process began with the passage of Laws No. 22 and 25 of 1999 and now includes Laws 32 and 33 of 2004. These laws provided the initial framework for the devolution of power to sub-regional governments, which began effective implementation in 2001, leading to significant changes in the political and economic life of the citizenry.

At the sub-regional level, district governments received the most power through decentralization, gaining concrete legislative and budgetary authority, whereas provincial governments assumed mostly supervisory functions. Local administrations were authorized to impose local taxes and issue investment permits, as long as such policies did not contradict national law (Oxford Analytica 2009). The legal framework further provided for provinces, districts, and sub-districts to be divided into smaller units "in the interests of better service delivery, more equitable resource distribution and more representative government" (International Crisis Group 2007). According to the World Bank, Indonesia has become one of the most decentralized countries in the world, and has accomplished this without major disruption in government services. To the contrary, a recent poll has shown that, following decentralization, the majority of Indonesians saw improvements in service delivery and access (World Bank n.d.).

For Indonesia, the transfer of authority from the center to regional and local governments has been key, given the thousands of local governments, 33 provinces, and 499 districts. Objectives of the decentralization process included bringing government closer to the people, strengthening transparency and accountability in the use of public resources, reducing corruption, improving participation in the policy process, and ultimately improving service delivery and access at the local level. Correspondingly, it was accompanied by public service reforms, implementation of the minimum service standard, and serious anti-corruption initiatives. Local governments are often more aware of and attuned to the needs of local populations, and may have a clearer sense of which projects and policies people living in their jurisdictions would favor. When resources are managed at the local level, local populations are also more able to rapidly identify when these resources have not been effectively dedicated to the purposes for which they were earmarked or intended.

However, the transition to the increased autonomy of local governments has not been without hiccups. In many cases, there are still overlapping claims of authority, different regulations to be followed according to the local government, and challenges by the central government as to the legality of local regulations. A related issue has been the growing number of districts themselves, since these frequently have distinct regulations. According to Oxford Analytica (2009):

> Another cause for uncertainty is the continuing division of districts and, to a lesser extent, of provinces. When Suharto fell in 1998, Indonesia had 27 provinces and 292 districts; ten years later, the number of provinces has risen to 33 and districts to more than 500. Splitting territories has been a popular and effective way for local elites to gain control over resource-rich areas or to obtain political office in smaller administrative units after they failed to build a career in their "mother provinces" or districts.

The same report concludes that these issues have created legal uncertainty and an absence of predictable procedures, impacting foreign investment practices within Indonesia and leading to confusion and occasional conflict between law enforcement officers, politicians, and investors. To follow up on the decentralization reform measures, a clear definition of power of different levels of government must still be further refined to enable better coordination and cohesiveness of policy both between local governments and with the central government.

Decentralization and civil servants' pay scales

In Indonesia, the decentralization process coincided with civil service reform, and particularly changes to pay scales for civil servants. Prior to the implementation of decentralization measures beginning in early 2001, one issue of concern had been the extremely low salaries for government employees, which were considered to give an insufficient incentive for work in public service while minimizing the temptation of corruption. As a result of decentralization policy, the increased ability to legislate at the local level has now given local governments the ability to increase salaries, employ new incentive structures to reward performance, and increase the differential between the highest- and lowest-paid civil servants. For example, as of December 2006, a decree by the governor of Riau Province in West Sumatra gave the lowest-ranking civil servants (Ia) an additional Rp$1.6 million (approximately US$160) per month, while the highest ranking (IVe) received a pay increase of Rp$4.5 million (approximately US$450) per month.

In addition to regional civil servants being paid more in line with their rank, functional professions are also recognized by means of additional functional allowances. For example, in East Kutai Regency in East Kalimantan Province, since 2006, elementary and high school teachers have been paid an additional allowance of Rp$1.2 million (approximately US$120) per month. Consequently, teachers at the rank of II or III now receive monthly incomes of approximately US$250–290, which is significantly higher than the province's minimum wage, which was set by government decree at roughly US$150 per month.

However, the changes in salary levels at the regional and provincial level, which relate to the resources and wealth of the respective area, and particularly the discrepancy between the lowest- and highest-paid civil servants have created some problems. Whereas civil servants at the regional level may receive additional bonuses and allowances, civil servants within central government must be satisfied with the salaries given according to the law. Thus, the most senior civil servants in Riau are paid more than twice the basic salary received by central government civil servants of the same rank, which is only around US$207 per month. With a salary of US$657 (base pay of US$207 plus US$450) per month, civil servants in Riau earn almost as much as middle managers in the business sector in Jakarta, the capital.

Public sector reform and capacity

Since the 1980s, many countries within Asia and internationally have engaged in major efforts to promote administrative reform, focusing on the openness, transparency, and accountability of government administration. All countries, regardless of their economic situation or stage of development, need good governance. For some Asian countries, this need became particularly important after the 1997 Asian financial and economic crisis.

In Indonesia, following the end of the New Order Government in 1998, a political movement emerged that pursued reforms in relation to politics, the economy, the judicial system, and public administration. Law No. 22/1999 on Regional Autonomy, which was amended by Law No. 32/2004 on Regional Governance on Decentralization and Law No. 43/1999 on Civil Service Administration, opened up possibilities for public service reform in Indonesia, but the country still has a long way to go in relation to having a high-quality civil service. As with any reforms, strong and determined leadership is crucial. Although good governance is a central pillar for dealing with competition in a globalizing world, Indonesia must also undertake civil service reforms to achieve a clean and efficient bureaucracy in order to maintain trust in government. These reforms are needed in addition to other innovative efforts to ensure that civil society has trust in the government.

The public service currently prioritizes five managerial dimensions as a means to improve transparent and accountable governance in Indonesia: (i) development of accountability for performance; (ii) state financial management; (iii) development planning; (iv) control and oversight; and

(v) human resource management within the state apparatus (Mohamed 2007).[2]

First, to improve performance accountability for state institutions, Indonesia adopted a Government Agency Performance Accountability System, which identifies several stages of the accountability process: strategic planning; a performance plan and agreement; performance measurement, evaluation, and analysis; and a performance report. The Government Agency Performance Accountability System should be coherent with the budgeting system, planning system, treasury system, government accounting system, and auditing system.

Second, to improve state financial management, Indonesia implemented performance-based budgeting and also established a Government Accounting Standard in accordance with general accounting practices, as well as with international public sector accounting standards. Performance-based budgeting is formulated through a simultaneous and interactive top-down and bottom-up process. State financial management is now also expected to reflect the principles of transparency and accountability, have an outcome-oriented focus, and emphasize the functions and activities of an organization.

Third, Indonesia instituted a National Development Planning System, which uses a mix of top-down and bottom-up planning, facilitated through discussions and consultations. On the basis of each institution's strategic plan, there must now be a correlation between its budget and performance expectations. Budget allocation must be confirmed with the performance of government institutions as the budget users, accompanied with program and activity plans, as well as their budgets and performance evaluation. The overall approach undertaken has emphasized harmony and approachability.

Fourth, to improve control and oversight, Indonesia now requires that each government institution submits a report on its budget management and performance achievements to ensure that it is accountable both financially and in terms of performance. This includes a report on the performance accountability of programs and activities. Each institution must conduct a development performance evaluation that is related to its functions and responsibilities. At the same time, Indonesia has strengthened its state financial management and accountability audit system. The role and authority of the Financial Auditing Board – the state auditor – have been enhanced. This dimension of control and oversight has had positive implications for service delivery and access, leading to a more transparent goods and services procurement system. Other institutions that have played an important role in this area include the General Service Provision Board and the Minimum Service Standard, an official government policy on the types and quality of basic services to which all citizens of

Indonesia must have access. All services that are characterized as "basic" must by definition fall within this framework and become the obligatory responsibility of local governments to provide. This policy was designed to protect the constitutional rights of citizens.

Finally, alongside these measures, Indonesia has worked to enhance the quality of human resources within the public sector. These efforts have focused on improving the work ethic and professionalism of public servants; improving the remuneration system; requiring government officials to submit income statements to the Corruption Eradication Commission so that inappropriate sources of income may be detected and addressed; and promoting civil service ethics.

Despite these advances, some future challenges remain. First, there is additional need for harmonization between laws and regulations to ensure that all are complementary and mutually reinforcing. Second, the further development and implementation of public accountability are required. Third, there could be improvement of strategic planning formulation competencies. Fourth, there is the need for the development of performance information and measurement systems. Additional challenges that will need to be addressed in the future include the need to reinforce the reporting system through a management style that recognizes the value of "openness," financial accountability, while providing a medium for ensuring performance accountability, developing a performance agreement with an effective incentive system, and revising civil servant management systems.

The five managerial dimensions explored above are a reflection of the commitment of the government of Indonesia and its serious efforts to introduce sustainable reform measures that improve transparent and accountable governance. These efforts have produced good progress on several levels. Nonetheless, there are still many challenges, both in technical and managerial terms as described, as well as in other more complex aspects of the state administration system.

Pending initiatives in public sector reform

Currently, a number of new initiatives are planned to accomplish further changes to the incentive system, the size of the civil service, recruitment, performance management, remuneration, and probity as part of the overall civil service strategy, in line with recommendations by a World Bank report for the Indonesian government (World Bank 2001: 10). For example, pilot reform initiatives are planned for the ministries of Finance and Education, including a new merit-based pay initiative under Teacher Law No. 14/2005. In addition, an independent remuneration commission will advise on pay scales and on modernizing the pay structure for senior officials; a review of the legal framework for the civil service is ongoing; a number of sub-national reform initiatives are taking place in Yogyakarta, Jembrana in Bali, Solok in West Sumatera, and elsewhere; and a cabinet-level unit to help implement reforms is planned (World Bank 2006).

A remaining issue involves the establishment of a civil service commission (CSC). Despite the improvement that followed implementation of the Regional Autonomy Law – Law No. 22 of 1999, revised by Law No. 32 of 2004 – Indonesia's public sector still needs to undergo substantial change, especially towards improving governance and enabling the country to compete in the global arena. To have an effective and efficient public service, most governments have set up a civil or public service commission as a special institution responsible for human resource management. For example, the Republic of Korea established a CSC in 1999, which has been leading the country's major civil service reform initiatives. In 2004, those personnel management functions that still remained under the purview of the Ministry of Government Administration and Home Affairs were transferred to the CSC, thereby resulting in a single, central personnel authority for the government (Kong 2006). In New Zealand, in 1999 the state service commissioner asked to be given responsibility for developing a solution to the lack of corporate capacity in the public service. Since that time, New Zealand's public service has increasingly moved to address a wide range of service and human resource management issues from a corporate perspective (United Nations 2005).

In the case of Indonesia, there is no such body. Even though Law No. 43/1999 of 2000 called for the establishment of a civil service commission, the government does not currently have any plans to establish such a body. Due to this, the division of responsibilities in relation to human resources among line ministries and other public sector entities is as shown in Table 9.2. This table also illustrates that human resource management within the civil service is being carried out not by an independent body that reports directly to the president, but by institutions that are part of the government bureaucracy. Therefore, more innovative actions are still needed in relation to the governmental institutions setting in Indonesia.

Once a civil service commission has been established, questions often arise pertaining to the commission's relationship with line ministries and agencies. Therefore, once a government decides to establish a CSC, it must clearly delineate the division of responsibilities in relation to resource management among central government departments and agencies. In many countries, responsibilities for human resource management in the civil service are along the lines shown in Table 9.3. The structure outlined in Table 9.3 resembles the model prevalent in the Commonwealth of Nations, especially with respect to the role of the CSC, but

Table 9.2 Institutions responsible for human resource management in Indonesia

Agency	Function
Office of the President (State Secretariat and Cabinet Secretariat)	Overall government policies
Ministry of Finance	Civil service pay and pensions (state-owned enterprises are responsible for their own pay and pensions under the supervision of the State Ministry for State-Owned Companies)
Ministry of Administrative Reforms	Supervision, coordination, monitoring, and evaluation of all civil services matters, including supervision and coordination of the National Agency for the Civil Service and the National Institute of Public Administration
National Agency for the Civil Service	Appointments, promotions (except at the highest levels, which are managed by a team chosen by the president), and transfers
National Institute of Public Administration	Education, training, and organizational design

Source: Author.

Table 9.3 Responsibility for human resource management in central government agencies: A general model

Agency	Function
Office of the Prime Minister	Overall government policy
Ministry of Finance	Pay and pensions
Ministry of Public Service	Deployment and conditions of service for civil servants
CSC	Appointments, promotions, transfers, and discipline
National Administrative Staff College	Staff training and development

Source: Adapted from United Nations (2005: Table 6).

countries such as the Republic of Korea and Thailand have similar arrangements in place.

Anti-corruption initiatives

To complement decentralization and public sector reform in improving transparent and accountable governance, Indonesia has also implemented a series of recent measures designed to combat corruption during the same period. The Corruption Eradication Commission (KPK) was formed in 2003 to coordinate and supervise anti-corruption efforts, while focusing on eliminating and preventing corruption and conducting a system review. It undertakes this mission on the assumption that a comprehensive, systematic, and long-term approach is needed to achieve a corruption-free Indonesia, which must by definition include the holistic participation of all stakeholders. As such, its aim is to become a driver of change in cultivating a culture of anti-corruption in Indonesian society, government, and the business world (see Sunaryadi 2007).[3]

The KPK is independent from the executive, legislative, and judicial branches and is responsible to the general public. It receives funding from the state budget and from donors. In terms of staff, it has 5 commissioners, 2 advisors, and 600 staff members. These human resources face a population of over 220 million people, 4 million of whom are public servants, within the many provincial and local governments.

The KPK's duties include the supervision and coordination of institutions authorized to eradicate corruption; the investigation, indictment, and prosecution of corrupt acts; preventive action against corrupt acts; and monitoring state governance. To perform these duties, the KPK is authorized to coordinate investigations, indictments, and prosecutions against criminal acts of corruption; implement a reporting system for the purposes of eradicating corruption; request information from relevant institutions for the purpose of eradicating corruption; arrange opinion hearings and meetings with institutions authorized to eradicate corruption; and request reports from relevant institutions pertaining to the prevention of criminal acts of corruption. Law No. 30/2002 on the Corruption Eradication Commission provided the basis for the functions, authority, and duties of the institution.

One initial challenge in the fight against corruption related to the way in which it was defined. Over the 1971–2004 period, laws and regulations tended to address only those types of corruption that represented a direct loss to the state apparatus. As of 2006, a publication called "Memahami Untuk Membasmi" now identifies 30 distinct types of corruption, many of which were previously overlooked. In addition to defining 2 types of corruption representing a loss to the state, other major categories of corruption include 12 types of bribery, 5 types of embezzlement, 6 types of procurement fraud, 1 type of procurement conflicts of interest.

The KPK also faced other challenges. Its establishment followed a long history of anti-corruption measures, most of which had focused primarily on investigation of existing cases of corruption rather than on prevention (see Table 9.4). As a result of this lack of emphasis on prevention, many of the lessons learned from early efforts were not applied on an ongoing basis. Consequently, Indonesia found that the same kinds of corruption were equally prevalent over the course of decades. For example, people

Table 9.4 History of key anti-corruption measures in Indonesia, 1957–1999

1957	Order to fight corruption (Military Commander)
1967	Presidential Decree to fight corruption through prevention and repression (Corruption Eradication Team)
1970	Presidential Decree to assess corruption and its solution (Commission of Four)
1977	Presidential instruction to take disciplinary action in operations & administration (Disciplinary Team)
1987	Ministry of Finance order for a special operation on corruption in taxation (Special Re-Audit on Tax Return)
1999	Asset examination and disclosure law for public officials (Public Official Wealth Examiner)
1999	Government regulation to investigate complex corruption (Corruption Eradication Joint Team)
2003	**KPK established**
2005–2007	Timtas/Corruption Eradication Coordination (Attorney General, Police, Auditor)

in high-level positions were arrested for comparable offences in the 1950s, 1970s, 1980s, and again in the 2000s. Similarly, the same types of procurement corruption happened in 1983 and 2003. Areas perceived as highly corrupt in the 1970s continued to give the same impression.

To address this situation, the KPK has aimed to use an integrated program implementation approach, which includes capacity development, prevention, repression of corruption, and public involvement and participation. This entailed a shift in focus for programs to combat corruption. The KPK placed attention on the issue of bribery, catching "big fishes" in order to win public trust, using court video recordings, and bureaucratic reform through integrating investigation and prevention measures. These policies have resulted in many highly publicized cases where senior officials were caught "red-handed" on videotape in the process of conducting an illegal act. At the same time, court video recording helped to increase transparency and public awareness of court procedures and decisions. By 2010, significant anti-corruption reforms are expected to increase legal certainty, reduce budget leakages, increase investment, and increase state revenues. The ongoing commitment to combat corruption is expected to gradually increase citizen trust in government, while additionally improving investor confidence.

Recent cases in the fight against corruption

Three recent examples in the press have highlighted the advances that continue to be made in the promotion of accountability and transparency at both the national and sub-national levels. At the municipal level, the City of Surabaya developed an e-procurement system under the newly elected Walikota (mayor) in response to Presidential Decree No. 80/2003 on government procurement procedures. To set up the system, the city government conducted its own research and tried to incorporate best practices in procurement from Hong Kong and Singapore. It also received assistance in setting up the computer system from students at the local school of engineering. Initially the government faced resistance from big vendors, who relied on payments and collusion to win their contracts. Since the implementation of the e-procurement system, the savings have been substantial and have been allocated to other city projects. In addition, the application of e-procurement increases the opportunity for small and medium vendors to participate in the bidding process. As a result, a big portion of the city's projects now are won by small and medium-sized vendors (Hafild and Hanu Yulianto 2004).

At the district level, the fight against corruption has also gained credibility, as shown by the case of Kabupaten Solok. In this district, Gamawan Fauzi, Head of the Regency (or "Bupati") and now the Governor of West Sumatra, took the initiative to implement a new policy, following his participation in a 2003 Transparency International workshop. He required all civil servants and suppliers to sign an "Integrity Pact," which obliges them to refrain from corruption, not to receive or provide bribes, to provide transparency to the public, and to avoid collusion or cronyism. The Bupati has also reformed the rules for the procurement of goods and services in the Regency, simplifying documentation, reimbursement of funds, and correspondence in the procurement process. In early 2004, Solok eliminated civil servants' honoraria – the salary supplements received by government staff for working on specific projects. The objective was to reduce corruption as well as to improve employee welfare overall, since the honoraria collected had been distributed equally among public officials.

Finally, the level of central government has also demonstrated its commitment to anti-corruption initiatives and the strengthened role of the KPK. On November 27, 2008, the KPK arrested the former deputy governor of the Central Bank (Bank Indonesia) for the alleged misappropriation of Rp$100 billion (US$83 million) in Central Bank funds in 2003. Despite the fact that the person charged was related by marriage to the presidential family, President Yudhoyono took a widely commented upon stance of non-intervention in the case. The administration has won credit both at home and internationally for its anti-corruption drive, which political analysts have said contributed to the president's re-election in 2009. A survey in 2008 found Yudhoyono had regained popularity, thanks in part to his non-intervention in the case (*The Jakarta Post*, November 29, 2008).

The emergence of these and similar cases implies that anti-corruption policy is now being taken seriously by citizens and legislators, and accepted within the popular consciousness as a priority. Although this does not mean that work in this area is by any means complete, it does demonstrate a trajectory of improvement in restoring public trust.

Conclusion

Important steps toward restoring trust in government have been accomplished during and since Indonesia's Reformation Era by improving democratic and local governance, moving governance closer to the people, and committed efforts to strengthening transparency and accountability within the country. A global public opinion survey carried out in December 2005 for the World Economic Forum found that Indonesia was, in fact, one of the few countries in which trust in the national government had held steady in the new millennium, whereas the majority of others that were examined (including both developed and developing countries) experienced declines by "statistically significant margins" (World Economic Forum 2005).

However, building trust in government is an ongoing process, where complacency is unwelcome. This chapter illustrates that, although many gains have been made in improving governance, resulting in improvements in public confidence, there are still areas that need to be addressed in order to ensure that this positive trajectory continues in the right direction. As such, we make the following recommendations:

1. a clear definition of the power of different levels of government to enable better coordination and policy cohesiveness between local governments and with the central government;
2. additional attention to incentive and pay structures within the civil service;
3. the introduction of a civil service commission as a single institution responsible for human resource management; and
4. continuing support to the fight against corruption.

In each of these objectives, the role of leadership will be key in building the credibility of new reforms, providing the populace with an overall vision of a future in which government earns and fully merits citizen confidence, and helping to commit different socioeconomic actors and resources to this long-term goal.

Acknowledgements

This chapter is based on a paper presented at the Workshop on Promoting Trust in Government Through Innovations in Governance in Asia and the Pacific, held at the East-West Center, Honolulu, Hawaii, January 28–30, 2008.

Notes

1. The previously existing Ministry of Information was also disbanded.
2. More information on Indonesia's recent public sector reforms is available by visiting the National Institute of Public Administration online at <http://www.lan.go.id>.
3. More information on the KPK is available by contacting the office of the KPK at <http://www.kpk.go.id>.

REFERENCES

Hafild, Emmy and Hanu Yulianto (2004) "Hasil Assesement Penerapan Pakta Integrasi Kabupaten Solok," paper prepared by Transparency International Indonesia for the Workshop "Mewujudkan Sistem Pengadaan Barang dan Jasa yang Effisien dan Bebas KKN," Jakarta, August 25, 2005.

Hood, C. and M. Jackson (1991) *Administrative Argument*. Brookfield, VT: Dartmouth.

Huther, J. and A. Shah (1998) "Applying a Simple Measure of Good Governance to the Debate on Fiscal Decentralization," World Bank Policy Research Working Paper 1984, Washington, DC.

International Crisis Group (2007) "Indonesia: Decentralisation and Local Power Struggles in Maluku," Asia Briefing No. 64, May 22. Available at: <http://www.crisisgroup.org/home/index.cfm?l=1&id=4849> (accessed 8 February 2010).

Kaufmann, D. (2003) "Governance Redux: The Empirical Challenge," in M. E. Porter et al. (eds) *Global Competitiveness Report 2003–2004*. New York and Oxford: World Economic Forum and Oxford University Press.

Kong, D. (2006) "Reinventing South Korea's Bureaucracy Toward Open and Accountable Governance," paper presented at the Asian Public Reform Forum, Nanning, China.

Mohamed, Ismail (2007) "Reforms to Build and Sustain Transparency and Accountability in the Public Sector: The Indonesian Experience," Country Presentation at the Regional Forum on Reinventing Government in Asia, Jakarta, November 14–16. Available at: <http://unpan1.un.org/intradoc/groups/public/documents/ungc/unpan028302.pdf> (accessed 8 February 2010).

Oxford Analytica (2009) "Indonesia: Local Governments Prove Difficult Partners," OxResearch, January 9.

Sunaryadi, Amien (2007) "Indonesian Experiences: Programmes to Combat Corruption," Context Presentation at the Regional Forum on Reinventing Government in Asia, Jakarta, November 14–16. Available at: <http://unpan1.un.org/intradoc/groups/public/documents/ungc/unpan028309.pdf> (accessed 8 February 2010).

United Nations (2005) *World Public Sector Report 2005: Unlocking the Human Potential for Public Sector Performance*. New York: United Nations Department of Economic and Social Affairs.

United Nations Commission on Human Rights (2003) "Report of the Special Rapporteur on the Independence of Judges and Lawyers Dato' Param Cumaraswamy, Submitted in Accordance with Commission on Human Rights Resolution 2002/43: Report on the Mission to Indonesia, 15–24 July 2003," E/CN.4/2003/65/Add.2, January 13.

World Bank (n.d.), "Decentralization in Indonesia," <http://go.worldbank.org/P65PRQ0VV0> (accessed 8 February 2010).

World Bank (2001) *Indonesia: The Imperative for Reform*. Report 23093-IND. Jakarta: World Bank.

World Bank (2006) *Country Assistance Strategy Progress Report for Republic of Indonesia*. Washington, DC: World Bank.

World Economic Forum (2005) "Trust in Governments, Corporations and Global Institutions Continues to Decline: Global Survey Ahead of World Economic Forum Annual Meeting in Davos Shows 'Trust Deficit' Deepening," Press Release, December 15, Geneva, Switzerland. <http://www.weforum.org/en/media/Latest%20Press%20Releases/PRESSRELEASES87> (accessed 8 February 2010).

10

Building trust in government in Timor-Leste: The roles and strategies of United Nations missions

Sukehiro Hasegawa

In a post-conflict country such as Timor-Leste, the trust of people in government depends on the government's ability to maintain security and stability in the country. Furthermore, people's trust in the government is determined by the extent of their confidence in the functioning of the various state institutions in delivering public services and in maintaining the transparency and accountability of governmental operations, the protection of human rights, and the rule of law. This chapter discusses how the United Nations helped, first, to establish and strengthen the capacity of a national law enforcement agency, Policia Nacional de Timor-Leste (PNTL); secondly, to deliver public services during the initial post-conflict period and build institutional capacity; and, thirdly, to establish national institutions concerned with transparency and accountability, i.e. the Offices of the Inspector General, the Prosecutor General, and the Ombudsman (Provedor) for Human Rights and Justice, as well as the Courts, so that they can function effectively to discharge their responsibilities.

The United Nations missions in Timor-Leste

The strategies of the United Nations were drawn up based on resolutions of the Security Council. These resolutions also established UN peace-keeping and peacebuilding missions, namely the United Nations Transitional Administration in East Timor (UNTAET), established in 1999; the

Building trust in government: Innovations in governance reform in Asia, Cheema and Popovski *(eds), United Nations University Press, 2010, ISBN 978-92-808-1189-6*

United Nations Mission of Support to East Timor (UNMISET), which replaced UNTAET in 2002 and completed its mandate in May 2005; the United Nations Office in Timor-Leste (UNOTIL), a one-year follow-on special political mission established in April 2005; and the United Nations Integrated Mission in Timor-Leste (UNMIT), established in August 2006. The goals of these UN missions were to help the Timorese government and other state institutions build their institutional capacity so that they could maintain the security and stability of society, protect human rights, sustain the rule of law, and provide a basic livelihood to the people. The missions had specific objectives that were relevant to the attainment of these goals.

The first priority objective of the United Nations in the immediate period after the restoration of the political independence of Timor-Leste in 2002 was to achieve the security and stability of the independent country of Timor-Leste by contributing to the maintenance of the external and internal security of the country. The second objective was to help establish core administrative structures critical to the viability and political stability of the nascent country. The third objective was to provide interim law enforcement and public security and to assist in the development of a new national law enforcement agency (Resolution 1410, UN Security Council 2002). These objectives reflected the concern of the UN Security Council about the possible threats posed by former militia and other elements residing in the Indonesian part of Timor Island and politically motivated issues groups active in Timor-Leste itself. The Security Council was also concerned about the need to build up the administrative and operational capability of the government to maintain political stability and public security, and recognized the need for continued international engagement in support of institutional capacity development.

During the subsequent three years until 2006, the United Nations shifted its attention from peacekeeping to peacebuilding and devoted most of its manpower and resources to strengthening the capacity of national institutions. In 2004, for example, the Security Council mandated UNMISET with the task of supporting public administration and the justice system of Timor-Leste, while continuing to develop a law enforcement capacity and safeguarding the security of the country. For this purpose, UNMISET was provided with 58 civilian advisers, 157 civilian police advisers, 42 unarmed military liaison officers, 310 formed troops, and a 125-person International Response Unit (Resolution 1543, UN Security Council 2004). By April 2005, contrary to the advice of the Secretary-General, the Security Council determined that the current situation no longer posed any serious threat to the external and internal security of the country. The Council decided to remove all armed forces and establish a special political mission (UNOTIL), with a view to transferring the capacity-building tasks to the United Nations Development Programme (UNDP) and other UN agencies. The key members of the Security Council considered that this transition to a development framework was possible because the Timorese appeared to have achieved security and stability. UNOTIL was entrusted with the task of providing civilian advisers to carry out training and the "proper transfer of skills and knowledge in order to build the capacity of the public institutions of Timor-Leste to deliver their services in accordance with international principles of rule of law, human rights, democratic governance, transparency, accountability and professionalism" (Resolution 1599, UN Security Council 2005). Thus, the Security Council decided to reduce the total number of civilian advisers but asked that advisers be deployed to assist the police and critical state institutions. The Security Council also approved 10 human rights officers to provide training in the observance of democratic governance and human rights. The transition from peacekeeping to peacebuilding and then to a development assistance framework was regarded as a logical and effective way to accelerate the process of helping the new country to achieve democratic governance and sustainable development, resulting in increased public trust in the Timorese governance structure.

There is a direct link between the trust that citizens are willing to give to their government and the overall physical security a government is able to provide. In a post-conflict country such as Timor-Leste, this link becomes the essential component, the very milestone against which to determine the level of trust of its citizens. Building an independent and professional police force that could protect Timorese citizens while abiding by rule of law principles thus became a crucial element of the United Nations missions in the Timorese nation-building process.

Building a national law enforcement agency

In recent years, many civilians around the world have become the target of violence in regional and intra-state conflicts. In order to protect civilians from armed conflict, the United Nations embarked upon the formation of national police forces, starting in Somalia in 1994. Since then it has become a common approach in peacekeeping and peacebuilding operations.

During the immediate period following the end of the Indonesian occupation until the restoration of political independence in May 2002, the government and the people of Timor-Leste relied entirely on the UN peacekeeping forces and the UN Police (UNPOL) for the external and internal security of the nascent country. The law enforcement component of the UN mission, UNPOL, carried out executive policing activities until a local law enforcement agency was able to takeover.

The establishment of a law enforcement agency – a national police service – that is professional and independent and capable of withstanding political pressure and manipulation was one of the priority tasks in Timor-Leste. Successive UN missions attached importance to the strict observance of human rights because ordinary people had been subjected to arbitrary arrest and imprisonment and even torture during the 24 years of Indonesian occupation. In Timor-Leste, furthermore, the United Nations became actively engaged in training the Timorese national police force (Policia Nacional de Timor-Leste: PNTL), which was established in May 2002, and provided technical and material support to its development. Adequate resources were provided for rehabilitating a major training complex equipped with classrooms and training facilities. UNPOL coached and mentored PNTL police officers and they shared police office premises throughout the country until UNPOL handed over executive policing responsibility to PNTL on 20 May 2004.

The number of UN police officers was reduced from more than 1,000 in 2002 to 157 in May 2004 and then to 60 unarmed training officers in May 2005. Meanwhile, the PNTL grew in size to 3,300 officers with the addition of specialized units; it replaced the UN police officers completely by May 2004. Since then, with the support of UN Civilian Police, the PNTL has made significant progress in organizing itself and strengthening the professional caliber of its officers. The nature of the UN police officers' assignment was also changed to solely that of the capacity-building of PNTL officers. The UNPOL training advisers, as they were now called, made concerted efforts to fill the gaps in capacity-building of the PNTL but also to develop its managerial capabilities. In 2003, Australia and the United Kingdom joined in assisting the development of a national capacity for the planning, management, and administration of the PNTL as an independent agency. The Timor-Leste Police Development Programme (TLPDP), funded by these two countries, concentrated assistance on crime prevention and community safety, training in investigations and operations, development of the Police Training College, and PNTL organizational finance and human resources management.

By 2005, the majority of Timorese police officers had acquired an adequate understanding of human and civil rights and became aware of the need to respect these rights while exercising their power. When demonstrations organized by some of the Church leaders took place in 2005, the PNTL contained them successfully without using excess force. This led many to believe that the PNTL had attained the necessary maturity in law enforcement. Yet this proved to be an optimistic assessment, as the PNTL disintegrated a year later in May 2006 when a peaceful demonstration against the government over the issue of personnel management staged by former military officers in the Timor-Leste Defence Force (F-FDTL) turned violent. Some of them were then engaged in shooting incidents, resulting in armed confrontation between the PNTL and F-FDTL and causing the death of 30 people. Because the UN peacekeeping forces had been withdrawn from Timor-Leste, there were no impartial forces that could restrain the national military and police forces from engaging in armed conflict. As a result of the armed conflicts, as many as half of the civilian population in the capital city of Dili fled either to areas outside of the capital city or to more than 50 camps created for internally displaced persons. Fearful for their personal safety, many of them were still in these camps a year later.

The United Nations missions in Timor-Leste were not involved substantially in building the managerial capacity of the national military force, the F-FDTL (established in 2001), until a mandate to do so was provided to UNMIT in 2006. The training of national military personnel was carried out by Australia, Malaysia, Portugal, and other bilateral partners. One civilian officer was recruited by the United Nations during the period of UNMISET and UNOTIL and advised the Minister for Defence in formulating the overall defense policy and the institutional requirements of the military establishment. However, the extent of his involvement in the management of F-FDTL as an organization was negligible. As a result, when the dispute erupted over the issue of personnel management in 2006, the F-FDTL was not able to address and resolve the issue until it had reached a crisis situation.[1]

The security incidents that took place in April and May 2006 further revealed the need for the United Nations to maintain adequate peacekeeping forces until the managerial capacity of the national military and police forces had been built up sufficiently so that they could manage themselves as professional and independent security agencies and avoid any major mismanagement. The outcome of the UN involvement in the capacity-building of the Timorese police force showed that full professionalization cannot be achieved in isolation and without comprehensive development of the democratic culture of political leadership. These incidents revealed the difficulty and the necessity of changing the mindset and mentality of security personnel in a post-conflict country such as Timor-Leste.

Government capability in delivering essential public services

The second critical requirement for enhancing trust in government in post-conflict countries is the establishment of a governmental capacity to deliver essential public services, particularly healthcare, food and education. For the nascent independent state of Timor-Leste, the Security Council recognized the importance of the newly established state institutions being able to deliver basic public services to improve the livelihoods of the people. Through its resolutions 1272, 1410 and 1599, the Security Council made this task one of the three basic mandates of the subsequent peacekeeping and peacebuilding missions, UNTAET, UNMISET, and UNOTIL. It called for the establishment of an effective administration to provide assistance that would be crucial for ensuring the stability of East Timor and the viability of its emergent public administration. The UN experience, however, showed that this was easier said than done.

With regards to the civilian administration, following the departure of international civilian administrators with the completion of UNTAET in May 2002, the Security Council decided first to maintain 100 "stability" advisers funded through assessed contributions. Along with 200 "development" advisers, to be provided through bilateral and multilateral voluntary contributions, these advisers carried out essential line functions and coached their Timorese counterparts in acquiring the technical skills necessary for the proper functioning of the newly created state systems and institutions in their respective areas.

The international advisers performed their pioneering tasks of capacity-building in democratic governance with varying degrees of success and failure.

- *Legal advisers* played a key role in drafting, revising, and submitting legal frameworks and other legislation for government ministries and other state institutions such as the judiciary and national parliamentary commissions. They worked at the level of the Council of Ministers where draft legislation is reviewed prior to approval by the Council of Ministers and/or submission to the parliament for adoption. The advisers also helped establish the basic legal frameworks for such new bodies as the Council of State and the Superior Council for Defence and Security. Although most of the advisers maintained their impartiality and professionalism, some were criticized for becoming a tool of the government to help it enact laws that were considered undemocratic.

- *International advisers engaged in the justice sector* included judges, court administrators, prosecutors, and public defenders, as well as advisers for the prison service. Apart from performing line functions, the international judges, prosecutors, and public defenders were also involved in formal training of Timorese court actors as part of the Judicial Training Centre Programme in Dili.

- *Financial management and audit services* were provided in the Ministry of Planning and Finance and line ministries, as well as the Office of the

Inspector General (OIG). Advisers in this area ensured the smooth functioning of the national financial system. International advisers who were engaged in audit services in the OIG and in the internal audit unit of the Ministry of Planning and Finance made attempts to enhance transparency and accountability in financial transactions. However, it should be recognized that their efforts did not produce the desired results owing to limited commitment at the highest level to achieving transparency and accountability.

- *National policy development* was supported by international advisers who assisted the Secretary of State for Defence with defense policy development and the Office of the Prime Minister with the development of foreign investment, petroleum fund management, and export development. The advisory services provided by Norwegian experts proved effective in the establishment of a "Norway-plus" system of managing revenues from natural gas resources. In 2005, on the advice of the UN Special Representative of the Secretary-General, both President Xanana Gusmão and Prime Minister Mari Alkatiri committed to achieving the Millennium Development Goals (MDGs). They worked on aligning their development policy towards attainment of the MDGs and proudly announced in their policy document that the share of national budget resources for health had been increased by 46 percent and the share for education by 12 percent for fiscal year 2005.

Promoting transparency and accountability

In the short time since independence, Timor-Leste has established the basic institutional infrastructure capacity to perform the functions of democratic governance. The democratic governance system was threatened by security incidents several times between 2002 and 2008, but it overcame the challenges and the various state institutions functioned more or less adequately, although they were far from perfect. The negative impact of corrupt practices, however, had more detrimental effects in eroding the confidence of people in the government. As Timor-Leste moves into the next phase of its institutional development and challenges, the country will need to ensure that the key institutions can perform their functions in the way intended by the constitution.

For the conflict-prone country of Timor-Leste, the demanding and critical phase of democratic institution-building required strong leadership and the commitment of the government as a whole to the democratic system of governance. It also required continued support from donors and the strong growth of civil society and the private sector. A crucial aspect of what remained to be done concerned the extent to which the key institutions of governance could be made more transparent and accountable to the basic welfare of the people.

The promulgation of the concept of transparency and accountability has had a significant impact on enhancing trust in the governments of post-conflict countries, particularly Timor-Leste. Here, when I refer to "transparency and accountability" I mean not only financial accountability and anti-corruption measures but also, more broadly, the need for full transparency of the government decision-making process and the accountability of government officials for their conduct. For this, the independence of the judiciary had a significant and positive influence in fostering a culture of transparency and accountability.

In Timor-Leste, former Prime Minister Mari Alkatiri asserted that his government placed a high priority on ensuring transparency and accountability. At the national level, he created several institutions to play a central role in promoting transparency and accountability. These included the Offices of (a) the Inspector General, (b) the Prosecutor General, (c) the Provedor for Human Rights and Justice, and (d) the Adviser on Human Rights to the Prime Minister. The mandates of these bodies to promote good governance through transparency and accountability were laudable and the officials occupying the positions did their best to fulfill their responsibilities with the assistance of international advisers.

The UN strategy was to build the national institutional capacity to ensure transparency and accountability by first developing an internal audit and evaluation system centered around the Office of the Inspector General and then strengthening the authority and capability of the judiciary to bring cases of criminal violation for indictment. More specifically, UNMISET and UNOTIL assisted the Prosecutor General and the Court in acquiring the technical expertise to act independently and effectively. For this purpose, UNMISET brought two advisers who were assigned to the Office of the Inspector General. They assisted in the completion of 69 reports covering the Office's activities since its inception in October 2000. The majority of cases involved non-criminal offences such as negligence by public officers, irregularities, and administrative deficiencies. Also reported were five cases of criminal offenses such as bribery, theft, and document falsification. In addition, the advisers organized monthly national seminars on auditing and investigations for both public officials and civil society, in cooperation with the Office of the Inspector General, as well as the Office of the Provedor and the Office of the Prosecutor General, and Office of the Adviser on Human Rights to the Prime Minister, the Timorese national police and civil society organizations. It was assumed, however, that the Office of the Inspector General would continue to require further support in the form of training in law, accounting, auditing, and engineering, as well as in other areas, in order to strengthen its human resources capacity.

UNMISET also brought several advisers to take up the posts of prosecutors and other positions within in the Office of the Prosecutor General. Furthermore, UNMISET recruited several judges and legal staff from Brazil and Portugal to serve in the district courts and the Court of Appeal. The mission undertook a diverse range of important initiatives in order to foster a culture of transparency and accountability. The number of advisers provided by UNMISET not only in the Office of the Inspector General and the judiciary but also in other public institutions was substantial: 14 advisers were assigned to the Ministry of Planning and Finance, two to the parliament, and two to the Council of Ministers. In addition, the mission provided an adviser to the Prime Minister on enhancing human rights. Specialized units within UNMISET were also actively engaged in fostering the culture of transparency and accountability, including the Human Rights Unit and UNPOL Technical Advisers.

Professional assistance included the establishment of a system of controls on financial expenditure and procurement, the drafting of appropriate regulatory documents, implementation of the Civil Act of Ethics, the drafting of a Code of Conduct for civil servants on the basis of which income and asset declarations were to be made. In addition, seminars or workshops were organized to publicize the concept of transparency and accountability; technical assistance was provided for the creation of the Office of the Provedor; and government staff (police and army included) were trained in ethics and other standards of transparency.

During the first few years, from 2000 to 2003, Timor-Leste remained more or less untouched by any major nepotism or corruption. This was owing mainly to the preoccupation of the Timorese leadership with the urgent task of achieving stability. But it was also owing to the scarcity of national budgetary resources. Revenues from natural gas in Timor remained relatively small during the first few years of the Mari Alkatiri government. The people began to lose confidence in the integrity of the government as stories of corruption, collusion, and nepotism prevalent during the period of Indonesian control began to permeate society. Many of the cases centered on public works and customs clearances.

By late 2003, it was clear that, if the situation were not contained, it would eventually bring the prime minister and the government down.[2] The United Nations organized a series of workshops with government representatives to identify mechanisms and approaches to enhance high standards of integrity among public officials. The United Nations considered it essential for the government, and more specifically the Inspector General and the Prosecutor General, to formulate an action plan for transparency and accountability and to indicate to the international community what assistance it required beyond May 2005. A systemic approach was required on the part of the government. It appeared that more momentum was needed so that the Security Council could be informed as to what the government was doing and would require after the departure of UNMISET.

To this end, Prime Minister Mari Alkatiri invited a UN Mission of Experts on Transparency and Accountability to Timor-Leste in January 2006 to assess the status of transparency and accountability in the public administration and to make recommendations on the way forward. The Mission was composed of senior experts from the United Nations Department of Economic and Social Affairs, the World Bank, the United Nations Development Programme, Transparency International, and the Government of Finland.

In its report, the Mission notes that:

> Based on wide ranging and exemplary consultation, a Petroleum Fund has been established to receive and invest all funds derived from oil and gas resources and to ensure that the benefits are available for future generations. An Investment Advisory Board to the Fund was established in 2005. The Fund should continue to adhere to the principles of transparency agreed at its establishment, which correspond to those subsequently adopted by the Extractive Industries Transparency Initiative (EITI). The Independent Consultative Council, which will include representatives of civil society, should be appointed by Parliament as soon as possible.

> According to the Constitution the financial audit function of Government is to be performed by the High Administrative, Tax and Audit Court. This Court is yet to be established, and [the Mission] rightly recommend[s] that this should be done as soon as suitably qualified personnel become available. The organic law of the Court will be able to ensure the independence of the Court in carrying out its functions. Until the Court is constituted, the Government – through the Ministry of Finance and Planning – should continue to engage an international firm of accountants to audit the State accounts. (UN Mission of Experts 2006: 12)

The formation of a reliable electoral system is the bedrock of a strong democratic state and one of the basic elements of accountability and transparency. The UN Mission thus emphasized in its report that it was vital that the electoral law, which was yet to be put in place, be developed in a consultative manner that took account of the views of all segments of society (UN Mission of Experts 2006). There were many issues to be considered. For example, despite greater financial costs, the UN Mission thought that it would be helpful to voters to hold the 2007 presidential and parliamentary elections separately on different days. In order to help sustain the transparency and credibility of the electoral process, the Mission recommended that the independence of the National Electoral Commission be safeguarded and that the Commission should be strengthened in terms of the financial and professional resources available to it. The Mission also considered it important that government and donors began to mobilize the resources required to prepare for and conduct the elections.

> The elections provide an opportunity for strengthening the operation of Parliament. Currently, the proper functioning of Parliament is constrained by a lack of office facilities and equipment; by an insufficient quantity and quality of translation and interpretation services; by capability limitations among parliamentarians; and by inadequate secretariat services. More importantly, however, parliamentarians are sometimes not given enough time to consider draft legislation and the national budget; and there tends to be insufficient opportunity granted to parliamentary committees for questioning senior members of government about such matters ... Suggestions for strengthening parliament in these respects included the necessity for the Executive to champion the independence and authority of Parliament, to require Ministers to attend committee discussions, and the desirability of providing various forms of capacity building support.

> ... Considerable strengthening is also needed in the legal system. An important aspect of this is clearly access to justice for ordinary citizens. It should be possible for them to engage with the legal system in a language that they understand. To facilitate this, [the Mission] recommend[s] that steps be taken to ensure that laws be published and legal proceedings be conducted in both official languages, even though the evolving language of Tetum had a limited technical vocabulary. Translation and interpretation services will need to be strengthened accordingly. (UN Mission of Experts 2006: 9–10)

> Freedom of information and the timeliness, comprehensiveness and validity of information that is made available to the public by Government are central to the functioning of society and the economy. Conscious efforts at maintaining an effective dialogue between government and civil society organizations are essential to promoting a culture of accountability and transparency in society as a whole. Inadequate or insufficient information can lead to mistrust of the intentions of government and the circulation of rumour and misinformation. (UN Mission of Experts 2006: 13)

The Mission therefore recommended that a freedom of information law be put in place and that the government should publicize its policies and programs more vigorously; that requirements for the registration of civil society organizations (CSOs) be publicized more widely and that consideration be given to extending the deadline for their registration; that consideration be given to including CSO representatives in national commissions such as the National Electoral Commission; that capacity-building support to CSOs from external donors should be encouraged; and that the coverage of the national broadcaster should be expanded to the whole country. The Mission also supported the formation by members of the media of a press council, which should set professional standards and provide advisory services to the profession. Journalists were in desperate need of training in investigative journalism and in ethical conduct, and the government was encouraged to endorse the channeling of donor assistance to them for these purposes. The Mission also felt that there could be some merit in the making of a media or press law that defines the rights and responsibilities of the media and confirms their right to freedom of expression guaranteed under the constitution.

The Mission's work closed in Dili on January 27, 2006 with a UNOTIL Consultative Group Meeting chaired by Prime Minister Mari Alkatiri. The meeting was designed to expose the Mission's findings to a wider audience and to provide a final opportunity for gaining feedback. In his opening remarks, the prime minister portrayed the country as one that was striving to be a model of good governance in terms of its transparency and accountability – for the region and possibly more widely. He reiterated his government's strong commitment to the ideals of transparency and accountability and to taking forward the recommendations contained in the Mission's report. At the same time, he acknowledged the considerable challenges posed by this ambition.

However, the collapse of the Alkatiri government within six months of the departure of the Mission did not allow Alkatiri to pursue any further the ideas embodied in the Mission report. If Alkatiri had been willing to act faster or had had more time, he might indeed have started implementing some of the measures recommended by the Mission.

Conclusion

Since independence, Timor-Leste has made considerable achievements in laying the foundation for democratic governance in spite of formidable challenges faced by the leaders and the people of this newly born country. The element of trust in such a newly formed government has become a driving force for the strength and sustainability of Timorese institutions. Long-lasting commitments to ensure security for its citizens, to deliver essential services, and to remain transparent and accountable are all fundamental elements for Timor-Leste in order for it to, in the long run, thrive on sound, inclusive, and people-centered development. Success depends as well on a joint partnership and constructive dialogues among the four state institutions of the presidency, the government, parliament, and the judicial branch, as well as civil society, business communities, and international development partners. It is essential that the international community continues to render all necessary assistance to independent Timor-Leste as it goes through the process of peacebuilding and sustainable development. The long-term and protracted commitment of international multilateral and bilateral development partners to Timor-Leste is required more than ever for the promotion and sustainability of citizens' trust in the government of Timor-Leste.

Notes

1. As Cheema points out (2005: 191–212), there is a distinction between the causes of conflict and conflict triggers. One of the structural causes of conflict in Timor-Leste was unfair treatment of personnel in the F-FDTL. A crisis situation was triggered in January 2006 when soldiers complained about this unfair treatment in a petition to the president and then deserted when they received little response.
2. The Customs Office was set on fire in August 2007, shortly after the elections that resulted in a change of government.

REFERENCES

Cheema, G. Shabbir (2005) *Building Democratic Institutions, Governance Reform in Developing Countries*. Bloomfield, CT: Kumarian Press.

UN Mission of Experts (2006) *Strengthening Accountability and Transparency in Timor Leste: Report of the Alkatiri Initiative Review*. Dili, Timor-Leste: United Nations Office in Timor-Leste, January 27. Available at: <http://www.globalpolicy.org/images/pdfs/jan2006accountability.pdf> (accessed 9 February 2010).

UN Security Council (2002) *Security Council Resolution 1410 (2002) on the Situation in East Timor*, 17 May 2002, S/RES/1410 (2002). Available at: <http://www.unhcr.org/refworld/docid/3d528a607.html> (accessed 9 February 2010).

UN Security Council (2004) *Security Council Resolution 1543 (2004) on Extension of the Mandate of UNMISET*, 14 May 2004, S/RES/1543 (2004). Available at: <http://www.unhcr.org/refworld/docid/411361714.html> (accessed 9 February 2010).

UN Security Council (2005) *Security Council Resolution 1599 on the Situation in Timor-Leste*, 28 April 2005, S/RES/1599 (2005). Available at: <http://www.unhcr.org/refworld/docid/42bc19ad4.html> (accessed 9 February 2010).

11

Conclusion: Trust is a must in government

Vesselin Popovski

A democratic government will not survive long if it does not build and sustain the trust of its citizens. Trust is a must in government, and not only for democratic government. Ironically, even rulers who may have come to power through a coup d'état or another form of unconstitutional seizure of power can gradually build trust among citizens, respect their rights, and enjoy popular support. In contrast, rulers elected through fair and free elections may rapidly lose trust if they do not deliver and live up to people's expectations. Trust in government is the central element of good governance – it can be built up with sound policies enhancing people's welfare and safety. But it can also be lost. It is not something a priori given. Our research that culminated in this book demonstrates in various examples how trust in government is difficult to build, and how it is easy to lose.

Governments need citizens, as much as citizens need governments. The glue of this connection is mutual trust, which legitimizes the government. Governments need citizens for economic reasons – to collect taxes – and for political reasons – to be elected and re-elected. Citizens also need governments for economic and political purposes – to ensure jobs, laws, regulations, safety, education, healthcare, and public services. Elected governments need people's trust both before and after elections. To ensure the trust of their citizens, governments have to deliver visible results on all the promises they have made. If governments make promises that are too large to be implement, they will lose people's trust and will not be re-elected. More importantly, when governments fail to live up to

Building trust in government: Innovations in governance reform in Asia, Cheema and Popovski (eds), United Nations University Press, 2010, ISBN 978-92-808-1189-6

people's expectations, when they betray their promises, people remain insecure and their welfare could be jeopardized.

It would be better if governments did not promise what they cannot deliver. Rulers should have the honesty to share the difficulties of governing, to speak openly, and to provide room for doubt about what they are planning and what they are able and competent to do. If the existing challenges are openly discussed and explained, people will not overestimate the role of government, they will know in advance the limits of government, and, accordingly, will create their own individual, family, or community "safety-nets." If they know the limits of government, citizens can plan in advance how to meet social, economic, cultural, humanitarian and other challenges and be ready to face negative consequences, such as poverty, economic recession, unemployment, a rise in criminality, old housing, the cost of children's education, health issues, and environmental hazards.

Citizens trust that the government, by collecting taxes, will fund all measures necessary for public security and will provide the laws, regulations, policies, and actions to implement these policies. Trust is both a precondition for, and a result of, good governance. As discussed in this book, various dimensions of effective and democratic governance and the promotion of trust in government are interdependent. We have examined how the nature of interdependence varies across Asia and the Pacific, depending on the sociopolitical context within a country and the nature of reforms undertaken to improve the governance of electoral, parliamentary, judicial, and public sector services.

After reviewing the literature on the concept of trust (and the decline in trust) in government, this book analyzed government reinvention and reforms in relation to four sub-regions of the Asia-Pacific – Northeast Asia, Southeast Asia, South Asia, and the Pacific Islands. We selected for analysis, discussion, and lesson-learning four country-specific experiences – from the People's Republic of China, the Republic of Korea, Indonesia and Timor-Leste – as examples of building trust in government.

In reviewing the literature on the concept of trust, our book has emphasized the comprehensive and unifying nature of trust: namely, that it exists in every society and at all times, right down to the level of the individual citizen. Despite the diversity of ways in which trust can develop and be sustained, at its heart high levels of trust are formed by good governance of institutions such as rule of law, an independent judiciary, and legitimate electoral and parliamentary processes. Importantly, the continuing challenge is to maintain these at a level where a culture of trust becomes the rule, and not the exception. Trust is a natural ingredient of every government, but it needs daily work to be sustained and promoted.

Our research examined the status of trust in governments in North and East Asia within the context of globalization, as well as the ways through which different dimensions of governance are affecting citizens' trust in government. We found that, even though Japan and the Republic of Korea have made significant progress in democratic governance and economic performance, trust in political parties and parliaments continues to be low. In contrast, in the socialist states of China and Vietnam, where politics and administration are controlled by the ruling party, there has been a commitment to reform and civil society engagement that has, along with remarkable economic performance, positively influenced citizens' trust in government. Despite overall progress in North and East Asia through active reforms, regardless of political ideology, continuing reforms are critical for maintaining, and in some countries recovering, public trust in government.

Analyzing the status of trust and governance in the countries of Southeast Asia, we suggested that there is greater trust in government and order institutions than in representative institutions. In our opinion, trust in government does not seem to be merited when viewed in the context of weaknesses in service delivery, equality of citizens' access, the performance of the police, and the provision of justice in most of the countries in the region. Governments in the region face many challenges in strengthening trust, especially in improving the performance, accountability, and transparency of service delivery. In such situations we found that it is possible that "trust begets trust" – some Southeast Asians have accorded trust even to governments that have as yet not shown themselves to be sufficiently trustworthy. Such governments, receiving the "benefit of the doubt," were encouraged further to enter the "politics of trust" by facilitating the more active involvement of their citizens in government and allowing themselves to accomplish better results by doing so. Certainly this spiral effect is welcome where the civil society and citizens are mature enough to provide the first step in trusting governments and receive in return stable legislation, equal opportunities, access to information, and everything else that is necessary for a stable society to flourish.

There are also examples where security, development, and participation factors are ignored and trust in government declines. Cynicism and impropriety in government programs and poor development performance can lead to the inequitable distribution of economic benefits, low effectiveness of participatory mechanisms, and other negative consequences at the local level. In South Asia (with the exception of India), for example, intra-state and inter-state conflicts and tensions contributed to a cycle of poor governance that encouraged alienated groups to challenge the authority of governments. Some political systems are struggling for stability and an underlying lack of trust from citizens in government remains problematic. Some positive political transition processes in Pakistan, Nepal, and Bangladesh have improved the prospects for democracy, accountability, and fighting corruption in these countries.

The traditional institutions of governance in the Pacific Island region represent a unique experience. Here one can observe emerging and enhancing links between globalization and government reinvention. We argue that local experiences need further encouragement: in a time of globalization, government reinvention processes should incorporate indigenous forms of governance, customs, and leadership. Although we caution that not all of the indigenous institutions are democratic, these institutions nevertheless in some cases serve as a source of stability and continuity by filling the gaps created by globalization and the universalization of government institutions. Overall, active incorporation of indigenous values and structures such as kinship that unify Pacific Island communities will help strengthen the capacity of states and public officials to improve public services. The building of trust should be viewed as an ongoing process. We acknowledge that changing government in ways that produce greater trust requires time and is dependent upon actions and assessments made by the Pacific islanders themselves.

The country-specific works on China, the Republic of Korea, Indonesia, and Timor-Leste bring additional assessments of how trust can be built and enhance governance. The chapter on China makes an interesting distinction between trust in central government, trust in local government, and trust in the Communist Party. Our research found that in China there is generally a popular trust in national leaders and political institutions, but frustrated citizens often show anger at local officials. Based on survey evidence, we noted that the younger generation in China, although it still appears to be very nationalistic, is less likely to offer blanket support for the Communist Party, as the older generation did. We anticipate that younger generations without a memory of socialist-era China will not hold the same expectations of the government to support individual social welfare. It could be that, in the future, people will have higher expectations of businesses and entrepreneurs than of local governments. Changes in political attitudes are usually difficult to predict, but trust in the central government in China is likely to be sustained.

The case of the Republic of Korea is another interesting country-specific analysis. It demonstrates how the building of trust in government was made possible through the purposeful introduction of the new National Tax Service. The Roh Moo-hyun administration (2003–2008) officially introduced a policy of "principle and trust" as a vision for government reform and innovation. The new tax reform was used as one of the key instruments to promote trust in government. Our analysis of the tax reform process in Korea found that participation, transparency, and the active championing of reform by the head of a government can have positive impacts on all levels of trust in government. Rebuilding trust levels takes time and it is often hard to measure. The Korean example offers some methodological suggestions on how to develop tools to measure the level of trust in government scientifically.

The Indonesian case study provides an instrumental overview of comprehensive changes implemented by a trust-building government in the so-called Reformation Era in Indonesia, which began in 1998. It examines key reforms related to constitutional change, democratization, decentralization, public sector reconstruction, and the fight against corruption, and their overall impacts on governance and, correspondingly, on trust in government at the national and sub-national levels. We found that Indonesia has made significant progress in increasing trust by moving government closer to the people and improving its transparency and accountability. Despite this progress, much work is still to be done to ensure that the level of trust does not decline and indeed rises further. We recommended that the responsibilities of the different levels of government should be better defined and suggested the creation of a civil service commission responsible for human resource management and the training of public officials.

The case of Timor-Leste is unique, first because it is a newly emerged country that did not exist before; second, because of the instability of the post-conflict situation; and, third, because a significant role is played in all elements of governance by an international administration – the United Nations. The issue of trust therefore applies not only to the national government but also to the international administration, and how the two coordinate their work is crucial. Trust in government in situations such as that in Timor-Leste nevertheless depends on more or less the same principles as elsewhere: the ability of government institutions to maintain security and stability, to deliver public services, to maintain the transparency and accountability of governmental operations, and to protect human rights and the rule of law. Also very important is the joint partnership and constructive dialogue among the state institutions of the presidency, the government, parliament, and the judiciary, as well as civil society, business communities, and international development partners. This partnership is a major contributing factor to building trust and to the survival and success of the government of Timor-Leste.

These are the messages, in summary, from our book. Trust in government is a must. It is the glue that seals and stamps the constitutional contract between the rulers – whether democratically elected or not – and the ruled. The dichotomy between benign authoritarianism and liberal democracy is not the only factor in understanding state–society trust relationships. The ability of governments to deliver services and improve people's economic opportunities is equally important. The role of leadership is crucial in building the credibility of new reforms, providing citizens with an overall vision of a future in which the government earns and fully merits citizen confidence. Trust can be built up through good governance, but it can also slip away through incompetent governance.

To sustain trust, governments need to limit their role to what they can efficiently deliver, and not intervene unnecessarily into people's everyday business. The best government is not the one that we have to see and examine every day, it is the one that remains unnoticed, whose policies run smoothly. Paradoxically, the best government is, in fact, the one that governs less. John Maynard Keynes (1926) wrote: "The important thing for government is not to do things which individuals are doing already, and to do them a little better or a little worse; but to do those things which at present are not done at all." Government does not need to be big. In fact, it should limit itself to the essential public roles. There is always a danger of expecting too much from government; such over-expectation can make government larger than necessary, threatening, over-powerful. Addressing a Joint Session of Congress in 1974, US President Gerald Ford said that "a government big enough to give you everything you want is a government big enough to take from you everything you have."

Our book demonstrates that the increase in income levels, in participatory activities, and in access to information leads to greater expectations of the government among citizens, who hold governments to higher standards of accountability. As governance becomes more effective and democratic, the challenge for governments is to continue to innovate in their relationship with citizens to meet these new challenges.

We have avoided making a general judgment about whether trust in government is increasing or decreasing, but our book emphasizes the need not only for democratic governance but also for effective governance that actively engages civil society and the private sector.

REFERENCES

Ford, Gerald (1974) "Address to a Joint Session of the Congress," August 12. Available at: <http://www.presidency.ucsb.edu/ws/index.php?pid=4694> (accessed 27 February 2010).
Keynes, John Maynard (1926) *The End of Laissez-Faire*. London: Hogarth Press.

Index